CONTESTED EMPIRE

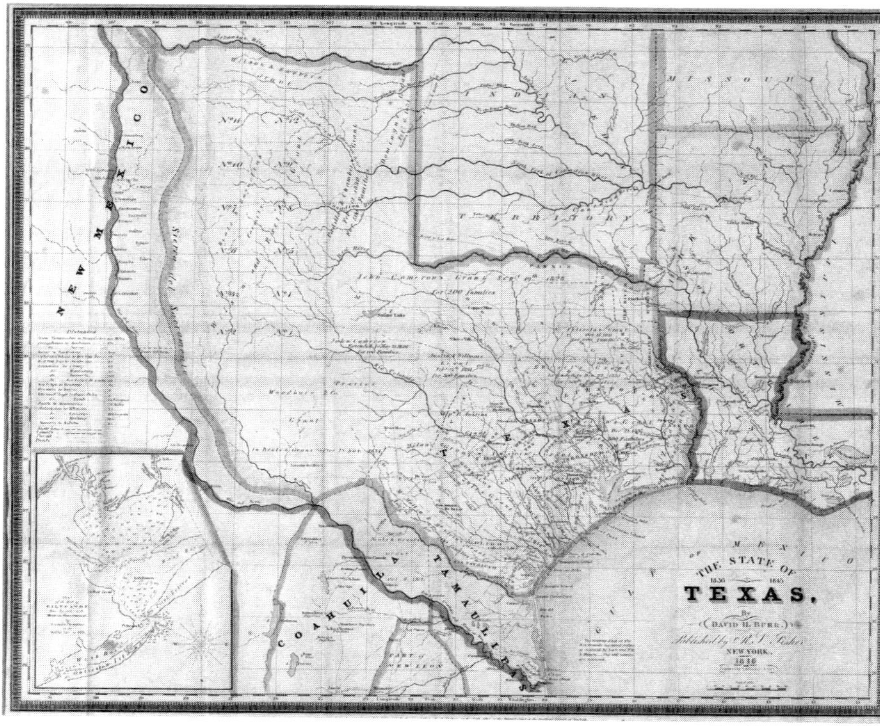

Courtesy Special Collections Library, University of Texas at Arlington

NUMBER FORTY-SIX

Walter Prescott Webb Memorial Lectures, published for the University of Texas at Arlington by Texas A&M University Press

A list of other titles in this series appears at the back of the book.

CONTESTED EMPIRE

Rethinking the Texas Revolution

EDITED BY SAM W. HAYNES AND GERALD D. SAXON

INTRODUCTION BY GREGG CANTRELL

Contributors

ERIC R. SCHLERETH

SAM W. HAYNES

MIGUEL SOTO

WILL FOWLER

AMY S. GREENBERG

Published for the University of Texas at Arlington by

TEXAS A&M UNIVERSITY PRESS

College Station

First edition

Manufactured in the United States of America
This paper meets the requirements of ANSI/NISO Z39.48–1992 (Permanence of Paper).
Binding materials have been chosen for durability.

LIBRARY OF CONGRESS CATALOGING-IN-PUBLICATION DATA

Contested empire : rethinking the Texas Revolution / edited by Sam W. Haynes and Gerald D. Saxon ; introduction by Gregg Cantrell ; contributors: Eric Schlereth, Sam W. Haynes, Miguel Soto, Will Fowler, Amy S. Greenberg.—First edition.
pages cm.—(Walter Prescott Webb memorial lectures ; number forty-six)
Includes bibliographical references and index.
Published on occasion of the 48th Annual Walter Prescott Webb Memorial Lecture, held at the University of Texas at Arlington in March, 2013.
ISBN 978-1-62349-309-7 (book/cloth : alk. paper)—
ISBN 978-1-62349-310-3 (e-book)
1. Texas—History—Revolution, 1835–1836. 2. Texas—History—To 1846. 3. Texas—Relations—Mexico. 4. Mexico—Relations—Texas. 5. United States—Politics and government—1815–1861. 6. Texas—Annexation to the United States. 7. Texas—Ethnic relations—Political aspects. 8. Irredentism. I. Haynes, Sam W. (Sam Walter), 1956- editor. II. Saxon, Gerald D., editor. III. Schlereth, Eric R., author. IV. Schlereth, Eric R. Voluntary Mexicans. V. University of Texas at Arlington, issuing body. VI. Series: Walter Prescott Webb memorial lectures ; 46.
F390.C77 2015
976.4'03—dc23
2015013394

CONTENTS

PREFACE

FEW EVENTS HAVE OCCUPIED as prominent a place in the American historical imagination as the Texas Revolution. Steeped in lore and shrouded in myth, the story of Texas's separation from Mexico has achieved iconic status, the subject of hundreds of books, not to mention more than a few Hollywood films. The events of 1835–36 have attracted more than their fair share of scholarly analysis, too. Some historians have sought, with varying degrees of success, to challenge popular notions of the rebellion, while others have tried to explain the enduring appeal of its more celebrated moments (the Alamo siege, for example) in American cultural life. Indeed, the story has been told and retold so many times that one might well ask if there remains anything new to say about the Revolution at all.

In March 2013, five historians from three countries—the United States, Mexico, and Scotland—met at the University of Texas at Arlington to reexamine the Texas Revolution. Each delivered papers at the Walter Prescott Webb Memorial Lectures, held annually by the university's Department of History. The 2013 conference, organized and presented by the department's Center for Greater Southwestern Studies, was intended to offer new perspectives of an event that has been studied by several generations of Texas historians, but that has rarely been the focus of historians of the United States and Mexico. Although scholars of Texas history have done much excellent work, a complete picture of the rebellion requires an appreciation for the roles played by both countries. To that end, the conference organizers sought to explore the causes and consequences of the rebellion in a broader, continental context.

In keeping with the transnational theme of the conference, the first two essays, written by US historians who study the early national period, seek to provide some insight into the mindset of Anglo-American colonists in

Texas. Eric Schlereth, of the University of Texas at Dallas, examines the concept of "voluntary allegiance" in order to better understand exactly what Mexican citizenship may have meant to the thousands of Anglo-Americans who abandoned their country of origin and settled west of the Sabine River in the 1820s and 1830s. As Schlereth notes, Americans regarded their allegiance as easily transferable from one country to another; it was such thinking that made Anglo colonization of northern Mexico possible. But they could just as easily withdraw their allegiance, and as tensions mounted in 1835, Anglo colonists ceased to view themselves as voluntary Mexicans and became voluntary Texans instead, thus giving the rebellion—in their own minds, at least—the stamp of legitimacy. Sam W. Haynes, of the University of Texas at Arlington, focuses on how Anglo-Americans's memory of the American Revolution informed their thoughts and actions during the war for Texas independence. Although a common commitment to federalist principles seemed to unite Anglo-American settlers and Tejanos at the outset of the conflict, the American Revolution provided a cultural frame of reference and a blueprint for armed resistance for the former citizens of the United States that Mexican-Texans did not share.

The next two essays examine the rebellion from a Mexican perspective. Will Fowler, of the University of St Andrews, challenges the widely held assumption that a Mexican national identity had its roots in the trauma of the 1846–48 conflict with the United States. Instead, he argues that Mexican intellectuals were already beginning to develop a sense of *Mexicanidad* by the time of the Texas Revolution, an identity formed partly as a result of an emerging anti-Americanism. While Mexican liberals like Lorenzo de Zavala may have admired the United States, conservatives such as Manuel de Mier y Teran, Lucas Alamán, and José Maria Tornel increasingly viewed Anglo-Americans with feelings of contempt—as an alien "other"—that enabled Mexicans to develop a clearer sense of who they were as a people and as a nation. Miguel Soto, of the Universidad Autónoma de Mexico, examines the role of prominent Mexicans in the land speculation schemes that accompanied the government's efforts to colonize Texas. Much like their Anglo-American counterparts, Mexican entrepreneurs who engaged in speculative activities in Texas sought to encourage Anglo-American settlement in the region. In so doing, they helped create the conditions that would lead to rebellion, prompting Soto to suggest that Texas may have been lost to Mexico well before the conflict began.

The final essay by Amy Greenberg, who delivered the conference's keynote address, provides a fitting postscript to these essays. A historian of nineteenth-century United States at Penn State University, Greenberg examines the consequences of the Revolution for the United States, as Americans wrestled with the prospect of incorporating Mexico's former province into the Union. Whereas scholars have traditionally cited Northern opposition to the acquisition of new slave territory to explain the failure of Texas's initial annexation bid in the late 1830s, Greenberg calls attention to a deeper sense of anxiety among American anti-expansionists. Drawing upon Thomas Cole's allegorical *Course of Empire* paintings depicting the rise and fall of ancient Rome, Greenberg argues that many Americans saw in the Roman experience a cautionary tale for the young American republic. If Americans balked at the prospect of annexing Texas, it was because they harbored misgivings about unbridled territorial growth, sensing, as Cole did, that conquest and empire would lead inexorably to decay and collapse.

A great many people helped to make the forty-eighth annual Walter Prescott Webb Memorial Lectures possible. The published Webb volumes are supported by a generous endowment from C.B. Smith Sr., a former student of Walter Prescott Webb, and supplemented by the Rudolph Hermanns Endowment for the Liberal Arts. We would also like to thank Marvin Dulaney, chair of the University of Texas at Arlington History Department, for providing additional financial assistance. Organizing any academic conference, and particularly one involving speakers from three countries, requires a keen attention to logistical detail. We were therefore fortunate indeed to be able to rely on conference coordinator Jennifer Lawrence and graduate student Karen Beazley, both of whom made sure that the conference went smoothly. We are grateful for the support of the Center for Greater Southwestern Studies staff, administrative assistant Elizabeth York and student assistant Rachel Makutuya. Alan Olson, director of Collections and Exhibits at the Dallas Historical Society, graciously loaned the Center its collection of Texas flag reproductions, some of which serve as illustrations in this volume. Introductions for the featured speakers at the conference were delivered by Chris Morris (Department of History, University of Texas at Arlington), Christopher Conway (Department of Modern Languages, University of Texas at Arlington), Sonia Kania (Department of Modern Languages, University of Texas at

Arlington), Sam W. Haynes (Department of History, University of Texas at Arlington), and Gregg Cantrell (Department of History, Texas Christian University). We would also like to thank Professor Cantrell who, though serving this year as president of the Texas State Historical Association, managed to find the time to write the introduction to this volume.

Finally, this collection of essays is dedicated to our friend and former colleague, Douglas W. Richmond. A scholar of revolutionary Mexico, Doug taught Latin American history at the University of Texas at Arlington for thirty-seven years. Prior to his retirement in 2012, Doug authored three books and a great many scholarly articles. Perhaps he is best known for his biography of Mexican president Venustiano Carranza (*Venustiano Carranza's Nationalist Struggle, 1893–1920*) and a textbook, *The Mexican Nation*, which has become a standard text in Mexican history classes in colleges and universities throughout the United States. More than just an able scholar and dedicated teacher, Doug also took an active role in the Center for Greater Southwestern Studies, where over the years he helped organize many conferences on the history of the US–Mexico borderlands. We wish him well.

—SAM W. HAYNES AND GERALD D. SAXON

INTRODUCTION

Gregg Cantrell

FEW EPISODES OF AMERICAN HISTORY have fired the imagination like the Texas Revolution. As of May 2014, a quick search of the online bibliographic catalog WorldCat revealed 2,471 books with the word "Alamo" in the title—and that is before we begin to count books on other aspects of the conflict apart from the fabled 1836 siege. Motion pictures had barely been invented when the first film about the Texas Revolution, *The Immortal Alamo*, appeared in 1911. It would be followed by more famous efforts, including D. W. Griffith's *Martyrs of the Alamo* four years later; Fess Parker's hugely popular Disney version, *Davy Crockett: King of the Wild Frontier*, in 1955; John Wayne's Hollywood epic in 1960; and, in 2004, Disney's big-budget Buena Vista production of *The Alamo*, starring Billy Bob Thornton. More than 1.4 million people visit the Alamo each year, according to the state, with another half-million or more visiting San Jacinto and other Revolution-related sites. Public art and monuments around the state celebrate the glories of the Revolution. Two full years (fourth and seventh grades) in the state public school curriculum are devoted to Texas history, where the Revolution continues to garner a disproportionate share of the time and attention. And the collecting of Texas Revolution artifacts and memorabilia has become big business, an obsession shared not only by free-spending Texas oilmen, but even by as unlikely an aficionado as British rock star Phil Collins, who now boasts one of the largest such private collections in the world.[1]

This has created problems for the academic study of the Texas Revolution. As the Revolution—particularly that portion of it that took place at a crumbling San Antonio mission in early 1836—gained resonance with people worldwide as a symbol of patriotic sacrifice and eventually became the key element in the Texas creation myth, historians have struggled to treat it objectively.[2] This is not to say that they have not tried. In the early twentieth century, the first generation of academically trained historians turned their attention to the Revolution, led by the University of Texas' Eugene C. Barker. Heavily influenced by Frederick Jackson Turner's "frontier thesis," Barker and his students and emulators depicted the Revolution as a natural step in the process of American westward expansion. But their work tended to be uncritical of that expansion and certainly uncritical of the major participants on the Texan side. Thus Barker's central subject, Stephen F. Austin, became the self-sacrificing "Founder of Texas," Llerena Friend's Sam Houston emerged as "The Great Designer," and the martyrs of the Alamo tended to remain just that—martyrs who perished at the "Shrine of Texas Liberty."[3] So thorough a job did Barker and his acolytes do that a 1991 essay by historian Paul Lack bemoaned the fact that three-quarters of a century after Barker, Texas historians were still laboring "In the Long Shadow of Eugene C. Barker."[4]

Lack was an appropriate scholar to write that 1991 historiographical essay on the Revolution and Republic era, because at the time he was working on one of the first truly revisionist treatments of the Revolution, *The Texas Revolutionary Experience: A Political and Social History, 1835–1836*. Using the tools of the social historian, he discovered a number of inconvenient truths about the brief conflict between Texas and Mexico. Texans, it turned out, were not particularly eager revolutionaries; indeed, there was considerable "tory" (pro-Mexican) sentiment throughout the war. Moreover, he found that recent arrivals from the United States—men who were little more than soldiers-of-fortune, if not mercenaries—figured heavily in the ranks of the Texan armed forces.[5] Over the next couple of decades, a number of other frankly revisionist works appeared, some better than others, to be sure, and these works took their place alongside the continuing torrent of books cast in the older, more celebratory mold. The role of slavery, the contributions of Tejanos and women, more frank assessments of the economic motives of Anglo settlers, studies of individual communities—all of these topics partook of the so-called new social history, which, by the time it made its way into Texas revolutionary historiography, was not all that "new" anymore.[6]

By the dawn of the twenty-first century, the limitations of this approach to new social history were becoming clearer. In their zeal to set the record straight, the social history revisionists had spent much of their time and energy refuting the traditionalists. In trying to peel back the stubbornly impervious layers of myth that still enveloped the Revolution, the revisionists had committed an error in some ways similar to that of the traditionalists: They had kept the focus of their studies largely on Texas itself, on people and events between the Sabine and the Rio Grande, contributing to a Texas-centric narrative that inadvertently reinforced the trope of Texas exceptionalism. In essence, the revisionists had met the traditionalists on the traditionalists' own turf, and to the extent that the revisionists emerged victorious, they found themselves in possession of the same old ground, the hallowed soil of the Lone Star State—a grand place, to be sure, but still largely cut off from meaningful connections to the wider historiographical world.

A few brave scholars sought a way out. Led by David J. Weber, whose innovative works in the 1980s and 1990s placed Texas in the broader context of the Spanish borderlands and the Mexican frontier, some twenty-first-century intellectuals began to expand the scholarly horizons of early Texas history. Significantly, historians of Texas American Indians were in the forefront of this new historiographical approach. Brian DeLay, Pekka Hämäläinen, Juliana Barr, and F. Todd Smith purposefully downplayed political borders and sought to view Texas events from perspectives other than those of the Anglo revolutionaries themselves. Andrés Reséndez and Raúl A. Ramos did the same in their studies of Tejano/Mexican/Texan identity.[7]

The new approach has been methodologically eclectic, frustrating scholars' efforts to place a label on it. Some stress the influence of postmodernism or post-structuralism, intellectual frameworks that treat historical reality as fluid, contingent, and constructed. Whereas the social historians tended to study individual ethnic or racial groups, genders, or communities in isolation, the new historians have often worked to understand the connections and interactions between multiple groups. In many cases, they have rediscovered both cultural and intellectual history, and they have expanded upon these methodologies, using them to delve into such questions as collective memory, the nature of citizenship, or what it meant to be white. And increasingly, scholars have realized the value in transregional and transnational history, going beyond the traditional concerns of diplomatic historians to explore cultural, intellectual, and economic themes across political borders. Lacking a better term, historian Walter Buenger has chosen the label "cultural constructionists" as a catch-all term for these post-social approaches to history.

If these new ways of writing history, whatever one chooses to call them, have come late to the study of Texas history (compared to American history generally), it should not surprise us that *within* the field of Texas history, they have come particularly late to the study of the Texas Revolution. The reasons are not hard to fathom. Looking for a way to get labeled "provincial" as a historian? Announce to the world that you plan to write about the Texas Revolution. Your book, then, for which you will easily find a publisher, can take its place alongside such dramatic titles as *Blood of Noble Men* or *The Blood of Heroes*, or perhaps even share a shelf with *The Mystery of the Alamo Ghost, The Alamo and Zombies*, or *Custer at the Alamo*.[8] But if looking to be taken seriously as a scholar, and to reap the rewards of prime academic jobs, tenure, promotion, prestigious fellowships, and the respect of one's peers, there are probably more promising career strategies than writing about the Alamo or San Jacinto.

All of which makes the five distinguished scholars and their works in this volume the more remarkable. Convening on the campus of the University of Texas at Arlington in March 2013 for the forty-eighth annual Walter Prescott Webb Memorial Lecture Series, these scholars delivered the lectures that are now published here in essay form. In the essays, they embrace the new approaches in American historiography described above, and they have intrepidly applied those approaches to the study of the Texas Revolution. A glance at the authors' biographies reveals the first significant fact about them: None grew up in Texas or received his or her undergraduate education there. Only two, Sam W. Haynes and Eric Schlereth, teach at Texas universities. The other three—Will Fowler, Amy S. Greenberg, and Miguel Soto—hail respectively from the University of St Andrews in Scotland, Pennsylvania State University, and Universidad Nacional Autónoma de Mexico in Mexico City. All have written books and articles on topics unrelated to Texas. To adapt a line from the old automobile ad, this is *not* your father's Texas history.

Although they vary greatly in subject matter and methodology, all five essays share one thing in common: They explore the Texas Revolution from perspectives broader than the borders of the Lone Star State. Two of the essays, those by Miguel Soto and Will Fowler, consider Texas in the context of Mexico and probe the connections between the two. In his piece, "Politics and Profits: Mexican Officials and Land Speculation in Texas, 1824–1835," Soto reveals the myriad ways in which the vast public lands of Texas shaped Mexico's policies toward Texas from the beginning of Mexican independence. Whereas traditionalist Texas historians have long noted the role that land policy played in the events leading to the Texas Revolution, Soto points out that Mexican speculators—sometimes acting in concert with Anglos, sometimes not—had a large hand in Texan affairs, including the policies that enabled Anglo immigration and that led to Mexico's eventual loss of Texas. As Soto provocatively speculates, "One may wonder if Mexican sovereignty over Texas was really lost by Santa Anna in San Jacinto in April of 1836 or whether it had not already been compromised long before then by the colonization policy and the various sales and dealings that the previous administrations from Mexico had done before then."

Will Fowler's essay likewise considers Texas in the Mexican context, delving into the complex question of Mexican national identity and its relationship to the events that unfolded north of the Rio Grande in 1835–36. In "The Texas Revolution of 1835–36 and Early Mexican Nationalism," Fowler takes on a widely accepted interpretation about when and how a sense of national identity developed among Mexicans. That interpretation suggests that the catalyst for the development of that identity was the US-Mexican War of 1846–48, "that a national consciousness started to emerge: in part, because Mexicans, in being confronted with an invading expeditionary army that spoke a different language, practiced a different religion, and, arguably, represented a different political outlook, started to think of themselves as Mexican vis-à-vis the hostile American 'other.' " By contrast, using the writings of Mexican intellectuals in the years *prior* to the 1846 war, Fowler discovers that "these intellectuals presented, by contrast, an early vision of *Mexicanidad* that highlighted their Hispanic heritage, Catholic faith, and more spiritual and less materialistic nature." He adds, moreover, that "by stressing that the Texan immigrants' secessionist drive stemmed from their threatened slave-holding entrepreneurial interests, . . . they also celebrated Mexico's contrasting caring and abolitionist values. The distinction that would emerge in their writings between what was foreign and national, and between what was considered to belong to Mexico (and not to the United States) would therefore contribute meaningfully to an awakening of an early form of Mexican nationalism." By underscoring the central role that the Texas Revolution played in the intellectual history of Mexico, Fowler, like his fellow scholars in this volume, helps to lift the Revolution from the parochial position to which the Texas-centric interpretations have so long consigned it.

If Soto's and Fowler's essays intellectually span the Rio Grande border between Texas and Mexico, those of Sam W. Haynes and Amy Greenberg do the same for the Sabine border between Texas and the United States. Both essays exemplify the best qualities of the so-called cultural constructionist bent, combining intellectual and cultural history in an interdisciplinary, transnational approach. Haynes explores one of the oldest topics in the historiography of the Texas Revolution—the question of the Texans' motives—and using the concept of collective memory discovers a previously underappreciated factor: the role played by Texans' memory of the American Revolution. What previous scholars had tended to dismiss as mere rhetoric, Haynes finds genuinely significant. From the earliest instances of conflict between Anglo-American settlers and the Mexican government, the Americans drew upon their memories of the "Spirit of 1776" not only as inspiration but to understand events and as templates for potential action. As Haynes explains, "Far from serving as a form of rhetorical window-dressing, their frequent allusions to the past reveal a fundamental connection between the political crisis in Texas and the American revolutionary experience." Thus, the runaway bestseller of the years prior to the Texas Revolution, William Wirt's *Sketches of the Life and Works of Patrick Henry*, in which Wirt quotes Henry's famed "Give me liberty or give me death" speech, becomes, according to Haynes, "the ubiquitous watchwords of Anglo resistance" to Mexico.

In her essay, "'Time's Noblest Empire Is the Last': Texas Annexation in the Presumed Course of American Empire," Amy Greenberg likewise delves into American culture to place the Texas Revolution in a broader, transnational context. As a point of departure, Greenberg creatively utilizes Thomas Cole's series of monumental paintings unveiled in New York in 1836, collectively titled *Course of Empire*, to make an important point about how Americans viewed the Texas Revolution and why so many of them so successfully opposed Texas annexation. Cole's exhibition, which became an overnight sensation just as the debate over annexation was beginning in 1836, ostensibly had nothing to do with Texas. The heavily allegorical paintings depict a seaport in ancient times, following its history through five stages: savage, arcadian, consummation, destruction, and desolation. Although the images evoke ancient Rome, Greenberg notes that most scholars who have detected a political message in the canvases have seen them as a commentary on domestic policy, "identifying the rampant speculation, urban poverty, and financial insecurity of the era, as well as Jackson's imperious actions as the objects of Cole's ire." By contrast, Greenberg argues, "This is a narrative about foreign policy, wrongly understood." She then goes on to reveal how the paintings tapped into a broad public concern about imperialism in Jacksonian America, a concern made concrete by the Texan victory at San Jacinto and the sudden application by Texas for admission to the Union. Acknowledging the standard explanation for northern opposition to annexation—opposition to slavery—Greenberg suggests that Texas spurred a greater fear "that annexation of Texas would lead to the internal collapse of the United States."

The cultural and intellectual approaches taken by Greenberg and Haynes, and the transnational perspectives of Soto and Fowler, are all evident in the contribution by Eric Schlereth, "Voluntary Mexicans: Allegiance and the Origins of the Texas Revolution." Schlereth focuses on the related concepts of expatriation and voluntary allegiance, key ideas in the early histories of the United States, Mexico, and the Republic of Texas. Prior to the American Revolution, most Europeans viewed citizenship as inseparable from one's place of birth. British common law, for example, featured a "doctrine of perpetual allegiance," in which "subjects born in the empire owed lifetime loyalty to the monarch." During and after their revolution, Americans rejected this doctrine, formalizing a right (and in many places, a process) of expatriation, whereby a person could renounce his citizenship in one country preparatory to establishing it in another. A similar theory developed in Mexico, contributing significantly to Mexico's adoption of the liberal immigration policy that led to the peopling of Texas by Anglo-American immigrants. As Schlereth explains, "Agreement that patriotism was transferable and patriotic duty a matter solely of establishing permanent residence and obeying local laws allowed Anglo migrants to become Mexican citizens according to their understandings of expatriation and Tejano officials to implement state-level colonization policy." As it turned out, these same ideas about the voluntary, transferable nature of citizenship could be used to justify rebellion against Mexico, immigration from the United States to the new Republic of Texas, and the transfer of Texas to the United States. However, as national identities increasingly coalesced in the decades following the Texas Revolution, the concept of voluntary allegiance became more complex, as more Americans and Mexicans alike began to view citizenship as being somehow caught up in culture, race, or blood. (The growth of national identity that Will Fowler detected in Mexico also happened in the United States—the "mystic chords of memory" of which Lincoln so eloquently spoke.) As Schlereth perceptively notes, "Had this principle [of allegiance as strictly a voluntary, legalistic matter] persisted, the later history of the US-Mexico border might have been shaped much more forcefully by assumptions that individuals have fundamental rights to move freely across international boundaries."

The essays in this volume, then, shed new light from an array of angles onto a topic that had become stale. The works presented here change the way we view the Texas Revolutionary era in some significant respects, but perhaps more importantly, they open the door to further research by showing that there are new *ways* of looking at an old topic. If the historiography of the Texas Revolution had in some sense reached a dead end, this volume serves to break through that barricade and clear the path for more, and even better, future work. Following the example set by these essays, future scholarship will continue to integrate the study of Texas history with that of Mexico, the United States, and the broader world, enriching our understanding of each.

NOTES

1. Don Graham, "Mission Statement: The Alamo and the Fallacy of Historical Accuracy in Epic Filmmaking," in *Lone Star Pasts: Memory and History in Texas*, eds. Gregg Cantrell and Elizabeth Hayes Turner (College Station: Texas A&M University Press, 2007), 242–44; Tom Benning, "Lines are drawn over plans for Battleship Texas at San Jacinto state historic park," *Dallas Morning News*, April 19, 2010, http://www.dallasnews.com/news/state/headlines/20100418-Lines-are-drawn-over-plans-for-8155.ece; Andy Greene, "Q&A: Phil Collins on His Alamo Obsession, Retirement," *Rolling Stone*, May 31, 2012, http://www.rollingstone.com/music/news/q-a-phil-collins-on-his-alamo-obsession-retirement-20120531#ixzz32ZTfiZYz.

2. On the Alamo as creation myth and its symbolic meaning to Texans and others, see Holly Beachley Brear, *Inherit the Alamo: Myth and Ritual at an American Shrine* (Austin: University of Texas Press, 1995); Richard R. Flores, *Remembering the Alamo: Memory, Modernity, and the Master Symbol* (Austin: University of Texas Press, 2002); and Randy Roberts and James S. Olsen, *A Line in the Sand: The Alamo in Blood and Memory* (New York: Free Press, 2001).

3. Eugene C. Barker, *The Life of Stephen F. Austin, Founder of Texas, 1793–1836: A Chapter in the Westward Movement of the Anglo-American People* (Austin: University of Texas Press, 1969), first published 1925 by Cokesbury Press; Llerena B. Firend, *Sam Houston: The Great Designer* (Austin: University of Texas Press, 1954).

4. Paul D. Lack, "In the Long Shadow of Eugene C. Barker," in *Texas Through Time: Evolving Interpretations*, eds. Walter L. Buenger and Robert A. Calvert (College Station: Texas A&M University Press, 1991), 134–64.

5. Paul D. Lack, *The Texas Revolutionary Experience: A Political and Social History, 1835–1836* (College Station: Texas A&M University Press, 1992).

6. The analysis of trends in Texas historiography in this paragraph and following three paragraphs are drawn heavily from Walter L. Buenger, "Three Truths in Texas," in *Beyond Texas Through Time: Breaking Away from Past Interpretations*, eds. Buenger and Arnoldo De León (College Station: Texas A&M University Press, 2011), 1–49. Copious examples of works from Buenger's three analytical categories—"updated traditionalists," "persistent traditionalists," and "cultural constructionists"—can be found in its footnotes.

7. David J. Weber, *The Mexican Frontier, 1821–1846* (Albuquerque: University of New Mexico Press, 1982); and *The Spanish Frontier in North America* (New Haven: Yale University Press, 1992); Brian DeLay, *War of a Thousand Deserts: Indian Raids and the U.S.-Mexican War* (New Haven: Yale University Press, 2008); Pekka Hämäläinen, *The Comanche Empire* (New Haven: Yale University Press, 2008); Juliana Barr, *Peace Came in the Form of a Woman: Indians and Spaniards in the Texas Borderlands* (Chapel Hill: University of North Carolina Press, 2007); F. Todd Smith, *From Dominance to Disappearance: The Indians of Texas and the Near Southwest, 1786–1859* (Lincoln: University of Nebraska Press, 2005); Andrés Reséndez, *Changing National Identities at the Frontier: Texas and New Mexico, 1800–1850* (Cambridge: Cambridge University Press, 2005); Raúl A. Ramos, *Beyond the Alamo: Forging Mexican Ethnicity in San Antonio, 1821–1861* (Chapel Hill: University of North Carolina Press, 2010).

8. These works and the 2,467 others with the word "Alamo" in the title can be found by performing a keyword search in WorldCat.org.

ONE

VOLUNTARY MEXICANS
Allegiance and the Origins of the Texas Revolution

Eric R. Schlereth

IN EARLY 1830, ASA BRIGHAM quit the United States for Mexico. Brigham was a New Englander who crossed the Sabine River into Texas after spending several years in Louisiana. He settled in Brazoria, where he followed successful agricultural and commercial pursuits. Brigham had a thriving family, especially measured by the values he acquired in the southern United States. He gloated over his daughter's marriage to a Virginia planter and beamed when describing his granddaughter. She was not even two years old, yet "she is mistress of all the chickens Pigs, Cats and negroes on the place." Brigham's standing also brought him political power. By 1835 he was the Brazoria *alcalde,* or mayor. Brigham signed the Texas Declaration of Independence within a year of his election as *alcalde,* but his early letters to family in Massachusetts offer no hints to his later life as an insurrectionary. Brigham missed New England, so he wrote to his siblings in 1832, but he had no desire to return. He felt "perfectly satisfied here and have settled for life in this country." Brigham anticipated that his decision to remain in Texas might perplex his relatives who stayed behind. So he elaborated. "You may ask why we leave the United States of America, for that of the United States of Mexico—in answer, I can only say, that it was through choice, with a view of bettering my fortune, which I consider has been realized."[1]

Brigham explained his motivations for settling in Mexico by answering one of his era's most important questions about the nature of political allegiance. Did a person owe allegiance to a nation for reasons of birth, custom, or culture—was allegiance coercive in one way or another? Or was national allegiance voluntary, an expression of personal choice? Brigham clearly held the latter view. By settling in Texas, Brigham had become a voluntary Mexican. Brigham's journey toward rebellion suggests the larger role of voluntary allegiance in the course of the Texas Revolution.

Over 20,000 Anglo settlers migrated to Mexican Texas. Many emigrated as families, often with their slaves, into a province already inhabited by nearly 3,000 Tejanos and powerful American Indian bands. Until 1835, the principle of voluntary allegiance provided a source of political and legal cooperation among elite Tejanos, Anglos, and Mexican officials. However, changing political conditions in Mexico fueled the rise of conflicting ideas about the meaning of voluntary allegiance. As this occurred, many Anglos increasingly viewed themselves as voluntary Texans rather than voluntary Mexicans. A breakdown in shared notions about the virtues of voluntary allegiance ultimately played an important intellectual and political role in the origins and course of the Texas Revolution.[2]

IN THE EARLY 1830S, voluntary allegiance was a long-standing albeit still controversial principle in the United States and Mexico. During the American Revolution, colonial Whigs justified rebellion against Great Britain by claiming a natural right to change political allegiance. As Thomas Jefferson argued in *A Summary View of the Rights of British America*, people were free to seek their happiness elsewhere in the world by leaving "the country in which chance, not choice, has placed them." This position gained added significance when the Whigs declared independence, an act that directly challenged the common law doctrine of perpetual allegiance. According to this doctrine, British subjects born in the empire owed lifetime loyalty to the monarch. Individual subjects could not unilaterally dissolve their bonds of allegiance. Voluntary allegiance gained theoretical legitimacy in the United States once it defeated Great Britain in the War of Independence.[3]

Mexicans inherited a notion of voluntary allegiance from their colonial rulers. According to prevailing legal opinion in early modern Spain, individuals had a natural right to change allegiance at will. This right entailed certain responsibilities. Writing in the eighteenth century, theologian and philosopher Benito Jerónimo Feijóo y Montenegro argued that "people who legitimately emigrate from their country of birth and fix their domicile in another dominion owe the same obligation to the new republic as to the one they had to the republic where they were born." Foreigners became full members of their adopted communities by behaving as "good" immigrants. In practice, individuals who established permanent residence in a new jurisdiction for which they cultivated genuine patriotic sentiments were good immigrants. Obeying local laws, paying taxes, and testimonies of strong moral character were all outward signs of patriotic love. Sufficient patriotic love transformed outsiders into citizens. An absence of patriotic love rendered one a dangerous foreigner who must be excluded from community membership. Authorities in Spanish America addressed the civil status of foreigners within their communities according to local needs, but they also recognized allegiance on fundamentally voluntary terms. Although the Spanish empire disintegrated in the early nineteenth century, the new republics formed in its place, including Mexico, preserved basic Spanish concepts of allegiance.[4]

The practical implications of voluntary allegiance proved equally controversial in the United States after 1776 and in Mexico after 1821. In the United States, debates surrounding voluntary allegiance commonly focused on the rights of expatriation. The term expatriation referred to a natural right under international law to unilaterally exchange citizenship in one country for that in another. Contemporaries described expatriation as the individual's right to "quit the nation" in pursuit of better fortunes elsewhere. Mexican controversies surrounding the implications of voluntary allegiance occurred in the context of developing and enforcing the nation's colonization policy. According to prevailing legal and political terms in the United States and Mexico, Anglo colonists such as Asa Brigham were thus expatriates who voluntarily became Mexican citizens. Nevertheless, the principle of voluntary allegiance incited debates in both countries over the nature and sources of patriotism.

In the United States, supporters of a robust right to expatriation understood patriotism in strictly legal terms. Loyalty and love for country required individuals to simply obey the law. From this perspective, law-abiding individuals could move throughout the world transferring their patriotism from place to place. A contributor to a New York newspaper in 1798 explained that a person has "a common claim for protection upon the society in which he lives. The duties he owes it in return consist in a due observance of its laws." Moreover, "When one deliberately quits a society, without having transgressed its laws, his subjection to them ceases, and his connection with, in the aggregate, is dissolved." Patriotic allegiance was not rooted in the moral obligations of nativity, religious traditions, family ties, or any sort of cultural sentiment.[5]

Commentators in the United States who identified the perils of expatriation held a strong belief that cultural sentiments underwrote genuine patriotism. A person who possessed "true patriotism" was unable "whatever may be his society, or in whatever distant land he may be thrown, to forget the country of his own and of his family's birth." For this reason, expatriates were, according to another critic, especially subversive. By "putting on and putting off his relationship to Government, according to his own whim and caprice," a voluntary citizen invited "upon his country all the horrors of dreadful anarchy and endless confusion." Luther Martin, a judge in Baltimore in the early nineteenth century, challenged the principle of voluntary allegiance more bluntly. Expatriation invited treason, Martin concluded. The jurist knew something about treason, for in 1806 he defended Aaron Burr against federal treason charges brought against him for his suspect activities in the Spanish Southwest. Yet in 1813, Martin dismissed expatriation's defenders who claimed that allegiance was a matter of choice and that nationality was an accident of birth. Following this logic, Martin argued, children owed no obedience to their parents who "in begetting them, were actuated by their own pleasure," rather than considering their future offspring's consent in the matter. Although absurd, expatriation's threat to parental authority paled when compared to its implications for religion. Martin argued that a person who cast aside allegiance to nation and home could use the same reasoning to cast aside duties to God, for "his existence was forced upon him, without his consent being first obtained or ever asked for!" Once obligation and obedience became matters of choice exercised according to personal measures of happiness, Martin warned, then no moral or legal brake existed to prevent a litany of crimes from perjury to murder. From this perspective, those who defended a right to expatriation colluded in an especially treasonous enterprise: the willful destruction of one's country.[6]

Several states took actions that allowed citizens to expatriate themselves despite divided opinions in the United States over expatriation's moral standing. Virginia and Kentucky passed statutes outlining procedures for expatriation. Petitioners in both places could surrender their citizenship before a county court or in writing before three witnesses provided they left the commonwealth immediately thereafter. The constitutions of many other states, western states formed before 1821 in particular, guaranteed the right to emigration, another term for expatriation according to prevailing legal opinion at the time. Increased Anglo migration to Texas after Mexican independence occurred at a time in the United States when the larger principle of voluntary allegiance held ambiguous moral standing but also more widespread legal recognition, especially in the states where many Texas migrants originated.[7]

The concept of voluntary allegiance fared similarly in Mexico. Mexican governments after 1821 adopted a series of colonization proposals. Each incorporated the notion of voluntary allegiance. Mexico's federal colonization law of 1824 and the state colonization law for Coahuila y Texas of 1825 both opened colonization to any foreigner who desired to settle in Mexico. Interested foreigners demonstrated their full intention of becoming Mexican citizens by affirming that they had left their homes in good faith, proving their good character, and establishing permanent residence in Texas. Mexico's colonization laws helped populate its northern frontier with the United States, but the vast majority of colonists by the 1830s were Anglo-Americans. As a policy, colonization raised troubling questions about the virtues of voluntary allegiance. Mexican observers debated if voluntary allegiance provided a basis for Anglo migrants to become loyal, patriotic Mexicans or if it actually encouraged self-interested actions akin to piracy.[8]

Despite similar concerns over the nature of voluntary allegiance on both sides of the Mexico-US border, voluntary allegiance was a principle central to political and social life in Mexican Texas. This is unsurprising, perhaps, as allegiance and patriotism always seemed rather flexible in borderland regions. In the late eighteenth century, Francisco Luis Héctor de Carondelet, the governor of Spanish Louisiana, worried that Anglo-Americans were too "accustomed to changing their place of residence as easily as they changed their shirts," whereas James Wilkinson, the Revolutionary War officer turned Spanish agent, held that patriotism never obliged one "to remain fixed like a vegetable." Under colonization laws adopted by the federal government in Mexico City and the state government of Coahuila y Texas, law-abiding Anglo settlers expatriated themselves from the United States to become patriotic Mexican citizens. In general terms, Anglos and Tejanos during the 1820s both embraced fairly strong notions of voluntary allegiance and similar understandings of patriotism.[9]

Promoters of Texas colonization, Tejano and Anglo alike, shared a view of patriotism that aligned with their acceptance of voluntary allegiance. Francisco Ruiz, a future signer of the Texas Declaration of Independence, proclaimed that "I cannot help seeing advantages which, to my way of thinking, would result if we admitted honest, hard-working people, regardless of what country they come from . . . even hell itself." Wealthy investors in New York and Boston created and financed the Galveston Bay and Texas Land Company, which recruited colonists to Texas with literature that tied Mexico's promise to its emergence from "the enthralling yoke of Spanish despotism" into a nation of "free constitutions and of wise laws." Noting that the Mexican Republic had benefited by emulating the constitution and principles of the United States, company boosters did not expect the colonists they recruited to transform Texas into an American outpost. Indeed, they warned that independence from Mexico would only harm Texas. Colonists would prosper, according to company literature, because the Mexican government recognized "that the freemen of all countries are patriots wherever their destinies fix or their interest call them."

The most quixotic proposal for settling Texas also advanced the most forceful repudiation of cultural sentiments as the source of patriotism. After founding an experimental community at New Harmony, Indiana, Scottish socialist Robert Owen turned his attention south. In 1828, he lobbied Mexican officials for full control of Texas. In exchange for this authority, Owen promised to create an entirely new society in Texas, free from violent revolutions, religious warfare, commercial competition, and economic inequality. According to Owen, a self-described "citizen of the world," this "society is to be formed of individuals of any country, whose minds have been enlightened beyond the prejudices of all local districts." Although Anglo ideas about expatriation and Mexican colonization policies were congruent in many ways, one event in the late 1820s exposed the social and political dangers of voluntary allegiance.[10]

In the winter of 1826 and 1827, Anglo-Americans and their Cherokee allies in East Texas rebelled against Mexican authority. Like many conflicts in colonial Texas, land was at issue. In November 1826, the state government of Coahuila and Texas revoked a colonization charter it had granted to the region's most influential *empresario,* Haden Edwards. Government actions infuriated Edwards and his settlers. Moreover, Cherokees in the region had their own difficulties securing land grants, so they concluded that the government's decision also jeopardized their Texas land claims. On December 21, 1826, Cherokee leaders Richard Fields and John Dunn Hunter joined the outraged Anglo-Americans in declaring independence for the Republic of Fredonia. Only a relatively small number of Anglos supported the nascent republic, while the Cherokee majority renounced the alliance of Fields and Hunter with the Edwards brothers. Nevertheless, the Fredonians had grand ambitions. Fredonia's boundaries would include all of Texas, divided into a northern region allocated to "Red People" and southern region for "White People."[11]

Opponents judged the Fredonians by the standards of legitimate expatriation. A diplomatic mission on behalf of Anglo colonists and the Mexican government traveled to Nacogdoches, Texas, in January 1827. The Fredonians flatly refused the government's amnesty and reiterated their view of a tyrannical Mexican government. The rebels' obstinacy was not surprising, the mission reported. "There is scarcely one of the perverse party that has any property; not one slaveholder among them, but many vagabonds and fugitives from justice, who have fled from the United States of the North, and who have so shamefully debased the American character." According to the report, the rebels lacked respectability that came from slave ownership, a value imported from the southern United States, and their behavior seemingly confirmed the fears of American critics of expatriation that lofty ideals about natural rights to move freely throughout the world actually provided cover to criminals. Inhabitants of the DeWitt Colony issued a series of resolutions condemning the Fredonian uprising as the actions of "those of bad character, whom we consider as refugees, and fugitives from justice." They hoped that the Mexican government would not confuse the rebels with the hardworking, "peaceable American emigrants" who had willingly exchanged citizenship in one republic for that in another. Further, the DeWitt colonists reaffirmed "that their great object in leaving their parent country, and migrating hither, was not for the purpose of unsheathing the sword of Insurrection, war, bloodshed, and desolation, but as peaceable and industrious subjects."[12]

By transforming voluntary allegiance from a pragmatic principle into justification for a visionary cause, the Fredonians voided their rights to the body politic. Stephen F. Austin, the region's leading *empresario*, worried that if the Fredonians were not stopped their actions would mar American character in the eyes of Mexican officials. With such valuable cultural currency at stake, could future colonists from the North possibly demonstrate their good morals and intentions as the colonization laws required? Austin did not believe so. He labeled the Fredonians "infatuated madmen" set on sowing disorder and violence, and, according to Austin, it was "our duty as Mexicans, to support and defend the government of our adoption." Although frightening to Anglo elites in Texas, the Fredonian Rebellion proved weak. National troops along with militias from the Austin and DeWitt colonies entered East Texas in pursuit of the rebellion's leaders, brothers Haden and Benjamin W. Edwards. Both escaped to Louisiana and the uprising ended within a few weeks.[13]

Anglo colonists joined Mexican troops to suppress the Fredonian Rebellion because their shared ideas of voluntary allegiance provided a legal framework for military cooperation. The same framework ordered daily life in Mexican Texas throughout the 1820s. Agreement that patriotism was transferable and that patriotic duty was a matter solely of establishing permanent residence and obeying local laws allowed both Anglo migrants to become Mexican citizens according to their understandings of expatriation and Tejano officials to implement state-level colonization policy. National political changes in Mexico beginning in 1830 weakened the legal framework for cooperation between Anglo colonists and Mexican officials, and, to a lesser extent, Anglos and Tejanos. The consensus on voluntary allegiance in Texas was the product of local autonomy allowed by Mexico's Constitution of 1824. Throughout the early 1830s, centralist politicians came to dominate federalist politicians in Congress. This shift culminated in 1835 when Congress, with the support of President Antonio López de Santa Anna, introduced a series of centralist constitutional reforms that significantly altered the Constitution of 1824, including limits on state power. This change intensified divisions between Mexico's northern states, especially the federalist stronghold Coahuila y Texas, and centralist authorities in Mexico City.[14]

As political tensions increased in Texas, Mexican centralists bolstered their own views that allegiance stemmed from race or culture, not solely respect for the law. Juan N. Almonte, a high-ranking Mexican official who led an inspection tour of Texas in 1834, believed that colonists in Texas would clearly prosper by remaining Mexican citizens, however they had acquired attitudes and values in their earlier lives that gave them a natural affinity for the United States. For Almonte, it was highly unlikely that Anglo settlers could become truly patriotic, loyal Mexicans. "It is necessary to understand," Almonte observed, "that compatriotism, similar customs, laws, religion, language, and government under which they have been educated and whose institutions are so familiar to them, can have a great hold on their spirit, and nothing, in their view, could compensate for those advantages." Almonte ultimately warned authorities in Mexico City that "foreigners . . . can never live in harmony with Mexicans" because immigrants are, by nature, self-interested. They emigrate "to improve their fortunes" and acquire land "whether it was under one government or the other," not for love of their new country. "And do we believe," Almonte asked rhetorically, "that the foreigners who will come to Texas will do so only because that territory is Mexican? Certainly not." [15]

Conflicts between federalists and centralists challenged older agreements about the nature of allegiance. Mexican centralists took a cautious view of voluntary allegiance; they were more likely to understand patriotism as a product of common culture. As a result, centralist officials expressed increasingly critical views about Anglo colonization. Although Anglo colonists and Mexican federalists cooperated to challenge centralism, by 1835 Anglo opinion in Texas also fractured over different views of allegiance. Moderate Anglos, eventually labeled "tories" or members of the "peace party," waged the political conflicts of the 1830s according to their standing as loyal Mexican citizens and good expatriates. More radical Anglo colonists also claimed the rights of voluntary allegiance, but as rights that only applied to Anglos. Ironically, then, pro-independence Anglos adopted a view of patriotism not unlike their centralist Mexican opponents. Once that occurred, by early 1836, older forms of Tejano-Anglo cooperation became far more difficult in Texas.[16]

The Law of April 6, 1830, posed the first serious centralist challenge to the principle of voluntary allegiance. The Mexican Congress adopted the law to assert more effective control over Texas. Inspired by recommendations from General Manuel de Mier y Terán, who toured Texas in the late 1820s, the law incorporated centralist reservations about the loyalty of Anglo colonists. Among other provisions, the law prohibited further immigration from the United States and voided unfulfilled *empresario* contracts. Supporters of the law also hoped to attract settlers to Texas whose cultural backgrounds might ensure a sentimental affinity for Mexico, thus confirming a view that patriotism was not entirely transferable. When federalists temporarily returned to power in Mexico City, Congress rescinded its ban on immigration from the United States in 1833.[17]

Despite repeal of a key provision, opposition to the Law of April 6, 1830, appeared in several important public complaints that Anglos issued to the Mexican government during the 1830s. In many instances, Anglos provided their grievances moral standing by appealing to their status as expatriates. They emphasized their previous behavior as law-abiding citizens of their "adopted country," loyal to the Constitution of 1824. Stephen F. Austin turned the logic of the Law of April 6, 1830, upside down. He argued that the prohibition on legal Anglo immigration would do nothing to stem illegal immigration, which brought people to Texas who had no civic incentive to think beyond personal interests and who might even "jeopardize the public tranquility." Moreover, colonization, or legal settlement, actually secured Mexico's northern boundary as the policy originally promised. Thus, Austin concluded, "by opening the door for admission of honest and honorable men of high character and property, the moral influence of such men will correct and direct public opinion, and make the moral tie, as well as that of interest, which does and ought to bind Texas to Mexico indissolubly."[18]

Questions of allegiance became urgent once more in the summer of 1835. Direct attacks on Mexican authority that summer compelled many Anglo settlers to publicly reaffirm their loyalty to Mexico. In June, William B. Travis led an armed force that seized the garrison at Anahuac. Mexican military officers initially responded to Anahuac by attempting to sort out the loyal colonists from the subversives in their midst. Other Anglos defended Travis and his band. In the aftermath of Anahuac, all sides posed questions about the Anglo colonists' true allegiances. Critics often cast the loyalties of Travis and those who seized Anahuac in the darkest tones. They were essentially pirates, since they had behaved without allegiance to a state or a sovereign.

Many Anglo settlers in the region quickly condemned the attack. Residents of Columbia, Mina, and Gonzales issued separate resolutions that shared much in common. Most importantly, they recognized that proof of their Mexican patriotism required them to remain expatriates in good standing. They had no recourse to cultural or ethnic bonds of allegiance, such as Mexican ancestry, birth, language, or even religion. After all, they were voluntary citizens of Mexico. Anglo residents thus disclaimed Travis and his followers by raising the standard of patriotic allegiance that all expatriates valued the most—"a strict adherence to the laws and constitution of the land," as expressed by the citizens of Columbia. The people of Mina affirmed a similar view. According to one of their resolutions, "We feel an entire confidence in the constitution & laws of our adopted country, & will at all times sustain the legal authorities in the exercise of their constitutional duties." Representatives from San Felipe assured Domingo de Ugartechea, the Mexican commander at Béxar, "that the citizens of Texas generally have become adopted citizens of the Mexican Republic from choice, after a full knowledge of the constitution and laws." On their foundation of sturdy Mexican patriotism, the representatives vowed to fulfill their duties as "Mexican citizens, in the enforcement of the laws and promotion of order, and respect for the government and its agents." On the other hand, Travis and his followers forfeited the possibility of remaining Mexican citizens. They were "foreigners," according to a resolution issued by the people of Columbia.[19]

Mexican authorities also addressed violence at Anahuac by distinguishing between loyal expatriates and subversive outsiders with allegiance to nothing but self-interest. From his perspective in Mexico City, the republic's head of foreign affairs, Manuel Diez de Bonilla, reminded Anglo colonists in Texas to remain good expatriates since "on adopting this for their country, subjected themselves to the alternations that, respecting the institutions, the majority of the nation may think fit to agree upon." The situation in Texas had greater urgency for Martín Perfecto de Cos, the commanding general of the Eastern Interior Provinces. He issued several statements during the summer of 1835 regarding Anglo actions in Texas. In a private correspondence to Domingo de Ugartechea, Cos explained that his order to disband Anglo militias in Texas targeted not loyal Mexican citizens, but "foreigners" with "no property save a gun and no occupation save hunting." Cos reiterated this distinction in a general proclamation to the people of Texas. He warned them to expect a military response if they forgot "their duties to the nation which has adopted them as her children" and pushed "forward with a desire to live at their own option without any subjection to the laws." Those Anglos "who are fauthful [*sic*] to their oaths and to the Laws" were obligated, Cos explained in another statement, to assist the Mexican government in punishing "the faithless adventurers who have nothing to risque [*sic*] in a revolucion." Cos included

Travis among the latter category for seeking to mobilize those in Texas "without a home, without moralities or any employment by which to subsist." Claiming to serve the Mexican government, Thomas M. Thompson issued a personal warning to the citizens of Anahuac in July 1835. "Beware!" Thompson exclaimed, "listen not to men who have no home, who have no family who have nothing to loose [*sic*] in case of civil war and who by merely crossing the Sabine, can put themselves out of the power of the Mexican Nation." Instead, Thompson advised the citizens of Anahuac to remain good expatriates: "Occupy yourselves in your daily avocations for the maintenance of your family, have confidence in the General Government and all will yet be well." In their responses to the uprising at Anahuac, Mexican officials from the nation's capital to its frontier relied on the principle of voluntary allegiance to reassure loyal Anglo settlers and punish the disloyal by treating them as subversive outsiders.[20]

Those involved in the attack on Anahuac disputed how their actions were portrayed by other Anglos and Mexican officials. Mexican authorities arrested and imprisoned Anahuac merchant Andrew Briscoe in 1835 for engaging in illegal trade. The attack on Anahuac bought Briscoe's freedom. This, along with Briscoe's existing opposition to Mexican customs policies in Texas, gave him good reason to seek public vindication for Travis and his supporters. Briscoe took special umbrage at claims by the people of Columbia that Anahuac had fallen to a band of foreigners. Rather, Briscoe charged in a letter to the Brazoria *Texas Republican* that "some twenty or twenty-five men were present, of whom but two were strangers or foreigners, and they both own land in the country and intend to become citizens." For Briscoe, the two individuals whose loyalty seemed most dubious were on a path to becoming good Mexican citizens by taking the essential steps of expatriation that supposedly severed prior national allegiances. Protestations of expatriate loyalty thus proved equally meaningful to Briscoe and his Anglo opponents. Moreover, Briscoe's position points to a view that became increasingly important among more radical Anglo settlers. Although colonists claimed their loyalty as Mexican citizens, revolutionary action might be necessary to protect their Mexican liberties from centralist corruption.[21]

Indeed throughout late summer 1835, the public and private statements of Anglos stretched the concept of voluntary allegiance to accommodate stronger claims about their rights in Mexico. Yet even then, the colonists' need to prove their good intentions as expatriates, as voluntary Mexicans, tempered their politics. The San Jacinto Resolutions of August 1835 declared that centralists in Mexico City destroyed the republic's social compact. Whether fueled by popular memory of the American Revolution, or an education in natural rights political philosophy, the Resolutions asserted the Anglo colonists' right to declare independence from Mexico. The people of San Jacinto demurred, however. Declaring independence would open them to charges of "parricidal ingratitude." Rather, "as adopted citizens, we ought to exercise even our absolute rights with some diffidence, and with a peculiar regard to the moral obligations that may rest upon us." A visit to New Orleans and an audience of US citizens put Stephen F. Austin in an insurrectionary mood befitting his eighteen-month detenion in Mexico. Austin wrote forcefully about his desire to see Texas "Americanized" in a series of letters he sent in August 1835. For Austin, Americanization would occur through increased but legal settlement under Mexican law, not an armed invasion. "A gentle breeze shakes off a ripe peach," Austin famously quipped. "All that is now wanting is a great immigration of good and efficient families, this fall and winter. Should we get such an emigration, especially from the western states—all is done—the peach will be ripe." Revolutionary gales were unnecessary while expatriation remained an option.[22]

When representatives of Texas colonists convened for the Consultation of November 1835, Texas was in open rebellion against Mexico but far from ready to declare full independence. The Declaration of the People of Texas, adopted by the Consultation on November 7, betrayed deep political uncertainty about Texas' future. Only a month earlier, the Mexican Congress abolished state governments and put governors under the control of the president. In response to this act, along with previous grievances, the delegates announced that centralists under President Antonio López de Santa Anna had "dissolved the Social Compact" binding Texas to the rest of Mexico. The people of Texas were thus free to assume their "natural rights" and proceed collectively in any way they saw fit. Notions of voluntary allegiance became more powerful amid the deep political uncertainty of the moment.[23]

After they asserted their right to act autonomously, the delegates at the Consultation issued several resolutions. They embedded the concept of voluntary allegiance in two of them. The first declared that Texans had armed themselves against the sitting national government in defense of the liberties granted them by the Constitution of 1824. Anglos interpreted this provision in a variety of ways until Texas declared formal independence in March 1836. The delegates also adopted a resolution designed to gain support for the Texas cause by promising to "reward by donations in land, all who volunteer their services in her present struggle, and receive them as citizens." Under this provision, the revolutionary leadership assumed the powers of naturalization but also validated the principle of voluntary allegiance. The delegates effectively called for expatriates to join the uprising. The November 7 declaration's provisions regarding allegiance to the Constitution of 1824 and its call for volunteers were related efforts to carry forth a rebellion in the most pragmatic way possible. However, these provisions also raised issues that divided Anglo opinion about the meaning of voluntary allegiance.[24]

By recognizing the Constitution of 1824, the Consultation reiterated the claim that Anglos were patriotic, voluntary Mexicans. This position appealed to Anglos who still wanted reconciliation with Mexico by providing an opportunity to form alliances with other Mexicans opposed to centralist policies. In a moment of moderation, Stephen F. Austin argued in December 1835 that Texas colonists should seek alliances with Mexican federalists in defense of the Constitution of 1824. With this position they could preserve their standing as loyal but aggrieved expatriates rather than belligerents in an independent republic. If independence became the Anglos' only demand, then the centralists could easily place the "Texas war on the footing of a national war against foreigners and adventurers whose object is to dismember the Mexican territory." The Consultation thus set a pragmatic course for its dealings with the Mexican government by recognizing a political conceit essential to notions of voluntary allegiance. Patriotism did not require seemingly immutable ethnic, religious, or cultural qualities; it meant simply obeying the Constitution of 1824.[25]

Loyalty to the Constitution of 1824 persisted into 1836. In January, James Kerr authored a strident statement rejecting calls for independence. His position rested on two claims, one practical and the other moral. In practical terms, Kerr argued, Texas could not survive as an independent republic. The financial burdens would be too great, war with Mexico would be persistent, the economy would suffer, and the nation's overall weakness would expose it to the depredations of foreign powers. In short,

Texas needed to remain in Mexico to prosper. Moreover, Kerr argued that Anglo colonists had moral reasons to remain loyal. Anglo colonists had sworn loyalty oaths in order to become Mexican citizens, thereby expatriating themselves from the United States. The current political crisis elevated the colonists' obligations to honor their oaths. A threatened nation needed loyal citizens. Anglo colonists should support their fellow Mexican citizens, the federalist insurgents fighting to defend the Constitution of 1824 in other parts of the Republic. Kerr warned Anglos in Texas not to "forget your duty as adopted citizens of Mexico." By abandoning their allegiance to Mexico, "christians and freeman" would treat the Texans "as a people not to be trusted, as having no respect for oaths, or compacts, or honor." Moreover, Kerr advised his fellow colonists that their actions had a global audience. Observers the world over were watching "your movements for the purpose of determining whether or not you have been governed by the selfish desire of promoting your own individual views, and robbing Mexico of her lands; or been influenced by the high, and laudable, and patriotic feelings, inducing a peril of life and property in defence of liberty and the Constitution of 1824." Thus for Kerr, Anglos had no choice but to fulfill their obligations as expatriates. Although some Anglos such as Kerr used the principle of voluntary allegiance in political arguments for continued loyalty to Mexico, others used it to justify more radical steps.[26]

Anglos who demanded full Texas independence in early 1836 also recognized the colonists' standing as expatriates. Members of the Committee of Vigilance and Public Safety from San Augustine acknowledged their emigration to Texas under Mexico's colonization laws, but attributed their success at building communities in the "uninhabited wilderness" to "individual enterprise, entirely unaided by succors of any kind, from the government." This statement contained no accolades to their adopted country or their duties as voluntary citizens. Rather, the authors indicted the Mexican government for its efforts to abolish slavery and passage of the Law of April 6, 1830. As a result, "Families and nearest ties of kindred and friendship were thus severed." William H. Wharton developed a similar argument in a series of newspaper articles written under the pseudonym "Curtius." He also found the Law of April 6, 1830, highly egregious even though it was consistent with Article 6 of the 1825 Coahuila y Texas colonization law, which reserved the government's prerogative to prohibit future immigration into the province. By forbidding only "North Americans" entrance into Texas, this law, Wharton exclaimed, "was enough to blast all of our hopes, and dishearten all of our enterprise." The law raised the frightening prospect that the Anglo colonists would "be cut off forever from the society of fathers and friends in the United States of the North." The San Augustine committee and Wharton interpreted the history of Anglo colonization in Texas in such a way to minimize the depth of their obligations as Mexican citizens.[27]

In denying their loyalty to Mexico, the San Augustine committee members and Wharton advanced an idea of patriotic allegiance that differed widely from the views of more moderate Anglos. The San Augustine Address completely elided Mexican Texas' complex politics. It ignored divisions between federalists and centralists as well as reference to the Tejano elites who made Anglo colonization possible during the 1820s. Instead, the authors derided all Mexicans. "The anglo Americans and the Mexicans, if not primitively a different people, habit, education, and religion, have made them essentially so. The two people cannot mingle together." For these reasons, the authors concluded, so "long as the people of Texas belong to the Mexican nation, their interests will be jeopardized, and their prosperity cramped." Wharton agreed, since "none of those ties which are necessary to bind a people together and make them one, existed between the colonists and Mexicans." Among the many intractable differences between the two peoples, several were cultural. Wharton believed that the colonists and Mexicans shared "no identity of pursuits, habits, manners, education, language or religion." The Anglos could not become voluntary Mexicans because respect for the law was a weak cohesive for people divided by vast cultural differences. Members of the San Augustine Committee and Wharton all concluded that Anglos migrated to Texas in order to strengthen the region's connections to the United States. In their estimation, Anglo colonists did not so much quit the United States for Texas as hope to re-create a familiar society there. They wanted to prepare the way for family and friends to follow, thereby populating Texas with like people. Once the Mexican government took steps to deny the colonists' ambitions, independence was their only recourse.[28]

The opinions of Anglo military leaders were also divided about the meaning of voluntary allegiance. Francis W. Johnson, the Anglo commander of Béxar, still maintained in early 1836 that the rebellion was a defense of the Constitution of 1824 and Texas' integral place as Mexican province. His call to arms in behalf of the volunteer army drew upon a concept of allegiance predicated on law-abiding citizens and commitment to principles of liberty. Anyone, in Johnson's view, could become loyal soldiers in the struggle to protect the Texans' Mexican liberties. This included Tejanos. As Johnson proclaimed, the people of Texas "invite into their ranks all friends to freedom, of whatever name or nation." The authors of a military report issued only a month earlier viewed the conflict in starkly different terms. Texans were in a battle for independence. After all, "The Mexican people and the Anglo-Americans in Texas never can be one and the same people. A civil compact can never bind together long people who differ so widely in their pursuits, their religion, their Languages and their ideas of civil liberty." From this perspective, patriotic allegiance to the Texas cause could only come from those bound to the Anglo colonists by blood and culture. A group of volunteers from the United States that arrived in February 1836 thus seemed fully justified in demanding local voting rights by "claiming Texas as our adopted country."[29]

The US volunteers who arrived in early 1836 entered Texas in response to the Consultation's request for foreign support from November 1835. Over the course of the Texas rebellion, over 3,500 men fought on the Texas side. Of this total force, nearly 1,000 were US volunteers. Anglo-Texans comprised the majority of the remaining forces along with roughly 138 Tejanos, who fought primarily under Tejano officers such as Juan N. Seguín. The vast majority of Anglos and Tejanos avoided participating in the conflict altogether. The composition of Texas' revolutionary army highlights the far-reaching consequences of the Consultation's decision to offer foreign volunteers citizenship. Despite the provision's universal language, the majority of volunteers came from the United States, ultimately comprising 40 percent of the total fighting force. Moreover, an additional 34 percent of the Texan army had immigrated to Texas no more than five years earlier. The relative newcomers and US volunteers who comprised such a large proportion of the fighting force exercised a strong influence over changing ideas of allegiance as the war progressed. For many Anglos who fought in the Texas rebellion, a notion that they were voluntary Mexicans had a weak to nonexistent hold on their understanding of the larger conflict. As the new volunteers declared in February 1836, they were voluntary Texans instead. George C. Childress's opinions suggest how volunteer Texans understood the cause they joined. Childress visited Texas for the first time in late 1834 and returned in December 1835. For him, any idea that Mexico was the colonists' adopted country seemed meaningless. Texas colonists should have declared their independence from the outset rather than maintaining their loyalty. As Childress explained to Sam Houston, "The contest for the Constitution of 1824 was, you know, but a mere *pretence* from the beginning," part of a deeply misguided hope for assistance from other parts of Mexico, from people who "are but a semi-civilized set, unfit to be free and incapable of self government." For a voluntary Texan, patriotism meant allegiance to people with ties of blood and culture to the United States, not support for a vanished political ideal such as loyalty to the Constitution of 1824.[30]

Anglos began to seek support from the United States even before the Consultation convened. In late October 1835, Richard R. Royall issued what might be called an expatriate's lament in pursuit of US support for a quasi-independent Texas. "We have wandered where danger and tyranny threaten us," pled Royall. Although Anglo colonists had "expatriated themselves from their native country, torn themselves from connexions dear, given up the conveniences and luxuries of life, and encountered for years back toils and dangers and privations of every sort," the centralist-dominated government of Mexico abolished the Constitution of 1824 that had secured their liberties as Mexican citizens. Royall reminded citizens of the United States that "You are united to us by all the sacred ties that can bind one people to another . . . we are alients [*sic*] to you only in country; our principles both moral and political are the same—our interest is one, and we require and ask your aid." Views such as Royall's became more pronounced once US volunteers began arriving in response to the Consultation's policy for recruiting them.[31]

The Consultation appointed a diplomatic mission to stoke support for Texas in the United States. The diplomatic delegation consisted of William H. Wharton, Branch T. Archer, and Texas' most prominent Anglo, Stephen F. Austin. The Texas diplomats left for the United States in late December 1835 and remained there until June 1836. During their six-month mission, they stopped in major western cities including New Orleans, Louisville, Nashville, and Cincinnati. They also fanned north and south along the East Coast. Austin drummed the Texas cause from Baltimore to New York. Archer sought support in Richmond, Virginia.

TEXAS!!

Emigrants who are desirious of assisting Texas at this important crisis of her affairs may have a free passage and equipments, by applying at the

NEW-YORK and PHILADELPHIA HOTEL,

On the Old Levee, near the Blue Stores.

Now is the time to ensure a fortune in Land: To all who remain in Texas during the War will be allowed 1280 Acres.

To all who remain Six Months, 640 Acres.

To all who remain Three Months, 320 Acres.

And as Colonists, 4600 Acres for a family and 1470 Acres for a Single Man.

New Orleans, April 23d, 1836.

FIGURE 1. TEXAS!! Courtesy Dolph Briscoe Center for American History, University of Texas at Austin

Wharton remained in Washington, DC, to measure official US opinion about events in Texas. The Consultation instructed the diplomats to muster money and men—by contracting loans, accepting donations, and recruiting volunteers. Texas' diplomatic delegation had limited success, yet enthusiasm for Texas in the United States certainly made their work less onerous.[32]

Observers in the United States quickly learned about growing political unrest in Texas. Segments of the US population just as quickly organized public meetings, donated money, and formed volunteer units that set off for Texas. The Texas diplomats attended these meetings whenever possible. New Orleans and Mobile, Alabama, hosted the earliest and some of the largest public gatherings. Texas boosters in the rest of the nation followed suit. Texas volunteers eventually organized themselves throughout the South and West, and as far north as New York and Boston. In an article for the New York press, a writer using the pseudonym "Citizen of New Orleans" explained the background and aims of the public meeting in his city. Although the Anglo colonists had "expatriated themselves to better their condition, and secure a patrimony for their children," recent developments in Mexican politics threatened to destroy the liberties that colonists once enjoyed. At such a dire moment in Texas, efforts to "prevent United States citizens from volunteering to assist their brethren and blood" were "Anti-American." Americans could not ignore the Texans' plight. According to a somewhat exaggerated New York newspaper report from autumn 1835, a "Very considerable number of men are leaving various parts of our country for Texas, taking with them the arms and munitions necessary for war. Some hundreds will leave the Atlantic coast within ten days, and a still greater number will probably go from the West."[33]

Despite passionate popular support, the Texas diplomats and the organizers of public meetings engaged in a legally dubious pursuit. Under an 1818 law adopted by the US Congress, it was illegal for citizens in the United States to volunteer or recruit for military service against a foreign power at peace with the United States; to set out on military expeditions from US territory; or to organize or provide support to any entity or group at war with a peaceful nation. Foreigners were also prohibited from recruiting US citizens for conflicts against peaceful nations. In 1835, Mexico and the United States were at peace, as recently affirmed in the 1828 Treaty of Limits. Under this agreement, the two republics confirmed the location of their international border as that set by the United States and Spain in 1819. Providing material support to the rebellious Texans potentially violated domestic and international law.[34]

US and Mexican officials responded to Texas enthusiasm in the United States by stressing its potential illegality. Strong public support for the Texas rebellion in New Orleans prompted US Secretary of State John Forsyth's instructions to Henry Carleton, the US Attorney for the Eastern District of Louisiana. Should the Texas conflict intensify, Forsyth predicted, "some of our citizens may form their connexion with the settlers there, and from their love of enterprise and desire of change, be induced to forget their duty to their own Government and its obligations to foreign Powers." According to Forsyth, the 1818 law required all US citizens to "abstain, under every temptation, from intermeddling with the domestic disputes of other nations." Forsyth ordered Carleton to prosecute any US citizen who violated their nation's treaty with Mexico by going to Texas with arms or otherwise supporting the rebellion. Louisiana governor

Edward D. White issued a public proclamation in November declaring that any US citizen who crossed into Mexico to aid the rebellion invited prosecution for violating the 1818 Congressional act.[35]

Officials in Mexico City protested that the Texas insurgency had already violated US and international law. José María Ortiz Monasterio, Mexico's foreign minister, wrote to Forsyth that the Texas uprising would not have erupted without moral, military, and financial support from sympathizers in New Orleans. Indeed, Monasterio claimed that foreign influence fomented Anglo disloyalty: "The Mexican colonists—for they are so and can be nothing else, since they have renounced their original nationality—would never dare to violate so openly their duties towards their adopted country, had they not the assurance that prompt and efficacious succors would be given them along their frontiers. These succors are furnished by American speculators who regard solely their own interest." Texas supporters in New Orleans ignored the basic legal fact that Anglo-Texans had expatriated themselves, that they were no longer citizens of the United States, Monasterio argued. Moreover, he accused the Texas supporters in New Orleans of merely claiming cultural allegiance to their supposed brethren in Texas in order to justify self-serving interference in Mexico's domestic affairs. Those in New Orleans sought "to give a color of American nationality to what is in fact a mere speculation of different adventurers of all kinds."[36]

By December 1835, centralist Mexican officials adopted strong measures against anybody from the United States who entered Mexico to support the rebellion in Texas. Secretary of War José María Tornel described such people as "speculators and adventurers" whose incursions into Mexico violated US laws. Tornel believed that US officials condemned the actions of individuals who entered Mexico illegally and would prosecute them if possible. There was precedent for this view. When armed US citizens attempted to foment rebellion in Texas years earlier, dominant opinion in Washington, DC, held that such individuals "forfeit the distinction of citizens," indeed "they denationalize themselves" by taking arms against a government at peace with the United States. Yet Tornel also advised Mexican authorities to take action. The government must, Tornel declared, treat and punish all foreigners who enter Mexico "armed and for the purpose of attacking our territory . . . as pirates, since they are not subjects of any nation at war with the republic nor do they militate under any recognized flag." From Tornel's point of view, and likely many in the US capital as well, the Texas insurgents fulfilled the worst fears of those critics who challenged notions of voluntary allegiance from the late eighteenth century onward.[37]

The national governments of the United States and Mexico converged on the opinion that Anglo colonists had expatriated themselves, thereby becoming Mexican citizens. This was a useful diplomatic position for both sides. It allowed officials in both countries to treat the Texas rebellion as a civil war. Federal officials in the United States could thus justify their country's neutrality. After all, by recognizing the legality of expatriation, they expected Anglo settlers in Mexico to behave as patriotic citizens who obeyed the laws of their adopted country. Those who did not should expect the Mexican government to punish them. The Mexican government also expected Anglo colonists to behave like law-abiding adopted citizens. By characterizing the rebellion as a group of Anglo settlers stirred to disloyalty by foreigners from the United States, Mexican officials felt confident that they could attempt to crush the domestic uprising while still expecting the US government to respect Mexico's national sovereignty.

Popular opinion in the United States divided over the legality of supporting the Texas colonists. Critics of US support largely agreed that aid to the Texas rebels in money, munitions, or volunteers violated international and domestic laws. Editors at two New England journals criticized resolutions in favor of the Texas revolutionaries adopted at the large public meeting in New Orleans. The editor of the *Connecticut Courant* argued that the citizens of New Orleans had "an evident design of waging war against a nation with which the United States are at peace." This position was "not only unauthorized, but absolutely illegal, and at war alike with the law of nations, and the spirit of the treaty existing between" Mexico and the United States. In a subsequent issue of the *Connecticut Courant*, the same editor reprinted parts of the 1818 Congressional act that Texas volunteers and supporters supposedly violated. The editor of the *Farmer's Cabinet* in Amherst, New Hampshire, admitted that although "the American residents of Texas are entitled to our sympathies, we cannot legally or justly engage in any warlike movements in their behalf without violating the treaty existing between the two nations." Those US citizens eager to volunteer under the mantle of shared political principles and lofty rights had suspect motivations. "They are not all Lafayettes who are such outwardly and professedly," concluded the *Cabinet*'s cynical editor. An article in the *New York Advertiser* described the Anglo-Texans' legal status in terms very similar to those used by Monasterio. Anglo-Texans should not expect support from the United States because they had severed their claims to protection by becoming Mexican citizens. "We hope, and trust, that our government will not involve themselves, or the nation in this controversy," the author pled. "Those inhabitants of Texas were once citizens of this country, voluntarily withdrew from their place, and put themselves under foreign jurisdiction. On them, of course, the consequence will fall, let them be favorable or otherwise." US critics of involvement in Texas affairs thus put their understanding of voluntary allegiance at the center of their arguments. It was an absolute change to the legal status of Anglo colonists—they had become Mexican citizens—so the people of the United States had no obligation to help them. Patriotic sympathy was undeniable but the law of nations was absolute. The first should be recognized but the latter could not be violated.[38]

In light of official and popular condemnations, some US citizens otherwise eager to volunteer in Texas hesitated from concerns about violating the law. New Yorker H. Meigs wrote favorably to Stephen F. Austin about armed resistance against the Mexican government. Yet he declined to become directly involved. "[B]y the Law of Nations, by Treaty with Mexico we cannot yet interfere," Meigs lamented. Near the rebellion's end, Stuart Perry of New Orleans celebrated growing popular opinion in favor of the Texas cause in the United States, but he admitted that "there has been much apathy and enmity here—people were afraid of prosecutions by the U. States." The Texas Declaration of Independence did not remove reservations about volunteering in Texas, especially if the US government did not recognize the new republic. As George C. Childress explained to David Burnet in a letter from Nashville, "Many persons, who now feel scruples volunteering to take part in the internal conflicts of a foreign country, would freely do so if the independence of the party with which they sympathize was recognized by the Government of their own."[39]

Texas supporters in the United States sought ways to provide assistance without violating the law. To some extent this was a moot concern by November 1835. That month, judges in the United States District Court for the Southern District of New York ruled that pro-Texas meetings and volunteer efforts organized in New York City did not violate the 1818 law. Yet pro-Texas forces in the United States still pursued their ambitions cautiously. The concept of voluntary allegiance provided them legal cover. It allowed them to honor patriotic sympathy with Anglo-Texans while opening a legal detour around the Congressional act of 1818 and US treaty obligations with Mexico. A writer in the New York press supported the rebellion and encouraged US citizens to participate. Indeed, it was "natural that the resistance of the settlers should be supported and maintained by thousands, not by the Government of the United States, but by thousands of individual American citizens." The contributor to another paper declared that "It would be a lasting stigma upon the US to suffer the tyrant *Santa Anna* to overrun with slaughter and ruin their brethren in Texas." However, this author clarified the nature of US support: "We do not mean that the Government need interfere—but volunteers!—volunteers! shoulder your rifles and march to Texas!" The *New Orleans Bee* called for "emigrant volunteers." In each of these instances, Texas supporters suggested an answer to legal doubts about volunteering. As free individuals, US citizens could migrate as they pleased; as "emigrants," they exercised their rights to change citizenship and allegiance. Since the United States was and would likely remain at peace with Mexico, volunteers to the Texas cause had good reason to turn concepts of voluntary allegiance and expatriation in their favor. If individuals chose to join the Texas fight and did so by abandoning their US citizenship, then they were no longer open to charges of violating US law.[40]

Proposals adopted during public meetings for Texas suggested that US volunteers exercised their right to expatriation by joining the Texas uprising. At the large New Orleans gathering, participants resolved to "aid and support" the Texas rebels "by every means in our power, consistent with duties we owe to our own government, to save them from the tyrant's military rule." Supporters in Nashville issued a public call for volunteers. However they noted that the "government of the U. States, as a government, is prohibited by the laws and policy of nations, from interfering in the internal conflicts of a foreign country, whatever be the merits of the controversy. If, therefore, they [Texans] are to receive any assistance from the people of the United States, it must be from them as individuals." In both instances, American citizens could abide by US law but still join the Texas war so long as they proceeded to Mexico and chose to grant their allegiance to Texas' provisional government once they crossed the border separating Mexico from the United States.[41]

Although the Texas Revolution effectively ended following Santa Anna's defeat at the Battle of San Jacinto in April 1836, support for the Texas cause remained strong in parts of the United States. In June 1836, a group of Nashville citizens petitioned Congress to recognize Texas independence. Yet regardless of congressional action, Texas "will draw from these States the means of conquering her enemy," the petitioners declared. This included money, arms, and most importantly, volunteers. As the petitioners asserted, "Every man in the Union has the undoubted right to emigrate to Texas if he chooses." This was especially important since the petitioners believed the situation in Texas remained dire. They accused the Mexican government of "savage cruelty" for its military actions at the Alamo and Goliad. In the wake of these events, "treaties are as cobwebs in the way of the torrent of popular opinion and will." The conflict in Texas thus was supported in the United States "as if the war had been our own. . . . [O]ur people felt all legal and moral obligations cancelled, and viewed the Mexicans as they did pirates on the seas—enemies to all mankind."[42]

Volunteers to Texas promised to expatriate themselves before joining the rebellion. Sydney S. Callender, a printer and occasional editor of the *Lafayette Gazette*, obtained a letter of introduction from L. R. Kenny of New Orleans to Stephen F. Austin. Kenny assured Austin of Callender's mettle. "Sympathizing in your Cause," Kenny announced, "he has determined to make Texas his adopted Country and to fight in her defence." On a single January day in 1836, over seventy volunteers from the United States swore an oath before Nacogdoches judge John Forbes that effectively dissolved citizenship in, and allegiance to, the United States, at least according to common understandings of the right to expatriation. Those who took the oath swore, in part, to "bear true allegiance to the provisional Government of Texas, or any future Government that may be hereafter declared."[43]

The revolutionary leadership in Texas adopted policies to welcome volunteers as expatriates. Sam Houston, as the commanding general of the Texas revolutionary army, quickly incorporated a notion of voluntary allegiance into his orders for recruiting volunteers. Houston reminded his recruiting officer Amasa Turner to "advise that all forces designed for Texas associate as emigrants." In another instance, Houston ordered a

Texas agent to visit New Orleans with the goal of "Recruiting 'Emigrants' for Texas." So it is unsurprising that authorities in Nacogdoches were well prepared to administer mass oaths of allegiance in early 1836. A month earlier, Houston had sent Captain Isaac W. Burton to the Sabine region to establish a "recruiting station." Houston supplied Burton, and presumably Nacogdoches officials as well, with blank enlistment forms to greet all volunteers who crossed into Texas. The enlistment forms contained the oath of allegiance, thus transforming these documents into citizenship papers and evidence of naturalization. Under this system, volunteers were considered "emigrants" to avoid prosecution in the United States, but they participated in a process of expatriation that had existed under American law since the late eighteenth century.[44]

As it transitioned from war to peace, the Republic of Texas incorporated the concept of voluntary allegiance into its own policy for populating the nation. The republic's constitution codified what might be called white man's expatriation. Section six of the General Provisions offered citizenship to any "free white" person who emigrated to Texas, established permanent residence and their good character, and swore a loyalty oath to the Constitution and the republic. The constitution allowed emigrants from the United States to bring their slaves into Texas, but free persons of "African descent, either in whole or in part," could emigrate to Texas only under special permission from Congress. Authorities in the Republic of Texas thus embraced voluntary citizenship as a principle to attract settlers provided they had the racial, and presumably, cultural qualities necessary for loyalty. When Asa Brigham, now treasurer of the Texas Republic, wrote his sister in Massachusetts in 1837, he boasted that "Emigration flows in rapidly, the country is improving beyond account."

Tejanos had good reason to remain skeptical about that aspect of Texas' revolutionary settlement celebrated by Brigham. In addition to the ordinary Tejanos who fought during the rebellion, prominent Tejanos José Antonio Navarro and Francisco Ruiz signed the Texas Declaration of Independence and were later elected to Congress. Tejanos participated in the rebellion and were also recognized as citizens of the republic after independence. Nevertheless, the voluntary Texans described in Brigham's letter were helping to create a society in which the terms of patriotic allegiance would prove far more exclusive than what had existed in Texas during the Mexican period.[45]

THE CONCLUSION OF THE TEXAS rebellion brought fundamental change to the meaning of voluntary allegiance in Texas. Throughout the Mexican period, Anglo colonists became, at least nominally, voluntary Mexicans. Soon after the rebellion started, Anglos, newcomers and some of longer residence as well, began to understand themselves as voluntary Texans. This transition from voluntary Mexicans to voluntary Texans nicely summarizes central themes in the history of Mexican Texas from 1821 through 1836. Voluntary allegiance was an important principle in creating the intellectual, political, and legal conditions in which Anglo colonization occurred. It was also a principle that influenced the choices of participants on both sides of the conflict, so it also affected the origins and course of the Texas rebellion.

Exploring the history of voluntary allegiance in Texas thus reveals important connections between life in the region before, during, and after the rebellion. This focus places developments in Mexican Texas in a larger context shaped by earlier political revolutions and international law without treating these developments as simply the prelude to Texas independence and eventually statehood. The Texas Revolution, like all events, was deeply contingent. Among its alternative outcomes, one is especially resonant. Voluntary allegiance was a powerful legal concept in Mexican Texas because it stemmed from political conditions common to the United States and Mexico. Had this principle persisted, the later history of the US-Mexico border might have been shaped much more forcefully by assumptions that individuals have fundamental rights to move freely across international boundaries.

NOTES

1. Asa Brigham to Brothers and Sisters, February 28, 1832. Asa Brigham Papers, 1832–1837, Dolph Briscoe Center for American History, The University of Texas at Austin. See also, L. W. Kemp, "Asa Brigham," *Handbook of Texas Online* (http://www.tshaonline.org/handbook/online/articles/fbr49), accessed August 14, 2013. Published by the Texas State Historical Association.

2. On the population of Mexican Texas circa 1836, see David J. Weber, *The Mexican Frontier, 1821–1836: The American Southwest Under Mexico* (Albuquerque: University of New Mexico Press, 1982), 177.

3. Thomas Jefferson, *A Summary View of the Rights of British America* (Williamsburg, 1774), 6.

4. Tamar Herzog, *Defining Nations: Immigrants and Citizens in Early Modern Spain and Spanish America* (New Haven: Yale University Press, 2003), 198, 73–75, and 118. Feijóo y Montenegro quoted in ibid., 74.

5. *New York Time Piece,* January 24, 1798.

6. *Political Observatory*, May 30, 1806; *Gazette of the United States*, December 20, 1799; and *The Charge Delivered to the Grand Jury* (Baltimore, 1813), 10–11. On Luther Martin's defense of Aaron Burr, see Nancy Isenberg, *Fallen Founder: The Life of Aaron Burr* (New York: Viking, 2007), 339–62.

7. For the Virginia and Kentucky statutes, see, respectively, "An act declaring who shall be deemed citizens of this commonwealth," May 1779, in William Waller Hening, *The Statutes at Large; Being a Collection of all the Laws of Virginia, from the First Session of the Legislature, in the Year 1619* (Richmond, 1822), 129 and *The Statute Law of Kentucky,* ed. William Littell (Frankfort, 1809–1819), 2: 580. On "expatriation" and "emigration" as synonyms, see James Kent, *Commentaries on American Law,* (Boston, 1826–30), 1: 49.

8. "General Law of Colonization, August 18, 1824," Article 1 and "Law of Colonization of the State of Coahuila and Texas, March 24, 1825," in ed. H. P. N. Gammel, *The Laws of Texas, 1822–1897* (Austin, 1898), 1: 97–98 and "Law of Colonization of the State of Coahuila and Texas, March 24, 1825," ibid., 99–106.

9. On the role of voluntary allegiance and patriotism in the Spanish borderlands during the late eighteenth century, see Sylvia L. Hilton, "Loyalty and Patriotism on North American Frontiers: Being and Becoming Spanish in the Mississippi Valley, 1776–1803" in *Nexus of Empire: Negotiating Loyalty and Identity in the Revolutionary Borderlands, 1760s-1820s*, ed. Gene Allen Smith and Sylvia L. Hilton (Gainesville: University of Florida Press, 2010), 8–36. Carondelet and Wilkinson quoted in, respectively, Hilton, 12 and 14. For a detailed study of the relationship between expatriation and colonization in Mexican Texas during the 1820s, see Eric R. Schlereth, "Privileges of Locomotion: Expatriation and the Politics of Southwestern Border Crossing," *Journal of American History* 100 (March 2014): 999–1020.

10. Francisco Ruiz quoted in Weber, *Mexican Frontier, 1821–1846*, 158; Galveston Bay and Texas Land Company, *Address to the Reader of the Documents Relating to the Galveston Bay and Texas Land Company* (New York, 1831) 3–5, 32; and Robert Owen, "Memorial to the republic of Mexico" in *Robert Owen's opening speech, and his reply to the Rev. Alex. Campbell, in the recent public discussion in Cincinnati* (Cincinnati, 1829), 178 and 181.

11. Andrés Reséndez, *Changing National Identities at the Frontier: Texas and New Mexico, 1800–1850* (Cambridge: Cambridge University Press, 2005), 40–45.

12. Richard Ellis, James Cummins, and James Kerr, "Report on the Rebellion," January 22, 1827 in "The Fredonian Rebellion Index," http://www.tamu.edu/ccbn/dewitt/fredonian3.htm and Dewitt Colony Resolution in Ethel Zivley Rather, "De Witt's Colony," *Bulletin of the University of Texas* 51 (Jan. 15, 1905), 18–19.

13. Stephen F. Austin to the Colonists of Victoria District, January 1, 1827, in Frank W. Johnson, *A History of Texas and Texans,* ed. Eugene C. Barker, (Chicago, 1916), 39–41.

14. Reséndez, *Changing National Identities at the Frontier*, 147–53.

15. Juan N. Almonte, *Almonte's Texas: Juan N. Almonte's 1834 Inspection, Secret Report & Role in the 1836 Campaign*, ed. Jack Jackson, trans. John Wheat (Austin: Texas State Historical Association, 2003), 214 and 223–24.

16. On centralist notions of allegiance, see Reséndez, *Changing National Identities at the Frontier*, 170.

17. Reséndez, *Changing National Identities at the Frontier*, 146–49.

18. Stephen F. Austin, untitled argument against the Law of April 6, 1830, in Independence Resolutions and Consultations Index: http://www.tamu.edu/ccbn/dewitt/consultations1.htm.

19. Columbia Citizens to the Citizens of Brazos, July 15, 1835, in ed. John H. Jenkins, *The Papers of the Texas Revolution, 1835–1836* (Austin: Presidial Press, 1973) 1:242 (hereafter cited as *PTR*); Mina Resolutions, July 4, 1835, *PTR* 1:191–92; Representatives of Brazos, San Felipe to the Commander at Bexar, July 17, 1835, *PTR* 1:250; and Columbia Meeting, June 28, 1835, *PTR* 1:169–71. See also, Gonzales Meeting, July 7, 1835, *PTR* 1:214–16 and Columbia Statement to delegates at San Felipe, July 14, 1835, *PTR* 1:240.

20. Manuel Diez de Bonilla to the Municipality of Gonzales, August 5, 1835, *PTR* 1:310; Martín Perfecto de Cos to Domingo de Ugartechea, July 7, 1835, *PTR* 1:214; Cos, Address to the Public in Texas, July 5, 1835, *PTR* 1:203; Cos to the Political Chief of Brazos, August 1, 1835, *PTR* 1:297–98; Cos, July 12, 1835, *PTR* 1:232–33; and Thomas M. Thompson to the Citizens of Anahuac, July 26, 1835, *PTR* 1:278–79.

21. *Texas Republican*, July 11, 1835.

22. San Jacinto Resolutions, August 8, 1835, *PTR* 1:318–20 and Stephen F. Austin to Mary Austin Holley, August 21, 1835, *PTR* 1:359–60. See also, Austin to H. Meigs, August 22, 1835, *PTR* 1:362–63.

23. "Declaration of the People of Texas," November 7, 1835, *PTR* 2:346–47.

24. Ibid., 2:346–47.

25. Stephen F. Austin to the Provisional Government, December 2, 1835, *PTR* 3:70–72.

26. James Kerr to the People of Texas, January 4, 1836, *PTR* 3:415–21.

27. San Augustine Address from the Committee of Vigilance and Public

Safety, December 22, 1835, *PTR* 3:287–92 and [William H. Wharton] "Curtius," *Texas. A Brief Account of the Origin, Progress, and Present State of the Colonial Settlement of Texas*, *PTR* 9:240–41.

28. San Augustine Address from the Committee of Vigilance and Public Safety, December 22, 1835, *PTR* 3:287–92 and [William H. Wharton] "Curtius," *Texas. A Brief Account of the Origin, Progress, and Present State of the Colonial Settlement of Texas*, *PTR* 9:239–40.

29. Proclamation of the Federal Volunteer Army of Texas, January 10, 1836, *PTR* 3:467; Military Affairs Committee Report, December 6, 1835, *PTR* 3:102–04; and Volunteers to the Convention, February 1836, *PTR* 4:473–74.

30. On the composition of the Army of the Texas Revolution, see Paul D. Lack, *The Texas Revolutionary Experience: A Political and Social History, 1835–1836* (College Station: Texas A&M University Press, 1992), 132–33. On Tejano participation, see Raúl A. Ramos *Beyond the Alamo: Forging Mexican Ethnicity in San Antonio, 1821–1861* (Chapel Hill: University of North Carolina Press, 2008), 149–53. George C. Childress to Sam Houston, February 13, 1836, *PTR* 4:322. On Childress' background, see Joe E. Ericson, "Childress, George Campbell," *Handbook of Texas Online* (http://www.tshaonline.org/handbook/online/articles/fch28), accessed August 14, 2013.

31. R.R. Royall to Citizens of the United States of the North, October 26, 1835, *PTR* 2:107–08.

32. Gregg Cantrell, *Stephen F. Austin: Empresario of Texas* (New Haven: Yale University Press, 1999), 343 and 334.

33. *Farmer's Cabinet*, November 13, 1835; "A Citizen of New Orleans," *New York Times* reprinted in *Richmond Enquirer*, November 13, 1835; and *Journal of Commerce* (N.Y.) quoted in *Richmond Enquirer*, November 6, 1835.

34. For the April 20, 1818 act, see "An Act in addition to the 'Act for the punishment of certain crimes against the United States,' and to repeal the acts therein mentioned" in ed. Richard Peters, *The Public Statutes at Large of the United States of America* (Boston, 1846), 3:447–50.

35. John Forsyth to Henry Carleton, October 27, 1835, *PTR* 2:234–35 and Edward D. White to the Public, November 13, 1835, *PTR* 2:404–05.

36. José María Ortiz Monasterio to John Forsyth, November 19, 1835, *PTR* 2:468–69.

37. *Daily National Intelligencer*, July 17, 1819, quoted in Ed Bradley, "Fighting for Texas: Filibuster James Long, the Adams-Onís Treaty, and the Monroe Administration," *Southwestern Historical Quarterly* 102 (Jan. 1999): 339 and *The Mexican Side of the Texan Revolution*, 2nd ed., trans. Carlos E. Castañeda (Austin: Graphic Ideas Incorporated, 1970), 55–56.

38. *Connecticut Courant,* November 2, 1835, and November 16, 1835.

Farmer's Cabinet, November 6, 1835, and November 20, 1835. *New York Advertiser* quoted in *Farmer's Cabinet*, November 6, 1835.

39. H. Meigs to Stephen F. Austin, November 15, 1835, *PTR* 2:424; Stuart Perry to David G. Burnet, April 16, 1836, *PTR* 5:490; and George C. Childress to David G. Burnet, April 18, 1836, *PTR* 5:501.

40. For the District Court opinion from the Southern District of New York, see *Richmond Enquirer,* November 20, 1835; *New Hampshire Sentinel,* November 19, 1835; *Richmond Enquirer*, October 23, 1835; and *New Orleans Bee* quoted in *Richmond Enquirer,* December 19, 1835.

41. New Orleans Meeting, October 13, 1835, *PTR* 2:116 and Nashville Meeting Address, November 17, 1835, PTR 3:56.

42. "Proceedings of a Meeting of the Citizens of Nashville, Tenn. in Favor of Recognising the Independence of Texas" in *Public Documents Printed by Order of the Senate of the United States, First Session of the Twenty-Fourth Congress* (Washington, DC: 1836), 6: document 418, page 4.

43. L.R. Kenny to Stephen F. Austin, October 20, 1835, *PTR* 2:171 and Voluntary Auxiliary Corps enlistees, January 14, 1836, *PTR* 4:13–14.

44. Sam Houston to Amasa Turner, December 5, 1835, *PTR* 3:73; Sam Houston to P.S. Wyatt, December 28, 1835, *PTR* 3:351; and Sam Houston to Isaac W. Burton, December 19, 1835, *PTR* 3:258.

45. Constitution of the Republic of Texas, *PTR* 5:113. Asa Brigham to Sister, April 4, 1837. Asa Brigham Papers, 1832–1837, Dolph Briscoe Center for American History, The University of Texas at Austin. The changing meaning of voluntary allegiance in the Texas republic provides an additional way to frame the problem of race in the Texas Revolution. Specifically, the widening gap between citizenship as a formal legal identity and patriotism as a cultural expression following independence suggests the role of legal ideas in bringing about racial tensions between Tejanos and Anglos. For two recent historiographic positions on the problem of race in the Texas Revolution, see Ramos, *Beyond the Alamo*, 155, and James E. Crisp, "Race, Revolution, and the Texas Republic: Toward a Reinterpretation" in ed. Joseph G. Dawson III, *The Texas Military Experience: From the Texas Revolution through World War II* (College Station: Texas A&M University Press, 1995), 38–46.

TWO

"IMITATING THE EXAMPLE OF OUR FOREFATHERS"

The Texas Revolution as Historical Reenactment

Sam W. Haynes

SINCE ITS INCEPTION on the banks of the Lower Brazos in the early 1820s, the colony of Anglo-American settlers founded by Stephen F. Austin had chafed at the presence of the indigenous tribal bands that had long inhabited the area. Accusing the Indians of a coordinated program of cattle and horse rustling and other depredations against the colony, Austin wrote to Mexican officials, calling upon the host government to drive them from the area. Lacking sufficient resources, Mexican authorities declined to take action, but by the spring of 1826 agreed to allow the American *empresario* to take punitive measures against the tribes living to the north along the Brazos River. In May, a militia company of less than two hundred men assembled in San Felipe de Austin to take part in an expedition against the Tawakoni and Waco Indians. Anglo-Americans all, Austin addressed them accordingly: "You are the descendants of freemen—the descendants of brave soldiers also American—the blood that fills your veins has warmed the hearts of those who fought in the American Revolution[,] fought and conquered the oppressors of American liberty. Perhaps the spirit of your Fathers watch over the conduct of their descendants, perhaps their eyes as well as those of your friends, your countrymen and your adopted Government are upon you[.]"[1] As it turned out, Austin's inspirational rhetoric proved unnecessary. Moving north along the banks of the river, the militiamen found both the Tawakoni and Waco villages abandoned, and they returned home a few days later, having not fired a shot.

Farther to the north later that same year, in the Piney Woods of East Texas, another empresario, Mississippi land speculator Haden Edwards, also saw fit to invoke the memory of those who had sacrificed their lives in the American Revolution. Edwards had recently run afoul of longtime local residents, refusing to recognize the validity of pre-existing Spanish and Mexican land claims. The Mexican government had sided against Edwards, revoking his contract and ordering his expulsion from Texas. Edwards promptly retaliated, urging newly arrived Anglo-American settlers to rise up in revolt against the Mexican government. The empresario-turned-filibuster declared East Texas to be in a state of rebellion and announced the creation of the grandiosely named Republic of Fredonia. In December, handbills urging residents to support the rebellion began to appear throughout Nacogdoches:

> *We knew you were Americans, the sons of those long departed patriots, who, when their rights were invaded, nobly grasped their arms, and planted the standard of liberty and independence in our native land. . . . Did our fathers, who are now no more, hesitate . . . when they were oppressed? No, their blood ran in willing torrents upon the altar of liberty. . . . Shall their sons do less?*[2]

Like the Austin colony's expedition against the Tawakonis and Wacos, the Edwards brothers' seditious enterprise ended anticlimactically. The residents of Nacogdoches ignored Edwards's call to revolution, and by the time Mexican troops sent to crush the insurrection arrived, the Fredonian rebels had fled into Louisiana.

As colonists and empresarios, Austin and Edwards had little in common. No American immigrant had embraced his Mexican nationality more unreservedly than Stephen F. Austin, whereas Edwards's loyalty to the Mexican nation-state existed only insofar as it served his pecuniary interests. Yet both men were shaped in part by their historical memory as Americans. In 1826, they invoked the American Revolution knowing the effect it would have on the Anglo-American residents of Texas, who were themselves recent arrivals from the United States, a country which was then celebrating the fiftieth anniversary of its independence from Great Britain. Anglo-Texans would continue to draw from the American story as their relationship with the host government deteriorated in the 1830s. Far from serving as a form of rhetorical window-dressing, their frequent allusions to the past reveal a fundamental connection between the political crisis in Texas and the American revolutionary experience.

For all the scholarly attention that the Texas Revolution has received, it is often viewed as an event somehow disconnected from the history of the United States. This is understandable, given the simple fact that Texas lay outside the nation's borders during what US historians refer to as the Early National period. As a result, they have generally tended to cede the study of these events to historians of the state, scholars such as Eugene C. Barker and William C. Binkley. In their extensive writings on the separation of Texas from Mexico, Barker and Binkley characterized the conflict as a clash of two opposing cultures, yet their exclusive focus on the region served to reinforce popular notions of a unique past. The work of subsequent generations of Anglo-Texan historians served to further seal this chapter of Texas history off from the larger American narrative. As a result, the most successful challenge to the idea of Texas exceptionalism during this period has been made by scholars of the American Southwest, who have sought to integrate the brief history of Mexican-held Texas into the larger structures of borderlands scholarship. Historian David J. Weber was one of the first historians to offer a counter-narrative to the "clash of cultures" thesis, pointing to the mutual interests that bound Tejano elites and American migrants. This thesis has been developed more fully with the work of younger historians, such as Raúl Ramos, who has argued that Tejano ranchers during the Mexican period served as cultural brokers for entrepreneurial Anglo colonists.[3]

Yet these constructive relationships quickly evaporated in the summer of 1835, as Anglo-Texans sought a cultural frame of reference with which to make sense of their brewing conflict with the Mexican government. This essay will focus, then, on the extent to which the shared memory of a revolutionary heritage shaped the behaviors of Anglo-Americans living west of the Sabine River. The trope of colonial resistance to British authority informed Anglo-Texan behavior in a number of meaningful and substantive ways. It fostered a sense of collective identity among a far-flung and disconnected set of Anglo-American communities; it provided a political language through which Anglo-Texans could articulate their grievances; and it endowed those inclined toward political activism with a ready-made ideology of opposition that lent their cause an instant legitimacy as new contretemps with Mexico City arose. Although Tejano elites initially shared Anglo opposition to Mexico City, their brand of republicanism differed markedly from those who drove the insurrection forward. The path toward secession for Anglo colonists—from initial expressions of alienation to armed resistance—was rooted in a historical memory that Tejanos did not share, precluding fruitful collaboration between the two anti-centralist constituencies. In the end, this revolutionary ideology ensured that the insurrection in Texas would bear a uniquely American stamp.[4]

To fully understand the importance of American historical memory on events in Texas, it is first necessary to review, if only briefly, the extent to which citizens of the United States were shaped by their nation's creation narrative. The mid-1820s saw Americans in the grip of a patriotic mania, occasioned by the approaching fiftieth anniversary of the nation's independence. In 1824 Gilbert du Motier, Marquis de Lafayette, who had served as Washington's aide-de-camp during the Revolution, crossed the Atlantic at the invitation of President Monroe for a yearlong tour of the country he had helped create. By some accounts, more than a million Americans saw the French aristocrat, now seventy years old.

In anticipation of Lafayette's tour, Americans sought to express their *amor patriae* in tangible and permanent ways. Towns through which he passed named streets in his honor; North Carolina settlers on the Cape Fear River renamed their town Fayetteville when he visited the area in March 1824. Elsewhere, communities raised money to erect Revolutionary monuments that would serve to memorialize both their national pride and their own unique contributions in the fight for independence. During a visit to Savannah the following year, the French visitor was called upon to lay the cornerstones at two monuments, honoring Nathanael Greene and Casimir Pulaski. In Boston a few months later, he performed the ceremony at the site of the Bunker Hill Monument, where Daniel Webster delivered one of his most famous orations. The monument building-mania continued after the Jubilee celebrations, with the completion, not only of these memorials, but of the Washington Monument in Boonsboro, Maryland (1827), the Washington Monument in Baltimore (1829), the Fort Griswold Obelisk in Groton, Connecticut (1830), and the Concord Monument in Concord, Massachusetts (1836).[5]

The adoring crowds that greeted the war hero wherever he went signaled a longing among Americans to reconnect with an idealized past. For underlying the frenzied jubilation was the melancholy awareness that the Revolutionary generation was passing from the scene. The anniversary prompted Americans to take stock of their society, and many wondered if they had fulfilled the promise of the Revolutionary era. Religious leaders issued jeremiads against the "anxious pursuit of gain" that seemed to afflict all classes and the unbridled license that had turned Independence Day celebrations into drunken revels. Social critics were particularly troubled by the complacent attitude of the younger generation, and predicted dark days ahead for a republic that no longer understood the true meaning of independence.[6]

This yearning for national renewal had begun long before the country's Jubilee celebrations, manifesting itself in virtually every aspect of American life. In the years after the nation's second war against Great Britain, a nascent publishing industry in Philadelphia and New York, which had once devoted itself almost entirely to producing facsimiles of British texts, now sought to capitalize on the public's fascination with the Revolutionary period. The postwar era saw the publication of a spate of works related to the Revolution, such as William Wirt's *Sketches of the Life and Works of Patrick Henry* (1817). American novelists, who had once aimed only to imitate their British counterparts, also joined in the cult of national devotion. James Fenimore Cooper first catapulted to national prominence with the release of his second novel, *The Spy* (1821), set in the so-called Neutral Ground in Westchester County, New York, during the Revolutionary War. Although he would subsequently gain lasting fame for the *Leatherstocking Tales*, he would return to the Revolution as the Jubilee approached, in such novels as *The Pilot* (1824) and *Lionel Lincoln* (1825).[7]

Political leaders of all partisan hues during this period claimed to be the legitimate heirs of the "sons of '76," invoking the memory of the Revolution to demonstrate their patriotic bona fides at every opportunity. The cult of personality that grew up around Andrew Jackson drew heavily from this swelling tide of patriotic emotion. We tend to forget that Jackson's supporters in the mid-1820s saw him not as a symbol of white male democracy—that would come later—but as the last remaining link to the Revolutionary generation. Jackson's campaign manager John Eaton played skillfully on the electorate's desire for a candidate who could assume the mantle of the nation's Revolutionary heroes, extolling Old Hickory as "the last of these valiant establishers of liberty" who had fought to create a nation. A Jackson victory, his supporters declared, would maintain the line of Revolutionary leaders in the White House unbroken for another four years. The Jackson machine was still exploiting Revolutionary nostalgia in the famously vicious rematch against John Quincy Adams four years later. As in 1824, the Jackson campaign characterized its candidate as both a symbol of republican renewal and a man who could drive the nation forward into a new golden age.[8]

Not surprisingly, the most important policy battles of the day were heavily imbued with the language of a Revolutionary past. The Nullification Crisis, which brought about the first rumblings of secession in South Carolina in the late 1820s and early 1830s, may serve as just one example. Both sides saw the conflict in terms of a broader historical narrative in which each claimed to be the authentic standard-bearer of the nation's Revolutionary legacy. Nullifiers staged elaborate July Fourth dinners and other celebrations that deftly fused past and present, conflating New England and Old England as twin symbols of oppression. One prominent nullifier at an anti-tariff dinner gave the following toast: "The stamp act of 1765, and the Tariff of 1828—kindred acts of despotism." Not to be outdone, unionists formed the Washington Society, which called upon citizens of the Palmetto State to carry on the great work bequeathed to them by their forebears.[9]

Ordinary Americans also used the narrative of colonial resistance to frame the struggles in their own lives. Many experienced various forms of marginalization as a result of the economic vicissitudes of the Jacksonian period, which they invariably regarded as an infringement of their historic "liberties." Craft laborers, mechanics, factory operatives, small farmers—indeed, anyone who found themselves disadvantaged by the power relations of the early republic—could find parallels in the experiences of their colonial ancestors. In the summer of 1835, a union of Boston-area carpenters, masons, and stonecutters met to formally declare their support for a ten-hour day, issuing what would become known as the "Ten Hour Circular," a statement that would spark a broad-based movement for a shorter work day among craft laborers in cities throughout the eastern seaboard. Tailoring the language of liberation to the labor struggle, the circular declared: "We claim by the blood of our fathers, shed on our battle-fields in the War of the Revolution, the rights of American freemen."[10] In short, one would be hard-pressed to find a single contest between competing political or economic groups during the early national period in which some or all of the actors involved did not at some point wrap themselves in the mantle of the Revolution to justify their actions.[11]

Anglo-Texans were no less inclined to look to the past to frame the world in which they lived. And none were more thoroughly influenced by their political heritage than a small group of radicals who would be the driving force behind the crisis in Texas. Termed the "war party" in 1835, the group's key figures had been agitating against a wide range of governmental policies since the early 1830s. Historians have tended to accept the thesis that the radicals were young, hailed originally from the Deep South, and were newcomers to Texas. These generalizations do not stand up under scrutiny.[12] What the radicals did have in common, however, was a deep connection to an American historical experience that served to compromise their loyalty to the Mexican republic. This was not true of all Texas colonists, of course; the province's leading moderates, most notably Stephen F. Austin, lent their full support to the Constitution of 1824, and evinced a genuine desire to participate fully in the obligations of Mexican citizenship. But those who gravitated to the radical camp in the early 1830s were willing only to pay lip service to the notion that republicanism transcended national boundaries. Even as they ostensibly disavowed seditious intentions during the Anahuac and Velasco disturbances of 1832, William H. Wharton, Robert M. Williamson, and others, not unlike Haden Edwards and the Fredonian rebels six years earlier, expressed political dissent in thoroughly American terms. They upbraided as "tories" those who did not share their stalwart opposition to the Bustamante government, and quoted liberally from the American Revolutionary canon in their public addresses and private correspondence.[13]

That expatriate Americans recently settled in a neighboring country should draw from their historical memory in a time of crisis is hardly surprising; as noted earlier, their compatriots east of the Sabine River were no less keen to legitimize all manner of behaviors by claiming the imprimatur of a bygone age. But as grievances accumulated against an alien and distant government, a growing number of Texans perceived an especially powerful symmetry between the Anglo-American settlements of Texas and the thirteen colonies. Texas radicals not only borrowed the language of their forebears, but to an ever-increasing degree sought to emulate them in their opposition to the national government. Anglo-Texan radicals drew inspiration from the American Revolutionary experience at every opportunity, discovering in the events of the past a rationale for secession and a blueprint for armed resistance.

This historical frame of reference appears especially significant given the absence of anything remotely resembling a unifying revolutionary agenda for the better part of 1835. Notwithstanding the aura of inevitability that has since attached itself to the secession movement, one finds no outpouring of popular discontent within the Anglo-Texas community as a result of the Plan of Cuernavaca issued by supporters of Mexican president Santa Anna one year earlier. The *pronunciamiento*, a conservative reaction to the anticlerical reforms implemented under Gomez Farías, would set in motion a chain of events that would lead Santa Anna to dissolve Congress and consolidate his political authority. Reports of political turmoil in the nation's capital and the subsequent subjugation of Zacatecas in May 1835 did indeed cause some anxiety in Mexico's northern provinces, but the centralist challenge to the Constitution of 1824 had yet to impact Anglo settlements in Texas in any meaningful way. As a precaution, those who would emerge as leaders of the radical faction established committees of correspondence to deal with future grievances modeled after those of the American colonial resistance. Still, as late as the summer of 1835, a far greater degree of public anger was directed toward the federalist state legislature in Monclova, which had recently engaged in a land giveaway to a handful of Anglo speculators. Even after the seizure of the Anahuac garrison in late June, Anglo sentiment was decidedly cool to the radicals' call for action, with localism, poor communication, and a general apathy all contributing to the absence of coordinated resistance.

Indeed, it could hardly be otherwise. On the eve of the rebellion the settled areas of Texas covered an area of some thirty-five thousand square miles. The Anglo population, estimated by some to have been no more than thirty thousand, was dispersed over this immense area, with no town consisting of more than a few hundred settlers.[14] During the crucial summer of 1835, Texas had but one newspaper, the pro-Wharton *Texas Republican*, published weekly in Brazoria. The *Telegraph and Texas Register*, which would begin publication in San Felipe de Austin shortly after the outbreak of hostilities, could claim a circulation of no more than five hundred by year's end.[15] While committees of correspondence occasionally issued handbills declaring their opposition to the centralist government, Anglo settlers had limited access to news and information. One finds little serious public opposition to the new regime in Mexico City until July, amid rumors that a contingent of troops would be sent to Texas in response to the Anahuac episode and forcibly quartered in settlers' homes. Even then, support for armed resistance did not crystallize until Mexican troops finally arrived in mid-September, only two weeks before hostilities began.[16]

How, then, did this fragmented and disparate population coalesce so quickly? The shift in public opinion toward the radical faction may be attributed in large part to its leaders' ability to frame the growing crisis between Texas and the new centralist government in terms that Anglos understood: as an extension of a struggle deeply rooted in their own historical memory. Although racially charged, anti-Catholic invective would suffuse Anglo-Texan rhetoric once the crisis erupted in violence, in the late summer and early fall of 1835 the radicals employed a very different lexicon, but one no less encoded with meaning for Anglo-Americans. "Despotism" and "tyranny" would serve as the shorthand by which they raised the stakes in their confrontation with Mexico City and roused a hitherto disengaged community to action. Although, at this early stage of the crisis, the political discourse in Texas still seemed to hinge upon the future of Mexican federalism, the radicals' appropriation of language associated with an American Revolutionary tradition proved enormously effective in undercutting Anglo-Texan loyalties to the Mexican nation. "Centralism," declared William Barret Travis in a letter to David G. Burnet in the summer of 1835, "is but another name for monarchy."[17] By conflating these terms as twin symbols of oppression, the radicals adopted an American nomenclature that assured their ascendancy.

It is worth noting, as further evidence of the extent to which historical memory shaped the thinking of Anglo colonists in Texas, that even conservatives who counseled caution invoked the American Revolution as they sought to undercut the radicals' insurrectionary message. Lavaca resident James Kerr, a prominent opponent of independence, urged Anglo settlers to work in concert with Mexican federalists to restore the Constitution of 1824. Anglo colonists who called for the province to separate from Mexico were in direct violation of the principles of 1776, he maintained; indeed, Washington, Hancock, Adams, "and the whole host of revolutionary worthies" would rebuke them should they violate their oath to uphold the principles of Mexican liberalism. Such reasoning would increasingly fall on deaf ears, however, as more colonists began to view the debate within Texas as a struggle between "patriots" and "tories."[18]

Isolated, too, were those Mexican federalists in Coahuila y Texas who had initially expressed support for the Anglo-American cause. Recent historians of the Texas Revolution have duly noted the political commonalities that linked Tejano elites and the new emigrants from the United States, and have tended to attribute the innate bigotry of Anglo-Americans to the failure of this once-promising alliance. But it is also important to recognize that racial identity presented only one of many obstacles to intercultural cooperation. Anglos may have shared with some Tejanos a common set of republican principles and a demand for greater self-government, but these putative connections have tended to obscure intrinsic differences in political culture. The ferment of participatory democracy had yet to be felt in the Tejano community, where a culture of deference toward a landholding minority prevailed. Though predominantly federalist, Tejano and Norteño elites acted upon a wholly disparate set of historical assumptions than their Anglo allies. While they could express deep admiration for Jeffersonian republicanism, the American Revolution remained for them a purely ideological abstraction, wholly divested of visceral meaning.

Anglo-Texas colonists, on the other hand, saw their own vivid reflection in the American creation narrative, for it had been fashioned by nineteenth-century Americans like themselves. Oaths of Mexican citizenship notwithstanding, the Anglo community in Texas continued to observe Independence Day and Washington's Birthday, celebrations that served to preserve their cultural identity and reinforce preexisting national attachments. As in the United States, these rites often became flashpoints for discontent, the opportunity for firebrands to inveigh against tyranny and despotism in all its many and nefarious guises. The July Fourth observances in 1835, which were held only days after Anglo colonists learned that a sizable contingent of Mexican troops was en route to Texas, seem to have been an important tipping point in galvanizing support for the radical agenda. Even the Alamo garrison would find time to honor Washington's birthday on the evening of February 22, 1836, only hours before the Mexican army arrived in San Antonio. Two days later, Travis would issue his famous appeal for aid "in the name of Liberty, of patriotism, & every thing dear to the American character," which he addressed to "The People of Texas and all Americans in the World."

Like Americans, too, Anglo colonists in Texas venerated historical figures who spoke directly to their own aspirations, such as Patrick Henry, whose place in the American national pantheon owed much to William Wirt's enormously popular biography. Wirt's romanticized portrayal of Henry as a working-class hero, a democrat more attuned to the will of the sovereign people than the seaboard gentry, struck a responsive chord among Americans of the Jacksonian period. Wirt's rendering of Henry's famous speech in the Virginia House of Burgesses on March 23, 1775, which Wirt re-created from the recollections of eyewitnesses, some forty years after the event, also captivated the national imagination. It seems doubtful that Henry ever uttered the famous cry, "Give me liberty or give me death!" in view of the fact that no earlier accounts record him delivering the line. Nonetheless, by the 1820s, "Liberty or Death" had become bywords of the Revolutionary struggle, emblazoned upon banners, transparencies, pamphlets, and other ephemera produced for national holidays in the United States. Between 1817 and the outbreak of hostilities in Texas, an astounding 42 editions of Wirt's biography were published. In Texas, as in the United States, oratorical skill was a prerequisite of political leadership, and as tensions with Mexico City mounted during the summer and fall of 1835, radical leaders all strove to emulate the Virginia firebrand's declamatory style, making his signature phrase, "Liberty or Death!" the ubiquitous watchwords of Anglo resistance.[19]

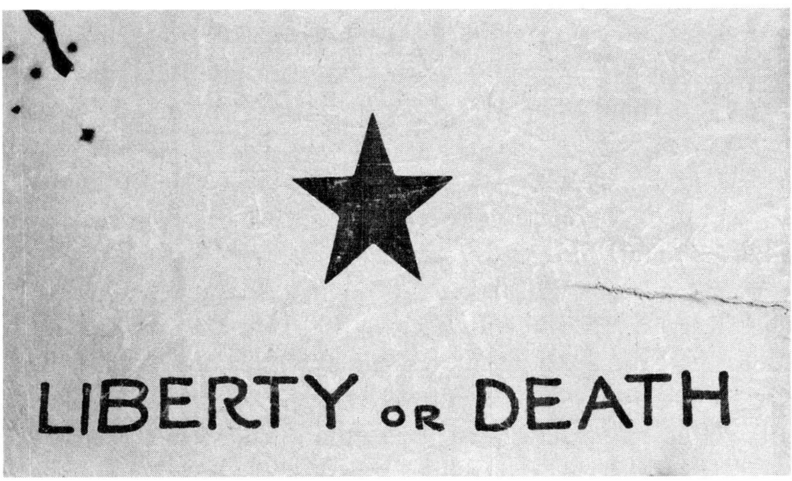

FIGURE 2. Troutman Flag. Courtesy Dallas Historical Society

Robert M. Williamson became known as the "Patrick Henry of the Revolution" after his July 4, 1835, address to a San Felipe de Austin gathering, widely regarded as one of the most effective in alerting colonists of the dangers to be apprehended from the change of government in Mexico City.[20] That distinction might also have been applied to itinerant Methodist minister William T. Smith. Arriving in the village of Gonzales on the evening of October 1, Smith found approximately 160 armed men engaged in a standoff with Mexican troops, having refused to relinquish a cannon that had been loaned to the colony in 1831. Smith delivered a rousing speech to the group, concluding as follows:

> *The same blood that animated the hearts of our ancestors of '76 still flows warm in our veins. Having waited several days for the Mexican army to make an attack upon us, we have now determined to attack them. . . . Let us go into battle with the words of the immortal Patrick Henry, before the Virginia House of Burgesses, deeply impressed upon our hearts, when, with arms extended towards heaven, and with a voice of thunder, he exclaimed in the most patriotic manner: Give me Liberty or Give me Death!*[21]

The skirmish the following day, which famously ignited the insurrection, offers an especially telling example of the ways in which the memory of the American Revolution informed the behavior of Anglo-Texas residents. As the men of Gonzales gathered along the banks of the Guadalupe River, they unfurled a large white banner on which had been drawn an image of a cannon and the challenge "Come and Take It." Here again their actions echoed those of their forefathers. In 1778, the defenders of Fort Morris on the Georgia coast had issued the same cry of defiance to the forces of Lord Cornwallis.[22] And while the few extant eyewitness accounts offer no direct evidence that the Gonzales volunteers saw themselves as the descendants of Lexington minutemen, it was a parallel that certainly occurred to many Anglos in the days and weeks that followed. Having learned of the skirmish on October 3, William H. Wharton dashed off a public call for volunteers, declaring that Santa Anna "will be made to feel and know from blood bought experience that a people who have adopted the motto of their ancestors, 'Liberty or Death,' will crush and laugh [at] his tyranic attempt to enslave them."[23]

FIGURE 3. Gonzales Flag. Courtesy Dallas Historical Society

With the spirit of '76 permeating the discourse of resistance against Mexico, it was no wonder that Anglo-Texan behavior had begun to take on a weirdly performative dimension, as colonists seized the opportunity to actually re-enact the events that had long been a conspicuous feature of their historical memory.[24]

These deeply held historical associations caused the lines of racial and cultural identity to quickly snap taut once the outbreak of hostilities occurred. Although ostensibly still a struggle on behalf of Mexican federalism, some Anglo secessionists now began to refer to themselves for the first time as Americans. Even as they appealed for support from Tejanos, they constructed their resistance to Mexico City in ways that deftly fused past and present.[25] The *Telegraph and Texas Register* filled some of its pages during the early months of the conflict with texts from or about the Revolutionary era, serializing John Dickinson's *Declaration of the Causes and Necessity for Taking Up Arms*, issued in 1775, and David Ramsey's popular *History of the American Revolution*, first published in 1789. While the Consultation, which convened in San Felipe de Austin in early November, reaffirmed Texans' loyalty to the Constitution of 1824, voting down independence by a 33–14 margin, the election of Branch T. Archer as president of the assembly assured the radicals a strong voice in that body's deliberations. Seemingly oblivious to the Tejanos in attendance, Archer declared in his opening remarks to the delegates: "Let our achievements be such that our mother country . . . shall proudly and joyfully exclaim, these are my sons!"[26]

In the face of this kind of escalating chauvinism, many Tejanos would abandon the revolutionary cause in the months that followed. Initially, some American insurgents seem to have made a sincere effort to appeal to the historical memory of both groups. After the battle of San Antonio in early December—a contest in which almost two hundred Tejano volunteers fought alongside Anglo colonists—Francis W. Johnson called upon all Texans to join him in an attack on Matamoros. Having assumed command of the volunteers at San Antonio following the death of Ben Milam, he invited Mexican federalists to carry "the banners of Morales [sic] and Hidalgo, inscribed with their own national mottoes," into Mexico, while urging Anglo-Americans to sustain "the principles of 1776."[27] Johnson's cultural sensitivity proved to be the exception, however. Denunciations of centralist tyranny were soon accompanied by a racially charged rhetoric that included blanket indictments of Mexican "priestcraft" that made it abundantly clear that Anglo objections to Mexican rule were not purely political in nature. By the spring of 1836, few Tejanos remained; the conflict had become for all intents and purposes a binary one between Anglo-Americans and the centralist government.

More than a justification for taking up arms, the public memory of the Revolution proved an equally potent recruitment tool once the war began. While continuing to inveigh against centralist tyranny, Anglo-Texan leaders now wove the familiar narrative of the thirteen colonies' struggle against the British Empire into their calls for community sacrifice. Echoing many of the same themes that had made the 1826 celebration a cultural touchstone for citizens of the American republic, Texan propagandists urged settlers to carry on the sacred legacy bequeathed to them by an earlier generation. For Anglo-Americans who had long stood in the shadow of their heroic forebears, armed resistance now became a matter of validation, an opportunity to match their accomplishments and, no less important, a duty that they owed to those who had forged a nation. Colonists who volunteered for military service were told that in so doing they would honor the heroes of the American Revolution; conversely, they would shame them should they fail in the endeavor. To drive the point home, Texas leaders invoked George Washington, the highest figure in the Revolutionary pantheon and the nation's patriarch. "Let us prove to the enimy [sic] that we are not unworthy decendants of Washington," declared Philip Dimmitt, commandant of Fort Goliad, three weeks after the clash at Gonzales.[28] Again and again, leaders of the rebellion asked colonists if they were the equals of their ancestors, while commanders in the field used the memory of the American Revolution to steel the resolve of volunteers, urging them on to greater acts of valor. By the end of the year, with the colony at peace following the defeat of General Cos at San Antonio, Texas leaders could aver with satisfaction that those who had taken up arms against Mexico were "worthy to have stood by Washington . . . and worthy to participate in the inheritance of the sons of such a Father."[29]

On the other side of the Sabine River, news of the revolt prompted a massive outpouring of support, which was strongest in, but by no means limited to, the southern states. In nearby Natchitoches, Louisiana, a mere five days after the outbreak of hostilities at Gonzales, the local citizenry met to endorse the actions of the Texas colonists, who were "engaged in the same cause in defence of which their and our forefathers bled and died—the great cause of constitutional liberty." Many towns and cities promptly established Texas Committees to raise money and volunteer companies for the insurrection, despite the fact that political conditions in Texas had received scant attention in the local press. New Orleans, the locus of commerce with the Latin American republics, was the exception. With its sizable creole population, it had long been the destination of choice for prominent Mexican federalist exiles, including Valentín Gomez Farías, recently deposed by Santa Anna following the Plan of Cuernavaca. Nonetheless, support for the Texan cause in the Crescent City also assumed an exclusively Anglo-American cast. When a pro-Texas meeting chaired by financier William Christy met at the Banks Arcade on October 13, it created a six-member committee to correspond with the provisional government; no federalists were nominated. The meeting's list of resolves declared as its purpose "the same sacred cause, which our fathers in '76 defended, and which we, their descendants are here assembled to support."[30]

Anglo-Texan leaders, mindful of the fact that a favorable outcome to the conflict was dependent upon financial and material support from the United States, did all they could to encourage American interest in their cause. The earliest appeals for men and supplies issued by the General Council in the weeks after Gonzales emphasized the ties that bound the insurrectionists to their country of origin. Declaring that it was their intention "to live free or die," the ad hoc body reminded Americans that "we are but one people," whose fathers had fought "side by side" in the Revolution.[31]

American males proved especially susceptible to such exhortative rhetoric. As news of clashes between colonists and Mexican troops spread through the southern states in the fall of 1835, thousands of young men enlisted in militia companies to aid the colonists' cause in a groundswell of martial enthusiasm that came to be known as the "Texas Fever." One Georgia editor lamented in December: "The Texas fever has treated us worse than the cholera. Our office is completely swept! Journeymen, apprentices, men and boys, devils and angels, are all gone to Texas! If our readers get an empty sheet, or no sheet at all, don't blame us."[32] Volunteer companies were still arriving along the Texas coast in the summer of 1836, long after hostilities had ended. By some estimates, more than 75 percent of all those serving in the Texas Army were Americans who entered the colony after January 1, 1836, making the independence movement what historian Robert E. May calls "the largest filibuster expedition in US history."[33]

A few Northern editors attempted to throw cold water on the Texas Fever, offering the opinion that the slaveholding colonists did not deserve American assistance, and that any material aid from the United States would be a violation of its treaty with Mexico. The thesis that the revolt had its origin in the growth of the cotton empire and land speculation would soon be developed fully by US antislavery leaders, most notably Benjamin Lundy and John Quincy Adams.[34] In seeking to undermine the argument that the revolution had been justified, antislavery pundits also turned to the Founders for a suitable analogy. "The Americans then fought for their own liberty," one Massachusetts editor opined, and by extension for the "liberty of the world." But the Texans fought for slavery, and if successful "will have fought for the perpetuity of slavery throughout the world."[35]

Southerners, however, were quick to point out that France had once played midwife to a new nation, and it was now incumbent upon the United States to do the same.[36] Supporters of the rebellion in the United

States were particularly fond of urging the nation's youth to follow in the footsteps of Lafayette, who at the age of nineteen had fought for liberty in a new country.[37] Nashville newspaperman George Childress, who sought to raise money and supplies before setting off himself for Texas, urged Tennesseans to consider the example of the Frenchman, who a decade earlier had returned as "the nation's honored guest, in one round of triumph by a grateful people."[38]

The widespread support for the Texas rebellion in the United States offers a glimpse into the ways in which American citizens continued to be conscious of their own revolutionary legacy. The Texas meetings held in scores of towns throughout the United States took on much the same character as the celebratory rites with which Americans commemorated their own history on national holidays, replete with banquets, speeches, parades, and the inevitable list of resolves. Rare was the orator on these occasions who did not regale his audience with allusions to the American struggle for independence. It is important to note that communities providing assistance to the Texas cause did not regard such efforts as evidence of their charity, but their own love of liberty—their patriotic validation as Americans. When the citizens of Macon, Georgia, rallied to support the rebels in the fall of 1835, the *Macon Messenger* noted proudly that the size of the pro-Texas meeting furnished ample evidence that "the spirit of '76 is still alive among us . . ." Elsewhere, communities that had not caught the Texas Fever were chastised for their lack of patriotic ardor. Pointing to the Texas meetings that were being held across the United States, one South Carolina citizen in November asked in a plaintive letter to the editor of the *Charleston Mercury,* "Why have we not called one also?" and urged the young men of the city to follow in the footsteps of Lafayette.[39]

In much the same way as they had erected monuments to their Revolutionary forebears during the Jubilee celebrations, Americans regarded the raising of volunteer companies to meet the crisis in Texas as a reaffirmation of their national pride. One Mississippi native who had emigrated to Texas urged the young men of that state—"brave descendents [sic] of worthy sires"—not to let their counterparts in Louisiana "bear away the palm" in the scramble to enlist.[40] Within a matter of days after the aforementioned meeting in Macon, a "Georgia Battalion" had been formed and was making its way to Texas. Feted in every town through which it passed, the battalion's ranks swelled as it picked up additional volunteers en route to the coast. At a public meeting in Knoxville, Georgia, its commanding officers received a silk flag sewn by local resident Joanna Troutman. With a five-pointed blue star on a white background, the flag is believed to be the first of the "lone star" flags flown in Texas. On one side the flag bore the slogan "Liberty or Death," on the other, a Latin phrase attributed to Benjamin Franklin, "where liberty dwells, there is my country."[41] The battalion arrived at Velasco on the Texas coast in December, and on Christmas day held a ceremony in which it consecrated the flag and formally placed itself under the command of Col. James Walker Fannin, a Georgia native who had moved to Texas in 1834. Fannin praised the volunteers, declaring that the group could claim a "legitimate descent from the true stock of 1776."[42]

The motives of American participants in the Texas secession movement, like the motives of those who participated in the innumerable filibustering expeditions during the antebellum era, are not easy to comprehend. It has been argued that a quest for romantic adventure led many to catch the Texas Fever, having been weaned on the novels of Walter Scott, James Fenimore Cooper, and William Gilmore Simms. Economic opportunity also served as an important motivating factor. Sam Houston had issued a call for volunteers with the promise of liberal land bounties as early as October 5, although the provisional government would not officially make such an offer until November 24, by which time the mass exodus of young men into Texas was already well under way.[43] But individual renown and economic opportunity by themselves were not enough. It was a paradox of the Jacksonian era that while young American males of the period embraced an ethos of unfettered individualism, they were very reluctant to acknowledge the impulse of self-interest. For all their overweening ambition, they remained bound to the eighteenth-century dictates that held that there was something unseemly in the quest for profit and personal ambition. They craved renown, but only if it could be gained in the service of a noble cause.

As a result, Anglo-American males who set off for Texas did not simply take pride in the fact that they were emulating their forebears. The need to live up to the legacy of '76, in their own minds at least, was for many the paramount reason for taking up arms. One volunteer wrote to his brother that, despite the privations of soldiering, "all was sweet when I reflected on our forefathers in the struggle of liberty."[44] Particularly poignant was the case of John Sowers Brooks, a twenty-one-year-old Virginia native. In 1835, Brooks had served a brief stint in the US Marines, a career choice that he soon had reason to regret. Homesick and unhappy, he secured a discharge on the grounds that he had been too young at the time of his enlistment. Brooks' letters to his family reveal his deep sense of shame at his failure to make a career in the Marines, and during the fall of 1835 and early part of 1836, he wrote frequently of his longing to do something of consequence.

> *I trust I have a holier motive than mere ambition, for abandoning my native country and the pleasures of social life to encounter the dangers and turmoil of war in a foreign land. There is something in the cause of the Texians that comes home to the heart of every true American. Its near similarity to the glorious struggle of our own ancestors in "Seventy Six" must produce a sympathy for them in every part of the Union which will result in something more than mere kind wishes for their success. I hope and I believe that there are many of the youths of our country who have inherited enough of the spirit of our forefathers to induce them to procure, like myself, a musket and a hundred rounds of ball cartridge and join the holy crusade against priestly tyranny and military despotism.*[45]

For Anglo-Americans, be they colonists already residing in Texas or, like John Sowers Brooks, adventurous newcomers, the conflict against Mexico and the earlier struggle against Britain were integral parts of the same historical continuum, making independence a foregone conclusion. Even delegates to the Consultation who opposed a break with Mexico in the early days of the rebellion had studied the American Declaration of Independence as they drafted their plan for a provisional government when that body met in November 1835.[46] The following month, the signatories of the Goliad Declaration of Independence invoked Washington's name as they explicitly called upon "the North Americans of Texas" to set the example for the "Creole population" in establishing a constitution and a bill of rights.[47] Weighing in on the debate over independence in late February, the *Telegraph and Texas Register* took a different tack. Mindful of the motives of young men like John Sowers Brooks, who yearned to attach themselves to a great and noble cause, it maintained that only a complete break with Mexico would attract the American volunteers Texas so urgently needed, for such a move would "put the contest on a footing worthy of their assistance."[48] Thus when the delegates gathered in the hamlet of Washington (only later would it come to be known as Washington-on-the Brazos), they wasted little time signing a document that borrowed the style, structure, and substance of the Declaration of Independence signed in Philadelphia in 1776. A constitution modeled on its American counterpart followed two weeks later.

As the colony moved inexorably toward independence, it would face a series of dispiriting setbacks as the centralist government in Mexico City took aggressive measures to reclaim it. Once again, Texas leaders harked back to the American Revolutionary experience to remind residents living east of the Colorado River that their travails were not without precedent. "Are there none in Texas to imitate the example of Washington and his illustrious associates?" the General Council asked upon learning that an army under Mexican president Santa Anna had crossed the Rio Grande and was advancing on San Antonio.[49] When the government devolved into chaos with the impeachment of Governor Henry Smith, Lieutenant Governor James Robinson reminded Texans that the First Continental Congress "was but little better than ours."[50] When the news of the capture of San Antonio reached the settlements in the interior, the government urged Texans to "imitate the example of our forefathers and hurl destruction" upon Santa Anna's advancing army.[51] And when news of the fall of the Alamo reached the Anglo settlements on the Brazos River, Richard Ellis, president of the Convention in Washington, penned a frantic open letter to remind the people of the United States that "the sainted spirit of Washington would rebuke your apathy," should they fail to come to the Texans' aid.[52] Meanwhile, David G. Burnet, the newly appointed interim president, sought to calm a panicked populace by observing that their forefathers had also "persevered through many reverses, surmounted many disasters," but in the end had "gloriously triumphed."[53] Such analogies offered little comfort to Anglo-Texans in the face of the advancing Mexican army, most of whom promptly took flight in a chaotic exodus known to Texas history as the Runaway Scrape. As soldiers deserted the army to accompany their families toward the safety of the United States, Burnet could only reproach them for exhibiting behavior unworthy of the "heroes of 76."[54]

In other ways, too, the insurgents sought to mimic their Revolutionary forebears. The more poetically inclined composed their own patriotic lyrics, such as "The Star of Texas" and the "Texian Banner," which were sung to the tunes of "Yankee Doodle" and "The Star Spangled Banner," patriotic airs that were a staple feature wherever Americans gathered to celebrate national holidays.[55] During the revolt against Mexico, "Yankee Doodle" appears to have been far more popular than Francis Scott Key's contribution to the national hymnody ("The Star Spangled Banner" did not become the official anthem until 1931). Based on a mid-eighteenth-century folk song, the tune had been adopted by American militiamen after the battles at Lexington and Concord.[56] Foreign travelers to the United States commented frequently on the American public's unfettered enthusiasm for the song—yet another way in which Americans called attention to their national pride. Visiting a theater in Cincinnati in 1832, Frances Trollope remarked, disapprovingly: "When a patriotic fit seized them, and 'Yankee Doodle' was called for; every man seemed to think his reputation as a citizen depended on the noise he made."[57] Little wonder, then, that less than a month after the outbreak of hostilities, the *Telegraph and Texas Register* unveiled a new version of the song, which substituted the tune's familiar refrain with the following bit of doggerel:

> *Huzza! For Texas volunteers, we are the boys so handy*
> *We'll teach the Mexicans to fear our Yankee Doodle Dandy.*[58]

While it is not known whether Texans who took the field against Mexican troops sang the new lyrics, the tune was certainly popular among Anglo-American insurgents throughout the conflict. At the Battle of Coleto Creek, soldiers in Fannin's army played the song on the morning of March 20, just prior to their surrender to General José de Urrea. And although a fifer in Houston's army reputedly played "Will You Come to the Bower" as it marched toward the enemy camp on the field of San Jacinto, several eyewitnesses attested that they heard "Yankee Doodle" as the Texans approached the Mexican picket lines. In describing the tune's stirring effect on him some months later, one of Houston's officers revealed the extent to which the two contests had become conflated in the minds of Anglo-Texan combatants: "What a crowd of recollections rushed on the mind as 'Yankee Doodle' greeted our ear;—my heart leaped for joy—new ardor seized my soul—my native country—her victories and her power, all greeted themselves at the same moment—I felt that I was an American citizen, and that under the protection of Yankee Doodle, no harm could befall me."[59]

While Anglo-Texan colonists and newly arrived US volunteers sought to beat back the advance of the Mexican army, a three-man commission consisting of Stephen F. Austin, William H. Wharton, and Branch T. Archer had embarked on a tour of the United States to solicit American support for the Texas cause. Authorized by the Consultation in November, the commissioners arrived in New Orleans on January 1, 1836, and for the next several months made their way through the western states en route to Washington, DC. Owing to internecine quarrels within the General Council, the trio received little in the way of news or further instructions from their government, greatly hampering their effectiveness as official emissaries. Nonetheless they urged the Jackson administration to recognize the new government, and even urged Washington to intervene in the conflict, suggestions which were given short shrift by the president and his advisers, who had no wish to upset diplomatic relations between Mexico and the United States.

On the public relations front, however, the commissioners enjoyed more success. The Texas Fever was in full swing upon their arrival in New Orleans, and even as the news from home grew less hopeful in the early months of 1836, the three men were met with enormous crowds in every city they visited. Austin had been reluctant to serve as a member of the commission, having quarreled with the radical firebrand Wharton. Ever the pragmatist, he was not yet convinced that Texas would be best served by declaring its independence. By the time he reached New Orleans, however, Austin had become fast friends with his former nemesis, and the three men declared that the time had come for Texas to sever all ties with Mexico. Austin now sought support for "the same holy cause for which our forefathers fought and bled." Speaking before huge crowds in the United States, the three men had the opportunity to flesh out the comparison to the American Revolution more fully. Austin distinguished between the "theory of oppression," which had compelled the sons of '76 to rebel, as opposed to the reality of oppression, citing as an example his own incarceration in La Accordada, the infamous prison in Mexico City. Unlike the Greeks and the Poles, who had also recently been engaged in struggles for liberty, "they are not the sons and daughters of Anglo-Americans," Austin declared. "We are."[60] Wharton echoed these sentiments, exclaiming that the Texas colonists were "now gallantly contending for the same sacred principles for which Henry thundered—Washington conquered—and Warren died."[61] The commission's appeals to consanguinity and a common heritage found a receptive audience in the United States. As in the days following the news of the outbreak of hostilities the previous year, the commission's tour sparked a new round of fund-raising and the formation of volunteer companies to aid the insurrection.[62]

During the course of the trip, the three men also collaborated on a new flag for the breakaway government. An early draft of the banner sketched by Austin featured a star on a background of thirteen stripes with the Franklin dictum, "Where liberty dwells, there is my country." Wharton objected to the quote on the grounds that its "frequent use by schoolboys as a motto & by Volunteer companies" (such as the Georgia battalion, presumably) had rendered it "stale." Never reluctant to draw attention to the insurrection's historical antecedents, he suggested an alternative: in place of the star, the head of George Washington encircled by a glowing nimbus, beneath which would be the phrase, "in his example, there is safety."[63] Austin endorsed the change, and during a visit to Lexington, Kentucky, in mid-March, he gave a sketch of the flag to his cousin, Mary Austin Holley, who promptly had it rendered on a silk banner by a member of the town's Ladies Legion. In June, her niece, Henrietta Austin, presented the flag to a local volunteer company as it prepared to set out for Texas. Reading a speech written by her aunt, Austin declared: "What tyrant would not quail before the light of that benignant countenance—the Light of Liberty which illuminates the world? What perjured soldier would not hang his head and drop his arms, in view of greatness like that of Washington, whose word was truth? . . . Let this beautiful banner, which fair hands have wrought for you[r] honor, and the thought of the youthful La Fayette, inseparable from the image of Washington, be your inspiration."[64]

With the victory at San Jacinto, and the realization that the Mexican government could not, at least for the foreseeable future, mount another attempt to subjugate its errant province, Americans' attention now turned to diplomatic recognition of the breakaway government. From across the country, citizens' committees sent petitions to the US Congress urging

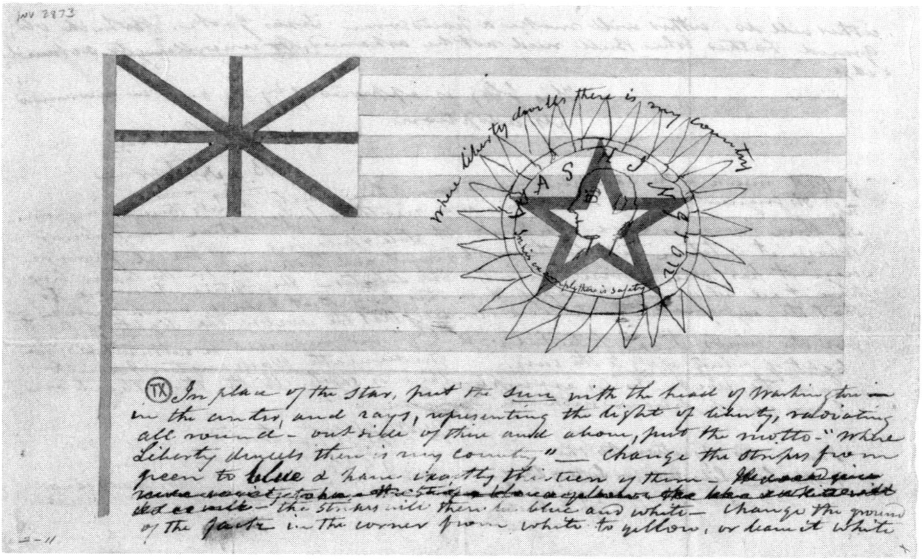

FIGURE 4. Austin-Wharton Flag. Courtesy Texas State Library and Archives Commission

Washington to acknowledge Texas' independence immediately. "She is in the same position that this nation was in 1776," one Lexington, Kentucky, memorial declared in April. "The heroes of that day are in their graves, but their spirits rest with their sons."[65] At another meeting a week later, Lexington residents drafted a resolution in a similar vein, comparing the motives of the Texas colonists to that same spirit that did battle for the rights of man on the fields of Trenton and Princeton; and achieved blessings for themselves and their posterity before the battlements of Yorktown."[66]

This overwhelming need to reprise the past is, of course, hardly unique to the Anglo-Texans who joined the insurrection against Mexico in 1835–36. At various times in their history, Americans have been prone to look to earlier generations for guidance, and never more so than when seeking to make the case for national renewal. Perhaps it might be helpful at this point to provide another, more recent example of the power of historical memory: the fiftieth anniversary of the D-Day invasion and its impact on the American response to 9/11. During the mid-1990s, the public fascination with the "greatest generation" appears to have been rooted in feelings of anxiety not unlike those that citizens of the republic exhibited during and after the 1826 Jubilee. The end of the Cold War had left the nation without a sense of geopolitical purpose, prompting foreign policy theorists to ponder the implications for an American superpower that, for the first time in half a century, found itself without a major adversary.[67] American social commentators also weighed in, deploring what they regarded as the self-indulgent narcissism of baby-boomers and Gen-Xers, who enjoyed the material benefits of American power with little appreciation for the sacrifices that had been made to attain it. Thus the commemorations and cultural productions honoring the nation's World War II veterans in the 1990s took on special significance for a nation that looked upon its storied past with feelings of inadequacy. By the end of the decade, World War II nostalgia had become something of a cottage industry, as a flood of best-selling books, films, and television series sought to tap into the era's enduring and sentimental appeal.[68]

The memory of World War II, so fresh in the minds of Americans as a new century dawned, would acquire a new resonance and meaning after 9/11, as several essayists have observed. Much as Anglo-Texans indulged their hero-worship of the "sons of '76" during the struggle with Mexico, Americans would discover in the greatest generation a model for emulation in the war on terror. And just as the inspirational oratory of Patrick Henry had a special meaning for Texans in the mid-1830s, the voices of Allied leaders could be distinctly heard in the rhetoric of US policy makers. Bush administration speechwriters turned, perhaps inevitably, to the wartime addresses of Allied leaders, who had rallied Americans and Britons some six decades earlier. President Bush's first speech to the nation after the 9/11 attack, his speech in the National Cathedral on September 14, 2001, contained deliberate echoes of an October 1941 address delivered by Franklin D. Roosevelt. Administration speechwriters were no less intent on channeling Winston Churchill, invoking the British leader not only by name but mimicking the cadence and style of his more memorable wartime addresses. In his speech to a joint session of Congress on September 20, the president drew from a BBC radio broadcast that Churchill had delivered in February 1941 (during the dark days of the London blitz), when he famously declared: "We will not tire, we will not falter, and we will not fail."[69]

Blurring the line between the two crises still further, US policy makers and pundits developed a new vocabulary that self-consciously recalled the demonology of an earlier time. Terms such as "Islamo-fascism," "axis of evil," and "de-Baathification" would become part of the national lexicon.[70]

As in the Texas Revolution, these were not mere rhetorical flourishes, but deliberate attempts to find in the past an organizing trope to make sense of a crisis Americans only dimly understood. Indeed, there can be little doubt that US policy makers believed such parallels to be an entirely appropriate reading of the crisis at hand. Tasked in December 2001 with writing a speech that would draw a clear connection between Al Qaeda and Iraq, Bush speechwriter David Frum coined the term "axis of evil," a phrase deliberately calculated to demonstrate the ideological linkage between those who had attacked the United States on 9/11 and what the administration perceived to be the bigger threat: Saddam Hussein. Frum turned to the historical record for guidance and inspiration. He found both in FDR's famous "day of infamy" speech, which first informed the nation of the attack on Pearl Harbor, even as it laid out the rationale for a war with Nazi Germany.[71] The Bush administration continued to draw on such comparisons as it prepared the nation for the invasion of Iraq. The belief that Nazi Germany and Iraq posed identical threats provided both a facile frame of reference—the labeling of antiwar opponents as "appeasers," for example—and a handy instruction manual with which to craft specific policies. Allowing the memory of World War II to intrude upon its own war effort at every turn, administration leaders were determined to show that they had "learned" the lessons of history.[72]

To be sure, such parallels have limitations, but at the very least they serve to draw attention to the extent to which the past—that is, a carefully constructed interpretation of it—can inform the behaviors of later generations. In both cases, an historical didacticism shaped Americans' actions as they searched for answers in the face of an entirely new threat (Mexican centralism, Islamic jihadism), the nature of which they did not yet fully comprehend. It mattered not at all that few Americans could remember the events upon which they framed their response to the crises at hand. On the contrary, Americans evinced little interest in comparisons to more recent, but less morally satisfying conflicts. Far from diluting their symbolic power, the passage of time invested both the American Revolution and World War II with an easy malleability, allowing a new generation to draw its own meaning from them. Stripped of any moral ambiguity and enshrouded in a set of comforting myths, both events offered Americans a means to legitimize their actions, to endow them with a momentous consequence. Finally, in both cases, an acute generational anxiety framed the response to the crisis at hand. Like Americans at the onset of the twenty-first century, Anglo-Texans were keenly aware of the achievements of their forefathers, their own "greatest generation." Americans framed their response to both crises as an opportunity to achieve their own defining—and redemptive—historical moment. For all these reasons, the urge to replicate earlier conflicts proved irresistible.[73]

In the immediate aftermath of separation from Mexico, Anglo-Texans continued the process of molding their rebellion into an exact likeness of the struggle that had brought about the independence of the thirteen colonies. In their postmortems on the rebellion, editorialists spared no effort in pointing out what they perceived to be similarities between the two events. One writer, who adopted the pseudonym "Patrick Henry," insisted that Anglo-Texans had shown clemency to Mexican troops at San Jacinto, much as the Continental Army had done at Yorktown, while another compared Santa Anna's capture to the surrender of Lord Cornwallis. And while Texas faced seemingly insurmountable obstacles as it sought to establish a fully functioning government, editorialists reminded their readers that the American republic in its infancy had faced similar challenges. Indeed, they confidently predicted that just as their forebears' experiment in republican government had influenced events in Texas, their own revolt would have equally favorable effects upon Mexico.[74] And, no less important, such a similarly bright future for the infant republic allowed Anglo-Texans to cloak their personal ambition with the mantle of a noble cause, the kind that had drawn thousands of young men like John Sowers Brooks. Just as in the United States, "Texas now presents to her patriotic citizens the same opportunities of acquiring fame, the same opportunities of serving their country."[75]

And yet, even as they delighted in pointing out these similarities, Anglo-Texans were already engaged in the process of decoupling their insurrection from its American predecessor. In the months prior to the onset of hostilities and during the conflict itself, Anglo-Texans and their supporters in the United States had worked to fuse the two events in the public consciousness of Americans on both sides of the Sabine River. In so doing, they had managed to legitimize the Texas revolt, thereby deflecting criticism of those who dismissed the independence movement as a naked land grab and proslavery conspiracy. By the fall of 1836, however, such comparisons had ceased to serve any useful purpose. Indeed, to belabor the historical parallels in the aftermath of the conflict would actually serve to diminish what Anglo-Texans thought they had achieved. As a result, the significance of 1776 in the Texas creation narrative would begin to recede as Anglo-Texans began to fashion their own unique story from the events of 1835–36. Their martial struggle could now stand alone, a narrative with its own fallen martyrs and heroic pantheon, in which the siege of the Alamo, the executions at Goliad, and the victory at San Jacinto featured prominently. When interim president David G. Burnet delivered his first and only message to the Texas Congress in October 1836, he made only a passing reference to American citizens' decisive role in the war effort, stating simply that the struggle for independence had led to "the diffusion of the great principles of '76."[76] The inaugural address of incoming president Sam Houston did not mention the American contribution at all. For Houston and for so many other Texans, the narrative had already become one in which a valiant "little band" of Texas colonists had managed to emerge victorious in the face of insuperable odds.[77] Tellingly, when printer Gail Borden reissued William Barret Travis's now famous "Victory or Death" letter, which had been addressed "To the People of Texas and all Americans in the World," the widely disseminated broadside bore the simple title "To the People of Texas."[78]

The need to disassociate the Texas insurrection from the US experience became even more desirable once it became clear that Texas would not fit neatly into the larger American political narrative of the 1830s. Most insurrectionists had assumed that Texas would be speedily incorporated into the United States, unaware that fierce opposition to the expansion of slavery would derail early annexation talks. When Texas voters approved an annexation referendum by an overwhelming margin in the fall of 1836, antislavery societies inundated the US Congress with petitions opposing the measure. In 1838, John Quincy Adams staged a twenty-two-day filibuster to prevent a resolution calling for the immediate annexation of Texas from coming to a vote, and the 25th Congress adjourned without taking any action on the matter. Unwilling to hazard a political firestorm over the issue, the Van Buren administration notified Texas diplomats that it would not pursue annexation in the next session.

Now that Texas had unexpectedly become a nation by default, its citizens had no choice but to craft a new creation narrative, one that de-emphasized the role of the United States. Resentment at Washington's rebuff helped to sever the "mystic chords of memory" that bound them to their country of origin. The result was a self-conscious nationalism, more ersatz than organic, that emphasized the region's exceptionalist character. And though Anglo-Texans never relinquished the goal of annexation, overwhelmingly supporting the measure when a second opportunity to enter the Union arose in 1845, they continued to build upon a narrative that focused on the uniqueness of their struggle against Mexico. Orations delivered during Independence Day observances during the Republic period, not surprisingly, tended to dwell upon the alpha male heroics of celebrated freedom fighters.[79] Early efforts to write a history of the Texas independence movement also downplayed the extent to which an American historical memory had shaped the Texan revolutionary ideology. Still believing it necessary to legitimize the events of 1835–36, Henry Stuart Foote asked his readers to ponder the many "curious coincidences" between the two rebellions in his *Texas and the Texans*, published in 1841. By the time Henderson K. Yoakum published his two-volume *History of Texas* in 1855, however, the American contribution to the Texas cause had all but disappeared.[80]

In their search for the Texas Revolution's underlying causes, historians have focused on the concrete, emphasizing the political tensions and racial animus that existed between Anglo-Texan colonists and Mexico. But perhaps we might be well served to look beyond specific issues of contention toward something more elusive, more opaque: the broader mindset through which these issues are filtered, perceived, and acted upon. In deciding upon a course of action in 1835, Anglo-Texans looked to the past. Eager to view the conflict as part of a broader historical continuum, they deliberately strove to mimic the behaviors of an earlier generation. But it was a narrative that could be easily discarded once independence had been achieved. And as Anglo-Texans set about to tell the story of their separation from Mexico, few could remember the extent to which they had once been, in a very real sense, re-enactors of the American Revolution.

NOTES

1. Stephen F. Austin to Militiamen, on or about May 1, 1826, *Papers Concerning Robertson's Colony in Texas,* Malcolm McLean, comp. and ed. (Arlington, Texas: UTA Press, 1983), 2:560.

2. "B.W. Edwards and H.B. Mayo to the Inhabitants of Pecan Point," December 25, 1826, ed. Eugene Barker, *Austin Papers, Annual Report of the American Historical Association for the Year 1919*, vol. II, Part 2 (Washington, DC: Government Printing Office, 1924), 1542–45.

3. David J. Weber, "Refighting the Alamo: Mythmaking and the Texas Revolution," *Myth and the History of the Hispanic Southwest, Essays* (Albuquerque: University of New Mexico Press, 1988), 138–151; Raúl A. Ramos, *Beyond the Alamo: Forging Mexican Ethnicity in San Antonio, 1821–1861* (Chapel Hill: University of North Carolina Press, 2009), 81–107. See also Andrés Reséndez, *Changing National Identities at the Frontier: Texas and New Mexico, 1800–1850* (New York: Cambridge University Press, 2004), 146–170.

4. Although the Anglo-Texan colonists' historical memory of the American Revolution has received scant attention, several historians have noted the similarities between the two conflicts. See, for example, Eugene C. Barker, "The Texan Declaration of Causes for Taking up Arms Against Mexico," *The Quarterly of the Texas State Historical Association*, 15 (January 1912): 174–85; Andreas Reichstein, *Rise of the Lone Star: The Making of Texas* (College Station: Texas A&M University Press, 1989), 194–95.

5. For more on the Jubilee celebrations, see Andrew Burstein, *America's Jubilee: How in 1826 a Generation Remembered Fifty Years of Independence* (New York: Alfred A. Knopf, 2001), as well as Fred Somkin, *Unquiet Eagle: Memory and Desire in the Idea of American Freedom, 1815–1850* (Ithaca, NY: Cornell University Press, 1987), 131–74.

6. Sam W. Haynes, *Unfinished Revolution: The Early American Republic in a British World* (Charlottesville: University of Virginia Press, 2010), 112.

7. Haynes, *Unfinished Revolution*, 61–62.

8. "Pennsylvania. Address of the committee of the Harrisburg convention . . ." in *Niles' Register*, March 20, 1824, 41; Haynes, *Unfinished Revolution*, 113–114.

9. Haynes, *Unfinished Revolution*, 144–45.

10. *The Man*, June 29, 1835. Quoted in ed. John R. Commons, *A Documentary History of American Industrial Society* (New York: Russell and Russell, 1958), 6:41.

11. Commons, ed. *A Documentary History of American Industrial Society*, 6:98. Sarah Purcell, *Sealed with Blood: War, Sacrifice and Memory in Revolutionary America* (Philadelphia: University of Pennsylvania Press, 2010).

12. The most influential of the radicals, William H. Wharton, fits none of these criteria. A native not of the Deep South but of Nashville, Tennessee, he was 33 at the outbreak of hostilities, and had been living in Texas since 1827. For a traditional view of the so-called war party, see Margaret Swett Henson, "Tory Sentiment in Anglo-Texan Public Opinion, 1832–36," *Southwestern*

Historical Quarterly 90 (July 1986): 9–10. During the early 1830s, the Whartons emerged as strong opponents of Stephen F. Austin. The terms "Wharton party" and "Austin party" were used to designate the two factions. J. H. Kuykendall, *Reminiscences of Early Texans* (Houston: Union National Bank, 1928), 17.

13. In a memorial to the Mexican Congress to protest Austin's 1834 arrest, for example, Wharton quoted from the US Declaration of Independence in pledging "their lives, their fortunes and their sacred honor," upon their word. Henson, "Tory Sentiment in Anglo-Texan Public Opinion," *Southwestern Historical Quarterly* 90 (July 1986): 7.

14. Henry M. Morfit to John Forsyth, August 27, 1836, *PTR* 8:335–38.

15. "Telegraph and Texas Register," *Handbook of Texas Online*. (http://www.tshaonline.org/handbook/online/articles/eet02), accessed June 11, 2014.

16. Paul D. Lack, *The Texas Revolutionary Experience* (College Station: Texas A&M University Press, 1992), 29; Linn to Miller, July 17, 1835, *PTR* 1:257–59; Ugartechea to Cos, July 25, 1835, ibid., 1:276.

17. William Barret Travis to David G. Burnet, August 31, 1835, *PTR* 1:379.

18. James Kerr, "To the People of Texas," January 4, 1836, *PTR* 3:416.

19. William Wirt, *Sketches of the Life and Character of Patrick Henry* (Philadelphia: 1817), 123–24. For more on Patrick Henry's relevance to Americans of the Jacksonian era, see Andrew Burstein, *America's Jubilee*, 39–46. Richard Beeman, *Patrick Henry: A Biography* (New York: McGraw-Hill, 1974). For more on the provenance of Henry's immortal dictum, see Judy Hample, "The Textual and Cultural Authenticity of Patrick Henry's 'Liberty or Death' Speech," *Quarterly Journal of Speech* 65 (October 1977): 300–310.

20. Williamson's speech is reprinted in full in Duncan W. Robinson, *Judge Robert McAlpin Williamson: Texas' Three-Legged Willie* (Austin: Texas State Historical Association, 1948), 106–12.

21. "An Old Soldier," *Texas Almanac*, 1861, 61. The author of the article was believed to be William P. Smith.

22. The phrase has its origins in classical antiquity. At the Battle of Thermopylae in 460 BC, Leonidas I was reported to have uttered the phrase "molon labe," (come and take), in response to the Persians' demand that the Spartans surrender.

23. Wharton to Public, October 3, 1835, *PTR* 2:31.

24. For comparisons to Lexington, see Wharton, *Texas*, 21; "Texas," *Georgia Journal*, November 24, 1835.

25. David Randon et al. to Public, October 2, 1835, *PTR* 2:16; Travis to Jones, October 2, 1835, ibid., 2:28.

26. H. P. N. Gammel, "Journals of the Consultation," *Laws of Texas, 1822–1897* (Austin: Gammel Book Company, 1898), 1:511.

27. "Proclamation of the Federal Volunteer Army of Texas," *PTR* 3:467–68.

28. [Dimmitt to Public], October 21, 1835, *PTR* 2:180.

29. "Goliad Declaration of Independence," December 20, 1835, *PTR* 3:265.

30. Edward L. Miller, *New Orleans and the Texas Revolution* (College Station: Texas A&M University Press, 2004), 60–61.

31. Richard Royall, "To the Citizens of the United States," October 26, 1835, *PTR* 2:225, 226.

32. *Georgia Telegraph*, December 7, 1835.

33. Robert E. May, *Manifest Destiny's Underworld: Filibustering in Antebellum America* (Chapel Hill: University of North Carolina Press, 2004), 9.

34. The *New York Courier and Enquirer*, a Whig paper, was among the first to criticize the revolt. *New York Courier and Enquirer*, October 31, 1836.

35. "From the Pawtucket Chronicle," *The Liberator*, July 28, 1837.

36. [Lexington Meeting], April 20, 1836, *PTR* 5:518. See also [Natchez Meeting], December 8, 1836, *PTR* 3:118–119. See also [Natchitoches Meeting], October 7, 1835, *PTR* 2:62–64.

37. "Report of Meeting at Nashville," *New Orleans Courier*, November 17, 1835; ed. Charles A. Gulick, *Papers of Mirabeau Lamar* (Austin: A.C. Baldwin, Printers, 1921–27), 1:253; [Steedman to Smith], December 30, 1835, *PTR* 3:378.

38. "Address" [11/17/35], *PTR* 3:58.

39. "Volunteers for Texas!" *Charleston Mercury*, November 10, 1835.

40. C. A. Parker to—, *PTR* 2:476.

41. "Texas," *Southern Argus*, December 4, 1835. For more on the Troutman flag, see Lucien Lamar Knight, *Georgia's Landmarks, Memorials and Legends* (Atlanta: Byrd Print Co., 1913–14), 1:34–36.

42. J. W. Fannin to Ward et al., December 25, 1835, *PTR* 3:322–23.

43. Sam Houston to Parker, October 5, 1835, *PTR* 2:46–47. On November 24, the Provisional Government offered US volunteers a land bounty of 640 acres, or one square mile.

44. [Carey to Carey], January 12, 1836, *PTR* 3:492.

45. John E. Roller, "Capt. John Sowers Brooks," *Quarterly of the Texas State Historical Association* 9 (January 1906): 163.

46. Eugene C. Barker, "The Texan Declaration of Causes for Taking up Arms Against Mexico," The *Quarterly of the Texas State Historical Association* 15 (January 1912): 179.

47. "Goliad Declaration of Independence," December 20, 1835, *PTR* 3:265, 67

48. "Communication: Shall We Declare Independence?" *Telegraph and Texas Register*, February 27, 1836.

49. Robinson Proclamation, February 12, 1836, *PTR* 4:313.

50. Ibid., 4:310.

51. Smith to Public, March 2, 1836, *PTR* 3:492.

52. "To the People of the United States," March 16, 1836, *PTR* 5:89–90.

53. [Burnet Proclamation] March 18, 1836, *PTR* 5:126.

54. [Burnet Proclamation] March 29, 1836, *PTR* 5:226.

55. *Telegraph and Texas Register*, September 27, 1836. American patriotic airs continued to be sung during commemorations of the Texas Revolution in the years that followed. See, for example, Francis Lubbock's account of a Liberty County banquet celebrating the one-year anniversary of the Battle of San Jacinto. Francis Lubbock, *Six Decades in Texas, or Memoirs of Francis Richard Lubbock, Governor in Texas in War-Time, 1861–63*, ed. C.W. Raines (Austin: Ben C. Jones, 1900), 61.

56. J. A. Leo Lemay, "The American Origins of 'Yankee Doodle,'" *William and Mary Quarterly*, Third Series, 3 (July 1976): 435–464.

57. Frances Trollope, *Domestic Manners of the Americans* (1832), ed. Donald Smalley (New York: Alfred A. Knopf, 1949), 134.

58. "New Yankee Doodle," *Telegraph and Texas Register*, October 31, 1835. The author would like to thank Jeff Dunn for bringing the Yankee Doodle references to his attention.

59. *Telegraph and Texas Register*, August 16, 1836.

60. All three Austin quotes are taken from *An Address delivered by S. F. Austin of Texas to A Very Large Audience of Ladies and Gentlemen in the Second Presbyterian Church, Louisville Kentucky, on the 7th of March, 1836* (Lexington: J. Clarke & Co., Printers, 1836), 9–10, 27–28. Writing to Andrew Jackson, Austin expressed similar sentiments. "Are not we . . . obeying the dictates of an education received here, from you, the American people, from our fathers, from the patriots of '76—the Republicans of 1836?" Austin to Jackson, April 15, 1836, *PTR* 5:478–79. See also Austin to Linn, May 4, 1836, *PTR* 6:160.

61. William H. Wharton, *Texas. Address of the Honorable Wm. H. Wharton, Delivered in New York* (New York: W. H. Colyer, 1836), 6.

62. For more on the commission's diplomatic errand, see Ethel Zivley Rather, "Recognition of the Republic of Texas by the United States," *Quarterly of the Texas State Historical Association*, 13 (January 1910): 155–256.

63. George P. Garrison, "Another Texas Flag," *Quarterly of the Texas State Historical Association*, 3 (July 1899-April 1900): 170–77.

64. "Address," *Kentucky Gazette*, June 20, 1836. The so-called Ladies Legion sailed to New Orleans, where its members were informed that the fighting in Texas had ended. Many returned home, although some members of the company sailed on to Galveston, where the group officially disbanded. *Kentucky Gazette*, October 27, 1836; Robert Bruce Blake, "Ladies' Battalions and Legions," *Handbook of Texas Online* (http://www.tshaonline.org/handbook/

online/articles/qj101), accessed June 9, 2014. James E. Winston, "Kentucky and the Independence of Texas," *Southwestern Historical Quarterly* 16 (July 1912-April 1913): 27–62. For more on the Lexington ceremony, see Rebecca Smith Lee, *Mary Austin Holley, A Biography* (Austin: University of Texas Press, 1962), 270–76.

65. "Cause of Texas—County and City Meeting," *Kentucky Gazette*, April 16, 1836.

66. "Texas Meeting," *Kentucky Gazette*, April 23, 1836.

67. This debate focused principally on the works of two political scientists, Francis Fukuyama, *The End of History and the Last Man* (New York: Free Press, 1993) and Samuel P. Huntington, *The Clash of Civilizations and the Remaking of the World Order* (New York: Simon Schuster, 1996).

68. In his best-selling book, *The Greatest Generation* (New York: Random House, 1997), Tom Brokaw examined the Americans who came of age during the Great Depression and World War II, and went on to transform the United States into a modern superpower. The book struck a responsive chord for many Americans, not only because it highlighted the sacrifices of an earlier generation, but because it revealed, at least by implication, the inadequacies of their own. The 50th anniversary commemorations of World War II also gave rise to several books that revisited the battlefield exploits of World War II veterans. These included works by Stephen Ambrose, a presidential biographer turned military historian who published from 1992 to 1999 five books on the subject, one of which, *Band of Brothers* (New York: Simon & Schuster, 2001), became a cable television series, premiering two days before the 9/11 attacks. Hollywood also sought to profit from the phenomenon with such films as *Saving Private Ryan*, 1998, and *Pearl Harbor*, 2001.

69. Although intended as a memorial service for those killed in the 9/11 attacks, the president's declaration that the conflict would "end in a way, and at an hour, of our choosing," recalled a speech delivered by Franklin Roosevelt following the sinking of the USS *Kearney* by German U-boats. David Frum, *The Right Man: The Surprise Presidency of George W. Bush, An Inside Account* (New York: Random House, 2003), 137–38.

70. The post-9/11 iteration of the term "Islamo-fascism" has been attributed both to Christopher Hitchens and Stephen Schwartz. It was reportedly dropped by the Bush administration because the term was meaningless in the Muslim world. Sheryl Gay Stolberg, "Islamo Fascism Had Its Moment," *New York Times*, September 26, 2006. For a strident defense of the term, and an argument for its utility as a comparative trope, see Norman Podhoretz's *World War IV: The Long Struggle Against Islamo-Fascism* (New York: Doubleday, 2007).

71. In his memoir, *The Right Man*, Frum states: "On December 8, 1941, Roosevelt had exactly the same problem we had. The United States had been attacked

by Japan, but the greater threat came from Nazi Germany. . . . And just as FDR saw in Pearl Harbor a premonition of even more terrible attacks from Nazi Germany, so September 11 had delivered an urgent warning of what Saddam Hussein could and almost certainly would do with biological weapons. The more I thought about it, the more the relationship between the terror organizations and the terror states resembled the Tokyo-Rome-Berlin Axis." Frum, *The Right Man*, 233–34.

72. Two months before the invasion of Iraq, the Department of Defense made what would prove to be one of the most important decisions of the war, insisting on a policy of "de-Baathification" in its plans for the country's postwar reconstruction. Based explicitly on the de-Nazification policy established at the 1945 Treaty of Potsdam, the purging of Hussein loyalists by some estimates resulted in the removal of between 50,000 and 100,000 Baathists from public office, a decision widely credited with fueling the Sunni resistance that followed. Asked about CPA Order No. 1, the directive that implemented the policy of de-Baathification decree, L. Paul Bremer stated: "Just as in our occupation of Germany we had passed what were called 'de-Nazification decrees' and prosecuted senior Nazi officials, the model for the de-Baathification was to look back at that de-Nazification." L. Paul Bremer III interview, "The Lost Year in Iraq," *Frontline*, PBS, October 16, 2006.

73. David Hoogland Noon, "Operation Enduring Analogy: World War II, the War on Terror and the Uses of Historical Memory," *Rhetoric and Public Affairs* 7 (Fall 2004): 339–64; Chris Hayes, September 8, 2006, "The Good War on Terror: How the Greatest Generation Helped Pave the Road to Baghdad," the Chris Hayes blog, http://chrishayes.org/articles/the-good-war-on-terror/, accessed June 13, 2014.

74. "Revolutionary Battles," *Telegraph and Texas Register*, September 6, 1836.

75. *Telegraph and Texas Register*, December 2, 1836.

76. "Journals of the House of Representatives of the Republic of Texas, First Congress, First Session," (Houston: Office of the Telegraph, 1838), 20.

77. "The President's Inaugural Address," *Telegraph and Texas Register*, November 9, 1836.

78. Michael Green, "To the People of Texas & All Americans in the World," *Southwestern Historical Quarterly* 91 (April 1988): 483–508.

79. See, for example, Henry Thompson, A. M. "Oration delivered the 2nd of March, 1839, on the Anniversary of Independence of the Republic of Texas" (Houston: National Intelligencer Office, 1839).

80. See, for example, Henderson K. Yoakum, *History of Texas from Its First Settlement in 1685 to Its Annexation to the United States in 1846* (New York: Redfield, 1856).

THREE

POLITICS AND PROFITS
Mexican Officials and Land Speculation in Texas, 1824–1835

Miguel Soto[1]

MEXICO'S INDEPENDENCE from Spain in 1821 and the creation of a new political order opened a path for opportunists in positions of power or with connections to profit from various sources. These potential paths to wealth included custom duties from the expanding trade, particularly with Great Britain and the United States; church tithes, which had been some of the largest of the Spanish Empire in the previous decades; and land distribution, especially on a huge scale like the one that was about to take place in Texas.

The new country confronted enormous challenges, among them the need to establish a new social and economic order to cope with the profound inequalities that prevailed during the colonial period, all within the context of heightened expectations. In the course of my research, I have become convinced that the Texas colonization process reflects vividly the opportunities and challenges that officials of independent Mexico confronted in trying to meet such challenges in rather complex and difficult circumstances. In fact, some of the conditions in which colonization and shared investments took place raise the question of whether Mexican sovereignty over Texas was not seriously compromised years before the military campaign of 1835. This chapter will try to address some of these aspects.

In the decades prior to the outbreak of the struggle for independence in 1810, Mexico, or New Spain as it was then called, experienced an economic boom, due mostly to the intensive exploitation of silver mines. Alexander von Humboldt, who visited in 1803, described Mexico as "one of the wealthiest, if not *the wealthiest,* land on earth." His comparative charts on silver mining seemed to prove his point, at least in the Western Hemisphere.[2]

While praising the natural bounty of the land, Humboldt also pointed out the enormous physical challenges that Mexico would have to confront—foremost, the Eastern and Western Sierra Madres—in order to profit from its abundant resources;[3] this, however, was something that Mexicans tended to overlook when they read or heard about Humboldt's views.

Abundant, fertile land, especially in Texas, was one of the untapped resources available to the young nation. Establishment of the new political order gave enterprising individuals an opportunity to take advantage of it to make their fortune. Before dealing with some of those wealth-seekers, though, it is important to point out several factors that contributed to Mexican prodigality in the issuing of land grants in Texas. These factors include two international treaties, the issue of border security, and the involvement of American speculators in land distribution in Texas.

Two international treaties contributed to a particular frame of mind among Mexican officials about the possibility of trading land on a large scale. The Louisiana Purchase was the first, in 1803. After trying unsuccessfully to subdue a revolution in Haiti, Napoleon Bonaparte decided to concentrate his efforts against Great Britain and other enemies in Europe; thus, he transferred the province of Louisiana to the United States "with all its rights and appurtenances" for $15 million. Even though the treaty did not state specifically the boundaries of the purchased territory, it was clear that it had more than doubled the size of the original thirteen colonies. The Louisiana Purchase has been properly called "the greatest real estate deal in American history."[4] The second was the Adams-Onís Treaty, also called the Transcontinental Treaty, which was signed in 1819 and ratified three years later. This agreement was a result of the strategic role that Florida played during the War of 1812 and its subsequent partial occupation by American forces. Thus, the Spanish government, in trying to save Texas, signed an agreement with Washington that implied the cession of both Eastern and Western Florida for a payment of $5 million. In return, the United States offered to renounce "forever"—that is how it is worded—"all claims west and south of the Sabine River."[5] This promise did, of course, not last long. Only six years later, the instructions to the first US minister to Mexico told him to explore the possibility of establishing a new boundary with that country, precisely west and south of the river. From then on, such efforts became a recurring topic in the early relations between Mexico and the United States.

While the Spanish Parliament discussed the ratification of the Adams-Onís Treaty in 1820, the press in Madrid debated the advantages of selling distant and unpopulated territories such as Florida *and Texas* in order to concentrate the resources obtained from such a transaction in other areas of the Spanish monarchy.[6] These arguments were known in Mexico following its independence. But even before then, as early as 1813, José María Morelos y Pavón, the second leader of Mexico's struggle for independence, considered exchanging Texas for American military and economic aid for the cause.[7] Thus, this factor lurked in the background as Mexican officials contemplated a land policy for Texas.

Another important factor in shaping Mexico's policy toward Mexican Texas concerned territorial security. In effect, during the war for Mexican independence, between 1810 and 1821, several filibuster expeditions had targeted Texas. The Bernardo Gutiérrez de Lara and Augustus Magee expedition in 1813, for example, led to the earliest formal proclamation of Mexican independence at San Antonio de Béxar in April of 1813.[8] Xavier Mina led another expedition that had a stronger impact in the central part of New Spain between 1816 and 1817. It reached the outskirts of the mining town of Guanajuato in 1817, but in the end, its leader was defeated and executed.[9] Thus, a national priority for Mexico after 1821 was the use of Texas as a buffer against potential aggressors. Spain, which refused to recognize the new country, and hostile American Indians in the north remained a constant menace. The notion that Anglo-Americans could help defend against American Indian attacks was used to support the policy of opening Texas to foreign immigration.

A third factor at play in Mexico's policy in Texas related to the interest of American businessmen, through various agents, in Texas land speculation. In fact, American designs on Texas preceded Mexican independence. The Aaron Burr Conspiracy in 1806 is one example of those early concerns. One of its objectives was the dismembering of both American and Mexican territories in order to form a different nation. At that time, a Mexican association was founded in New Orleans, most probably for speculating in lands that could be obtained from such a scheme.[10] Another case, certainly more important for its consequences, was the creation in March 1822 of the Texas Association, in Nashville, Tennessee. This was a joint venture of over sixty shareholders, including people like Sam Houston. While the ostensible purpose of this endeavor was to populate and protect the borderlands for Mexico, in fact, it was also a speculative scheme.[11]

From the outset, then, a combination of factors, local and international, personal and entrepreneurial, favored the exchange of enormous tracts of land in Texas, and in such exchanges there was almost invariably a combination of Mexican and American interests that participated in those ventures.

It was within the context of these factors that Mexican politicians took up the issue of colonization of its nearly unpopulated frontier. After considerable debate about the best way to address the demographic, economic, and security conditions of its borders, Mexico adopted a public lands policy based on the idea of exchanging land for population. Although it was aware of the dangers, Mexico invited foreign settlers of "industrious habits, good moral character," and Catholic religion into its territory. The inducement was land at cheap prices: 4,428 acres for a head of household at an average price of three or four cents per acre.

The colonization policy and associated land distribution program developed by Mexico contained three features that remained constant even as other aspects of the policy evolved: state control of the settlement process, the use of colonization agents to promote settlement, and the purchase of public lands by insiders. Beginning in 1824, Mexico's national government transferred to the states the authority to regulate and dispose of vacant public lands within their boundaries, subject to certain limitations. Settlement of land within twenty leagues (fifty-two miles) of any foreign nation and ten leagues from the coast, for instance, still required the approval of the central government.[12] With the exception of the 297 titles issued under Stephen F. Austin's first contract, the other titles issued in Texas under Mexican sovereignty were granted by the state of Coahuila y Texas.

A second constant was the government's use of colonization agents, known as *empresarios*. The colonization law adopted by the state of Coahuila y Texas in March 1825, granted the governor authority to enter into contracts with prospective agents, which were good for six years. As designed, the role of *empresarios* within the colonization scheme was that of agents who, at their own expense, would recruit and bring to Texas a specified number of families to be located in defined areas, commonly called "colonies" or "empresario grants," although it should be stressed that an *empresario* owned none of the land and could not issue titles to settlers. The issuance of titles was a prerogative of the land commissioners appointed by the governor for this purpose.[13]

The possibility of profiting from these *empresario* contracts was sensed at an early stage. Stephen F. Austin initially hoped to profit from collecting money for the land titles from his settlers. He pushed for and obtained a contract from the Mexican government in 1823. Other petitioners also gathered in Mexico City, including Robert Leftwich on behalf of the Texas Association, but they were forced to wait for the government of Coahuila y Texas to approve its own law.

Indeed, soon after the arrival of the Texas delegate Baron de Bastrop to the state legislature in Saltillo, the capital of Coahuila y Texas, the state issued its colonization law in March 1825.[14] This law clearly showed the eagerness of local officials to populate the area. Although in one article the legislature established that in spiritual matters the colonists should be Catholic—as it was the official religion of the country—in another article it only stated that the future colonists should be persons of "good manners" and "Christians," not specifically Catholics, as Professor Eric Schlereth rightly points out in his essay in this volume.[15]

The legislature's desire to attract as many settlers as possible can also be seen in the stipulation that only two hundred inhabitants were needed to set up an *ayuntamiento*, or municipal government. By way of comparison, the 1812 Spanish Constitution, which governed Mexico until 1823, required one thousand inhabitants for this purpose. With the adoption of a federal constitution the following year, that number was increased to two thousand inhabitants. The state of Coahuila and Texas reduced the requirement to 10 percent of that number.[16]

With enactment of the National Colonization Law in 1824, the action moved from Mexico City to Saltillo. The representative of the Texas Association, who had hoped to obtain a grant from the national government, along with other petitioners, moved to Saltillo in pusuit of their objectives. Thus, even before the representative from Texas arrived at the legislature, Robert Leftwich, Haden Edwards, and Benjamin Milam were applying for contracts from the government. As soon as the state Colonization Law was passed, the first two got contracts for 800 families each, and two other petitioners, Frost Thorn and Green De Witt, received one each for 400: in all, 2,400 families.[17]

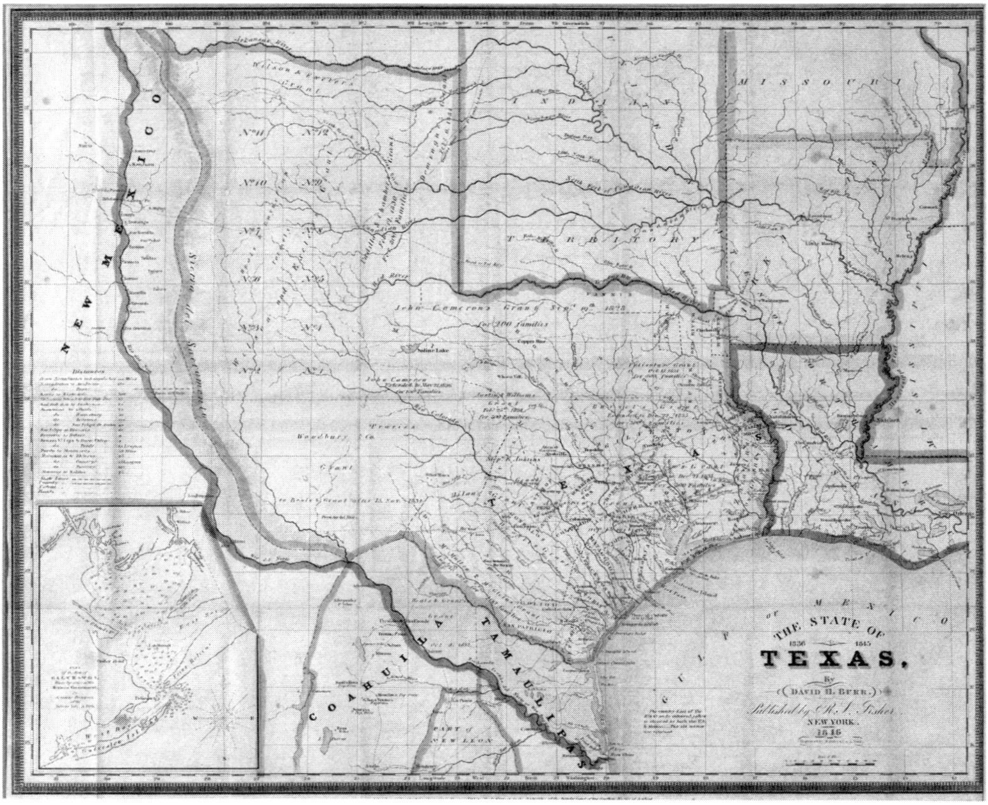

FIGURE 5. Map of the State of Texas by David H. Burr. Courtesy Special Collections Library, University of Texas at Arlington

State authorities would eventually approve close to forty contracts or agreements, and by the early 1830s, most of the Texas territory was covered by *empresario* contracts. Out of all of these contracts, Mexican officials and Texas land speculators were most heavily involved in the negotiations with Lorenzo de Zavala, who was destined to play a major role in Texas politics. Zavala was a public official from Yucatán who had been involved in local and national politics before developing an interest in Texas.[18]

Zavala's contract—which included some of the area formerly awarded to the disgraced Haden Edwards—involved a heavy element of national politics. The first presidential succession in Mexico in 1828 was decided by a military uprising, and Lorenzo de Zavala was one of its main leaders. He was awarded the Ministry of the Treasury for his role. The *empresario* contract was negotiated with the state of Coahuila y Texas, but because part of the land was in the border reserve controlled by the federal government, prior approval from the president was required before the contract could be made. Zavala's political standing gave him a decided advantage over other contenders, among them Peter Ellis Bean.[19]

An intriguing correspondence of the American minister in Mexico at that time, Joel R. Poinsett, suggests that Zavala sought this contract at the request of American speculators. Even before the contract was authorized, Poinsett mentioned to his associates that "the most valuable land in Texas" had been awarded to Zavala in the area next to the Sabine River; in other words, on the border with the United States. Poinsett also advised that it had cost money and that several people, including Zavala, were expecting "a handsome compensation" for it.[20]

As it turned out, being part of the Mexican political scene at that time could have its disadvantages, and Zavala soon suffered the consequences of its instability. The government in which he participated lasted less than a year, and because of his role in the violent seizure of power, he was forced into exile. While in New York, Zavala, along with two *empresarios* with adjoining land grants, David Burnet and Joseph Vehlein, sold their contracts to a venture known as the Galveston Bay and Texas Land Company, which came to include prominent citizens of New York and Boston.

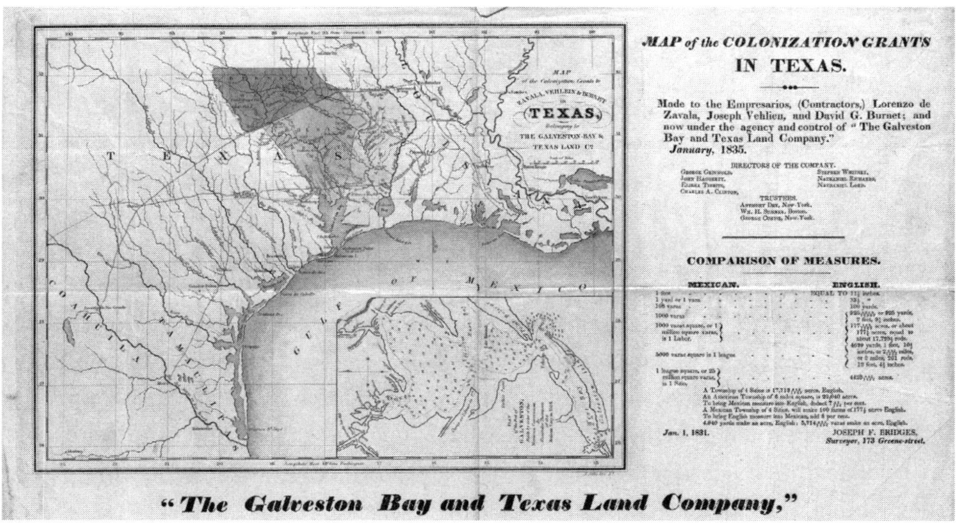

FIGURE 6. Map of Galveston Bay and Texas Land Company. Courtesy Beinecke Rare Book and Manuscript Library, Yale University, New Haven, Connecticut

The company encountered difficulties almost immediately. Mexican authorities disputed the right of the *empresarios* to sell their contracts, and the company initially failed to obtain recognition from the Mexican government. The Law of April 6, 1830, which restricted immigration from the United States, was used to thwart the company's initial attempts to place settlers in Texas. Even when officials' objections were finally overcome, the company's agents in Texas met staunch opposition from the thousands of settlers who had been occupying land in the area extralegally for years. The company felt frustrated at every turn.[21] The Texas Revolution dashed the company's last hopes for profiting from the venture, even when Burnet and Zavala became the interim president and vice-president of the Republic of Texas. True to their persistent nature, company officials sought for decades to recoup their losses by resorting to international claims commissions.

As far as other entrepreneurial ventures, by 1835, just before the outbreak of the Texas Revolution, other contracts had been sold to New York companies.[22] General Vicente Filisola, for example, received $2,000 from New York associates to form the "Filisola Association" in May of that year[23]; Filisola was the second in command of the Mexican army during the campaign of 1835–36, ordering the retreat of Mexican forces after the capture of Santa Anna at San Jacinto. I have questioned Filisola's motives for such a move elsewhere and mention it here in passing as another example of the kind of interests involved in land distribution in Texas.[24]

The third feature of Mexico's land distribution program that remained constant was that the colonization laws provided another avenue of potential profit to those in the know. The purchase of eleven-league tracts for resale to American speculators drew the attention of a group of government officials and their associates. Article 24 of the colonization law of 1825 contained the enabling provision. The article provided that Mexicans, and Mexicans only, could purchase up to eleven leagues (46,712 acres) directly from the state government at a price set by law.

I have compiled a list of over 160 Mexican purchasers of tracts of up to eleven leagues.[25] The list of purchasers includes an assortment of state and national officials and their associates, along with officers and soldiers serving at Nacogdoches and other towns of East Texas, and individuals recruited as "strawmen" in the speculation that surrounded these grants.[26] It is obvious that many of these purchasers did not plan to move to Texas. Instead, they made the purchase with the specific purpose of selling the land, generally to Anglo-American speculators, which the law did not forbid. As a result, between 1828 and 1834 there was an intensive exchange of these lands.

The list of purchases of Texas lands includes names such as Miguel Zaragoza, the father of Ignacio Zaragoza, the defender of Puebla in the 5 de Mayo battle against the French in 1862; and José Francisco Madero, the great-grandfather of Francisco I. Madero, the leader who started the Mexican Revolution in 1910. Buyers also included such prominent national politicians as Mariano Riva Palacio and Manuel Crescencio Rejón. The former was a member of the Ayuntamiento of Mexico City and later governor of the state of Mexico; the latter was a congressman and later minister of foreign relations. State politicians and officials who participated in the speculation included governors José María Viesca and his brother Agustín, vice-governor Víctor Blanco, and governor-secretaries Santiago del Valle and Juan Antonio Padilla.

Most of the purchased land ended up in the hands of a few American agents who again represented business interests from the North. More than one of the American speculators was left holding the bag because the grants were located within a restricted area, in the coast or border reserves established by Mexican laws. Because the buyers failed to obtain authorization from the federal government, the Republic of Texas declared them illegal.[27]

A notion common to both the large contractors or *empresarios* and the purchasers of speculative tracts was that Texas lands were a distant and disposable patrimony. The Spaniards had held a similar perspective years earlier. This is not to say that *all* Mexicans shared that view. Manuel de Mier y Terán, inspector general of Texas, was particularly zealous in the performance of his duties and warned the government of the increasing danger that Americans represented to national sovereignty. He tried with the limited means available to him to put into effect the prohibition of American immigration established by the Law of April 6, 1830.

It should also be pointed out that not everything regarding Texas lands was a search for easy profit; a review of the approximately 4,200 titles issued by the land commissioners of Coahuila y Texas shows that roughly 3,500 of them "retain their legal validity up to this day."[28] Thus, it is important to have a balanced view of the transfer and occupation of lands in Texas.

Mention can be made in passing of at least two other instances of important involvement of Mexican officials in efforts to sell Texas land on a large scale. The first one refers to Lucas Alamán, who was probably the most important statesman in Mexico at that time. In 1830, in response to the warnings of Inspector General Manuel de Mier y Terán, Alamán, then minister of foreign relations, pushed for the approval of the Law of April 6, 1830, which forbade American immigration into Texas.[29] Two years later, however, when the most conspicuous rebellious military leader at that time, Antonio López de Santa Anna, launched an uprising and seized the government's sources of income, like other politicians before him and in order to save his administration, Alamán seriously considered the transfer of Texas to the United States so he could obtain supplies and assistance.[30] This is significant, because Alamán had come to realize that both the unstable political conditions in Mexico and American immigration into such a distant province had made it impossible to maintain Mexican sovereignty over the region, despite his best efforts. As a result, as US minister Anthony Butler said, the Mexican statesman was ready to get something practical out of a lost situation.[31] In the end, these attempts came to nothing, but that one of the staunchest defenders of Mexican sovereignty should have adopted this attitude is very revealing.

The second instance refers to a dispute between the Coahuilan cities of Monclova and Saltillo in 1834 and 1835 over the seat of the state government. Their differences can be traced back to the colonial period, but with independence and especially with the establishment of the federal republic, the city of Saltillo—which was the home of the 1824 Constitution designer Miguel Ramos Arizpe—got the upper hand. Within a few years, however, according to the State Constitution, most of the legislature delegates (including the one from Texas) decided that the capital should be Monclova, as it was at the end of the Spanish rule; thus, for five years Coahuila y Texas had two capitals, Monclova and Saltillo. Finally, in 1833 the majority decided that the capital should be one: Monclova; that decision coincided with a series of strong secular reforms promoted by the federal administration of Valentín Gómez Farías and Antonio López de Santa Anna.[32]

The following year, though, the country experienced a counter-revolution, and Saltillo tried to use this to its advantage; it condemned the "radical" legislation passed in the previous months, particularly the removal of the state capital to Monclova. Thus, local disputes had national implications: The politicians from Saltillo renounced their earlier preferences for federal institutions and became strong supporters of centralism; on the other hand, the *Monclovenses* reached out to the foreign colonists in Texas and their entrepreneurial contacts in the United States in order to stop what they saw as the seizure of the state's public domain by the national government and the centralization of the political system. In order to achieve this goal, the legislature at Monclova passed a series of laws that authorized the state government to dispose of millions of acres, and between March and May of 1835, the acting governors signed several contracts with speculators that seriously imperiled the patrimony of the state. These actions were similiar to those of the late Spanish governor of Florida, José Coppinger, who sold huge tracts of land just prior to the formal American acquisition of that territory.[33] The Monclova sales were condemned not only by the Mexican govenment, but by many colonists in Texas as well. The constitution of the Republic of Texas declared several of these sales null and void. One of the beneficiaries of those sales was none other than the Federalist leader Valentín Gómez Farías.

Thus, in reviewing all of these issues, one may wonder if Mexican sovereignty over Texas was really lost by Santa Anna in San Jacinto in April of 1836, or whether it had not already been compromised long before by previous Mexican administrations and their colonization policies and various sales and dealings. This is not by any means an attempt to exonerate Santa Anna as commander of the Mexican Army and his poor performance during the Battle of San Jacinto.

Although Anglo-American immigration to Texas was not overwhelming in real terms (thirty thousand to forty thousand by 1835), it was more than enough to relegate the population of Spanish and Mexican descent to a minority. The failure to assimilate the new population into the social and economic fabric of Mexico soon became a problem for the young nation.[34]

In the end, it is clear that a decisive factor in the outcome of the Texas situation was the low population of Mexican society at that time, about six million people, compared to the enormous potential of the United States, which almost doubled its population every twenty years in those decades of the nineteenth century, starting with about five million in 1800. Obviously, this demographic imbalance is very different today, when Latinos can help decide the outcome of a presidential election, as happened in 2012.

Allow me to return to a point that has been mentioned earlier but should be repeated: that the drive for profit from Texas lands ran high on both sides of the border. Studies of recent years, like Gregg Cantrell's excellent biography of Stephen F. Austin and Edward L. Miller's work, *New Orleans and the Texas Revolution*, show us the role of this powerful factor in the colonization process and later in the events of the Texas Revolution.[35] But certainly, more work is needed along those lines to have a more realistic and complete view from a dual Mexican and American perspective.

Some decades ago, an essay by Holman Hamilton, entitled "Texas Bonds and Northern Profits," explored a similar eagerness for profit in the North and South during the negotiations of the Compromise of 1850, which finally set the terms of the incorporation of Texas into the Union.[36] Obviously, as new studies analyze various aspects of the complex relationship between Mexico and the United States, more questions are raised and new doors are opened to the understanding of the tangled relationship of our two countries. That is a common task that we have ahead of us, and I believe we should confront it together.

NOTES

1. The writing of this paper was part of a sabbatical at The University of Texas at Austin supported by a fellowship from the Universidad Nacional Autónoma de México, through the Dirección General de Asuntos del Personal Académico (DGAPA), between September of 2012 and April of 2013. I also want to recognize here the invaluable assistance of Galen D. Greaser, retired librarian of the Spanish Collections of the Texas General Land Office Archives in Austin, in reviewing and commenting upon the content of this text.

2. For Humboldt's appraisal of Mexican mining, see *Political essay of the Kingdom of New Spain. Containing Researches relative to the Geography of Mexico, the Extent of its Surface and its political Division into Intendancies, the physical aspect of the country, the population, the State of Agriculture and Manufacturing and Commercial Industry, the Canals projected between the South Sea and Atlantic Ocean, the Crown Revenues, the Quantity of the precious Metals which have flowed from Mexico into Europe and Asia, since the Discovery of the New Continent and the Military Defense of New Spain, by Alexander de [sic] Humboldt, with Physical Sections and Maps, Founded*

on Astronomical observations, and Trigonometrical and Barometrical Measurements, Translated from the . . . French by John Black (New York: I. Riley, 1811) 1:168–70. Regarding the prodigality of nature in these lands in general, Humboldt wrote:

"The vast kingdom of New Spain under a careful cultivation, would alone produce all that commerce collects together from the rest of the globe, sugar, cochineal, cacao, cotton, coffee, wheat, hemp, flax, silk, oils, and wine. It would furnish every metal without even the exception of mercury. Super timber and an abundance of iron and copper would favor the progress of Mexican navigation." Humboldt, *Political essay...* 1:61.

In fact, the Prussian scientist even suggested that the Spanish king should move the seat of government to Mexico City, stating:

"The physical situation of the city of Mexico possesses inestimable advantages, if we consider it in the relation of its communication with the rest of the civilized world [that is the western hemisphere]. Placed on an isthmus, washed by the South and the Atlantic Ocean, Mexico appears destined to possess a powerful influence over the political events which agitate the two continents. A king of Spain resident in the capital of Mexico, might transmit his orders in five weeks to the Peninsula in Europe, and in six weeks to the Philippine islands in Asia." Ibid., 1:61.

Oddly enough, this edition of Humboldt's text and another English version, *Political Essay on the Kingdom of New Spain, The John Black Translation*, ed. Mary Maples Dunn (New York: Alfred A. Knopf, 1972) do not include the referred charts; but they do appear in the Spanish and French versions: *Ensayo político sobre el reino de la Nueva España*, ed. Juan A. Ortega y Medina, 5th edition, (Mexico: Porrúa, 1991), 386–88; *Essai politique sur le royaume de La Nouvelle-Espagne; par Alexandre de Humboldt, avec un atlas physique et geographique, fondé sur des observations astronomiques, des mesures trigonométriques et des nivellemes barométrioques* (A Paris, chez F. Schoell, Libraire, rue des Fossés-Saint-Germain,-L´Auxerrois, No. 29, 1811, De L´Imprimiere de J.H. Stone), 1:505, 517–19.

3. Humboldt, *Political Essay*, 1:62.

4. "Treaty with France for the Cession of Louisiana, concluded at Paris, April 20, 1803," *American Historical Documents, 1900–1904*, ed. Charles Elliot, (New York: P. F. Collier & Son Corporation 1938); Víctor Arriaga Weiss, *La compra de Luisiana y las ideas sobre la expansión territorial en Estados Unidos* (México: CIDE, Miguel Ángel Porrúa, 1996), 250–54.

5. "Treaty of Amity, Settlement, and Limits Between the United States of America and His Catholic Majesty, Concluded at Washington, February 22, 1819," *American Historical Documents*, 268–276; the US pledge to renounce the said territory is in Article IV, 270.

6. [Comment on the Cortes or Congress session of July 9, 1820], *El Censor*, August 5, 1820, 12, 15. A copy of this Spanish newspaper is located at the José Fernando Ramírez Library, Biblioteca Central Pública del Estado de Durango José Ignacio Gallegos, Fondo Bibliográfico Antiguo.

7. "Morelos al mariscal [Ignacio] Ayala, le comunica cuáles son sus relaciones para proveerse de armamento y le informa sobre las naves de Filipinas," [Military headquarters of Yanhuitlán], February 17, 1813," in Juan E. Hernández y Dávalos, *Documentos para la historia de la guerra de independencia de México* (Mexico: Instituto Nacional de Estudios Históricos de la Revolución Mexicana, 1985), 4:859–60. Indeed, Morelos was not the only Spanish-American leader for independence who considered getting external support in exchange for strategic territory; Simón Bolívar thought of the same procedure by offering Nicaragua and Panama to England in 1815; Bolívar to Maxwell Hyslop, Kingston, Jamaica, May 19, 1815, eds. Vicente Lecuna and Esther Barret de Nazaris, *Simón Bolívar, Obras completas* (Havana: Ministerio de Educación Nacional de los Estados Unidos de Venezuela, 1947), 1:131–34.

8. Donald E. Chipman, *Spanish Texas, 1519–1821* (Austin: University of Texas Press, 1992), 234–35.

9. Ibid., 238–39; Iván Valdés Bubnov, "Galveston la Maldita o el Nuevo Argel" (BA Thesis in History, Facultad de Filosofía y Letras, UNAM, 1999), 80–81.

10. Ernesto de la Torre Villar, "Dos Proyectos para la Independencia de Hispanoamérica: James Workman y Aaron Burr," *Temas de la insurgencia* (México: Universidad Nacional Autónoma de México-Coordinación de Humanidades, 2000), 11–93, offprint of *Revista de Historia de América* 49 (June 1960): 57.

11. *Papers Concerning Robertson's Colony in Texas, Volume I, 1788–1822. The Texas Association,* ed. Malcolm D. McLean (Fort Worth: Texas Christian University Press, Arlington: University of Texas at Arlington Press, 1974–1992), 360–72. A specific proposal of this consortium can be found in the *Memorial que varios ciudadanos de los Estados Unidos de América presentan al Gobierno Independiente de México*, Mexico, Ofic. de Alejandro Valdés, Imp. de Cámara del Imperio, 1822.

12. "Decreto de 18 de agosto, 1824. Sobre colonización," eds. Manuel Dublán y José María Lozano. *Legislación mexicana o sea colección completa de las disposiciones legislativas expedidas desde la independencia de la república*, Ordenada por los Lics. (Mexico: Imprenta del Comercio, 1876–1911, 1876–1911), 1:712–13. The restrictions were established in article 4.

13. Galen D. Greaser, "That They May Possess and Enjoy the Land: The Spanish and Mexican Land Commissioners of Texas" (unpublished manuscript, Texas General Land Office, Austin, Texas), 16.

14. Philip Hendrik Nering Bögel, "Decreto No. 16. Ley de Colonización," Saltillo, March 24, 1825, J.P. Kimball, MD, *Laws and decrees of the State of Coahuila and Texas, in Spanish and English to which is added the Constitution of Said State, also the Colonization Law of the State of Tamaulipas and Naturalization Law of the General Congress* (Houston: Telegraph Power Press, 1839), 15–23.

15. The articles that referred to religious matters were 3 and 5, ibid., 16.

16. Article 41 of the same State law, ibid., 21.

17. "Actas del Congreso Constituyente del Estado Libre de Coahuila y Texas. August 15, 1824 to September 9, 1825," October 21, 1824, p. 45 of typed version. For the three grants issued see Mary Virginia Henderson, "Minor Empresario Contracts for the Colonization of Texas, 1825–1834," *Southwestern Historical Quarterly* 31 (Apr. 1928): 295–324; ibid. 32 (July 1928): 1–28; 298–99.

18. Lorenzo de Zavala had been secretary of the Ayuntamiento in Mérida in 1813–14. Because of his liberal views, he was prosecuted and put in jail for three years; then, in 1820, as the Constitution of 1812 was restored in Spain, he was a part of the Provincial Deputation in Yucatán, and later a representative to the Spanish Cortes. With independence he returned to Mexico and served in the first two congresses. Later he became governor of the State of Mexico, and in that position in 1828 he applied for the *empresario* contract in Texas. Betty Zanolli Fabila, "La alborada del liberalismo yucateco. El primer Ayuntamiento Constitucional de Mérida 1812–1814" (MA Thesis in History, Facultad de Filosofía y Letras, UNAM, 1993); Raymond Estep, *Lorenzo de Zavala. Profeta del liberalismo mexicano* (Mexico: Librería de Manuel Porrúa 1952), 195, 198–99.

Zavala's grant resulted from the first confrontation of a grantee—Haden Edwards—and the Mexican authorities in the area of Nacogdoches, during the so-called Fredonian Rebellion, after its leaders were denounced and attacked by Cherokee Indians who had previously been supporters of the rebellion. Cuauhtémoc Velasco, *La frontera étnica en el noreste mexicano. Los comanches entre 1800–1841* (Mexico: Instituto Nacional de Antropología e Historia, Centro de Investigaciones y Estudios Superiores en Antropología Social, Comisión Nacional para el Desarrollo de los Pueblos Indígenas, COANCULTA, 2012), 227–28.

19. Michael P. Costeloe, *La República Federal en México, 1824–1835* (Mexico: Fondo de Cultura Económica, 1975), 219. Jack Jackson, *Indian Agent: Peter Ellis Bean in Mexican Texas* (College Station: Texas A&M University Press, 2005).

20. Joel. R. Poinsett to [Thomas Luckett], Mexico [City], June 7, 1828, Anthony Dey Correspondence, Beinecke Rare Books and Manuscripts Library, Yale University.

21. Greaser, "That They May Possess and Enjoy the Land," 35.

22. This was a claim of several businessmen. James Prentiss, G[ilbert] L. Thompson to Anthony Butler, New York, July 17, 1835; Prentiss to Butler, New York, July 27, 1835; G[ilbert] L. Thompson, Thomas Davis, and James Prentiss to President Antonio López de Santa Anna, New York, 1835. All of these letters are in the Anthony Butler Papers, Briscoe Center for American History, The University of Texas at Austin. John Charles Beales, in particular, sold his contracts to New York investors who, in turn, created companies intended to profit from Texas lands.

23. Receipt for $2,000, New York, May 20, 1835, Samuel Swartwout Papers, Briscoe Center for American History, The University of Texas at Austin.

24. Vicente Filisola, *Memorias para la historia de la Guerra de Tejas,* (Mexico: Editora Nacional, 1973) [Tipografía de R. Rafael, 1849], 2:151, 177. In his *Memorias,* Filisola includes an extensive account of the various European seventeenth-century settlements in Texas, and then, after Mexican Independence, he deals with the various foreign colonists in the area. He neglects to mention, however, that he himself was a land grantee; so, when he condemns "the foreign adventurers" in Texas for their greed, he ignores his New York associates and the down payment that he got from them referred to in the previous note. Miguel Soto, "Vicente Filisola," in *El Surgimiento de la Historiografía Nacional* ed. Virginia Guedea, in *Historiografía Mexicana* (Mexico: Instituto de Investigaciones Históricas, UNAM, 1997), 201–10. A recent study recognizes the well-known Neapolitan background of Filisola, but also points out his partial Spanish origin; his complete name was Vicente Filisola Martínez; Juan Jiménez Vázquez, "Vicente Filisola y las Independencias Española, Mexicana y Centroamericana" (MA Thesis in History, Universidad Nacional Autónoma de México, 2008), 2.

25. Article 24 of the Coahuila y Tejas Law of Colonization, March 24, 1825, Kimball, *Laws and decrees,* 19.

26. "Record Translations, Empresario Contracts, List of Grants for Lands, and other Documents; made Under the Government of Coahuila and Texas, from 1825 to 1835, with Appendix," Texas General Land Office, Spanish Archives, Austin, Texas, 6–17.

27. Miguel Soto, "La otra pérdida de Texas. Venta y tráfico de los predios de once sitios, 1828–1834," in *El territorio disputado en la guerra de 1846–1848. Resistencia y asimilación de las comunidades mexicanas,* eds. Danna A. Levín Rojo y Martha Ortega Noriega México: UAM-Atzcapozalco (Dentro del Programa del Bicentenario del Natalicio de Benito Juárez, 2007), 15–45, 30, 33.

28. Greaser, "That They May Possess and Enjoy the Land," 14.

29. Jackson, *Texas by Terán,* 181.

30. Anthony Butler [to the interim Secretary of State Edward Livingston?],

Mexico [City], July 2, 1832, in Carlos Bosch García, *Butler en Persecución de la Provincia de Texas*, in *Documentos de la Relación de México con los Estados Unidos* (Mexico: Universidad Nacional Autónoma de México, Instituto de Investigaciones Históricas, 1983–1991), 2:290–92; "México. Conferencia número dos entre Butler y Alamán sobre la cesión de Texas," July 10, 1832, ibid., 2: 292–93; Butler to Jackson, México, July, 18, 1832, ed. John Spencer Bassett, *Correspondence of Andrew Jackson* (Washington: Carnegie Institution of Washington, 1931), 4:463–64. I have dealt with this unknown or little recognized attitude of Alamán in "Texas en la mira: política e intereses al iniciarse la gestión de Anthony Butler," in *Política y negocios. Ensayos sobre la relación entre México y los Estados Unidos en el siglo XIX, nuevas perspectivas*, eds. Ana Rosa Suárez Argüello y Marcela Terrazas (Mexico: Instituto de Investigaciones Históricas, UNAM, Instituto de Investigaciones José María Luis Mora, 1997), 19–62.

31. Butler to the interim Secretary of State Edward Livingston [?], Mexico [City], July 2, 1832, Bosch García, *Butler en Persecución de la Provincia de Texas*, 290.

32. Miguel Soto, "La disputa entre Monclova y Saltillo y la independencia de Texas" in *La independencia y el problema de Texas. Dos eventos en Coahuila*, ed. Carlos Valdés (Saltillo: Archivo Municipal de Saltillo, 1997), 45–109; the referred transactions appear in 90–95.

33. George C. Whatley and Sylvia Cook, "The East Florida Land Commission: a Study in Frustration" *The Florida Historical Quarterly* 50 (July 1971-April 1972): 39–52.

34. Manuel de Mier y Terán, *Texas by Terán. The Diary Kept by General Manuel de Mier y Terán on His 1828 Inspection of Texas*, trans. John Wheat, ed. Jack Jackson, with botanical notes by Scooter Cheatham and Lynn Marshall (Austin: University of Texas Press, 2000), 178–79.

35. Gregg Cantrell, *Stephen F. Austin: Empresario of Texas* (New Haven: Yale University Press, 1999); Edward L. Miller, *New Orleans and the Texas Revolution* (College Station: Texas A&M University Press, 2004).

36. Holman Hamilton, "Texas Bonds and Northern Profits: A Study in Compromise, Investment and Lobby Influence," *Mississippi Valley Historical Review* 43 (1957): 579–94.

FOUR

THE TEXAN REVOLUTION OF 1835–1836 AND EARLY MEXICAN NATIONALISM

Will Fowler

INTRODUCTION

Following the end of the Mexican-American War in 1848, moderate liberal politician Mariano Otero (1817–1850) famously lamented that Mexico's traumatic defeat, with the consequent loss of half of the country's territory to the United States, as stipulated in the February 2, 1848, Treaty of Guadalupe Hidalgo, was in no small measure the result of Mexicans not having yet acquired a common sense of national identity, or, as he put it: "There has not been, nor could there have been, a national spirit, for there is no nation."[1] It was a view discussed in the National Palace on May 20, 1847, following the debacle of Cerro Gordo (April 17–18, 1847) and Gen. Winfield Scott's occupation of Puebla (May 15). Mexico's top brass had held an extraordinary secret meeting to determine whether the time had come to count their blessings and surrender. Much to the gathered generals' dismay, Mexicans were quite simply not rallying behind their army. The general population was more concerned with resolving their personal, factional, and/or regional grievances than with defending their country.[2] Antonio López de Santa Anna would look back in anger on the eve of his departure into his second stint in exile, and retort in his *Manifiesto* of March 24, 1848, that their ignominious defeat was to be blamed on the "selfishness of the opulent classes," and the "inaction of the great majority of the Confederation's states . . . who did nothing to defend our country [*para la defensa común*]."[3]

As a number of recent studies have argued, it was only as a result of the Mexican-American War that a national consciousness started to emerge: in part, because Mexicans, in being confronted with an invading expeditionary army that spoke a different language, practiced a different religion, and, arguably, represented a different political outlook, started to think of themselves as Mexican vis-à-vis the hostile American "other."[4] Also, because the defeat inspired Mexican intellectuals and politicians to actively seek ways of correcting the noted absence of a national spirit by writing national histories (such as those Lucas Alamán, Juan Suárez y Navarro, and José María Tornel published between 1849 and 1853), or by organizing a series of nationalist events and festivities, including the commissioning of a national anthem in 1854.[5]

However, as will be argued in the present study, this interpretation of a late-1840s awakening of a Mexican national consciousness overlooks the impact the 1835–36 Texas Revolution had on the incipient nation's intelligentsia's emerging understanding of what it meant to be Mexican at the time. Therefore, after discussing the origins, themes, and context of early Mexican national identity, concentrating on the writings of individuals such as Alamán, Carlos María de Bustamante, Manuel Mier y Terán, and Tornel, this essay analyzes how, alongside Mexico's intelligentsia's damning account of the Texans' agency, an incipient sense of national pride and identity started to make itself heard. Arising from the indignation Mexican intellectuals and politicians felt toward the manner in which the "ungrateful" *foreign* immigrants who settled in Texas refused to comply with the laws of the land, and later turned against Mexico, the contemporary interpretations studied here started to develop an early version of that very national consciousness that would eventually become hegemonic after the Mexican-American War (1846–48). Focusing on how the Mexican intelligentsia of the 1830s depicted the Texan rebels as being foreign (and supported by the expansionist government in Washington, DC), English-speaking, Protestant, disobedient, and land-grabbingly selfish, this study proposes that these intellectuals presented, by contrast, an early vision of *Mexicanidad* that highlighted their Hispanic heritage, Catholic faith, and more spiritual and less materialistic nature. Moreover, by stressing that the Texan immigrants' secessionist drive stemmed from their threatened slave holding entrepreneurial interests, I contend here that they also celebrated Mexico's contrasting caring and abolitionist values. The distinction that would emerge in their writings between what was foreign and national, and between what was considered to belong to Mexico (and not to the United States) would therefore contribute meaningfully to an awakening of an early form of Mexican nationalism at a time when the Mexican nation-state was still very much in the making and *before* the Mexican-American War took place.

THE QUESTION OF NATIONAL IDENTITY IN EARLY REPUBLICAN MEXICO

That a sense of Mexican national identity was not widespread following the achievement of independence in 1821 should not surprise us. Notwithstanding Benedict Anderson's view that "creole communities . . . developed . . . early conceptions of nation-ness—*well before most of Europe*,"[6] Mexico was, in reality, as noted recently by Raymond Buve, "an archipelago of local societies."[7] As stressed by Eric Van Young, the War of Independence (1810–21) had not been driven by Enlightenment ideals or the examples of the US War of Independence (1775–83) and the French Revolution (1789), but by a conflagration of strictly local concerns and grievances: "Where collective political violence erupted in village Mexico, it was most often driven by local historical memory, local religious sensibility, local conflict, and local actors, and was not easily reframed in a discourse of providentialism, national or protonational political aspiration, or Enlightenment philosophical thinking."[8] It is because of this, as Van Young purports in a subsequent study, that "a central characteristic of the Mexican insurgency is that the very localist energies and diversity of circumstances that fueled the popular movements prevented them from coalescing ideologically or militarily for the capture of larger prizes, except under exceptional circumstances and for a limited period of time."[9] The size and geographical, cultural, and ethnic plurality and diversity of Mexico did not make for an easily constructed unifying national whole.[10]

Following its consummation of independence in 1821, after eleven years of civil war, what was Mexico, after all? To begin with, it was not a nation as such but an empire that included (until 1823) the present-day Central American countries of Guatemala, Nicaragua, El Salvador, Honduras, and Costa Rica, and whose remote frontier posts reached as far north as present-day California, Nevada, and Utah. Before Mexico became Mexico it was, as defined in the Plan of Iguala of February 24, 1821, the *América del Septentrión* (Northern America), and subsequently, as described in the

1824 Constitution, the *Estados Unidos Mexicanos* (The United Mexican States). Creole patriotism had certainly resonated with educated Mexican intellectuals like Servando Teresa de Mier (1765–1827) and Carlos María de Bustamante (1774–1848), and the war had given the army a definite patriotic rhetoric and discourse.[11] That much is true. However, this does not mean that for the majority of the population, living in remote sierras, barely speaking Spanish, with strong local, regional, and/or ethnic identities there was a clear sense of what it meant to be Mexican. Until independence, the people who inhabited New Spain and the Captaincy General of Guatemala owed their allegiance and obedience to the crown, not to Spain or their own nation. What was important to them was their families, their neighbors, their parish, and their *milpas* (fields of maize). Making that mental change, coming to accept that they now belonged to a country, a shared and abstract community that extended beyond their village, hacienda, or valley, that granted them rights but also expected them to fulfill certain responsibilities and obligations—to pay taxes, join its national army if they were of a certain age,[12] and abide by its laws—would most certainly not happen overnight and would take considerable time. With an ethnically diverse population of around six million, of which two-fifths were indigenous,[13] and of which only an urban minority could read and write,[14] a uniformly accepted idea of nationhood, of what it meant to be Mexican, would not come easy. By 1836, although the centralist constitution—the so-called Seven Laws—made a point of denoting who qualified as a Mexican (i.e., you needed to have been born in Mexico, or been a resident in Mexico at the time of independence in 1821, or be a naturalized foreigner), it nonetheless made a distinction between having Mexican nationality and being a Mexican citizen who could actually vote in popular elections (servants, criminals, drunks, vagrants, and anybody who earned less than two hundred pesos per annum was excluded).[15] As noted earlier, it would take the Mexican-American War of 1846–48 for Mexicans to begin to see themselves as belonging to a shared imagined community as they were pitted against another country and culture in the form of the invading US army.

Having said this, it would be misleading to claim that nobody had a sense of what Mexico was or what it meant to be Mexican. Anderson was not entirely wrong in suggesting that "pilgrim creole functionaries and provincial creole printmen played [a] decisive historic role" in propounding a patriotic view that distinguished the Mexican-born creoles from the peninsular-born Spaniards on the eve of the Spanish American Wars of Independence (1808–1826). The discriminatory laws of Bourbon Mexico, whereby "the accident of birth in the Americas consigned [the Mexican creole] to subordination—even though in terms of language, religion, ancestry, or manners he was largely indistinguishable from the Spain-born Spaniard," would prove determining—albeit unwittingly—in corroding, on the one hand, any sense of loyalty the creole may have felt toward the King of Spain, and in assisting, on the other, with the development of a new proto-national identity that was *not* Spanish. To quote Anderson one last time: "Hidden inside the irrationality [of the creole's exclusion to positions of power or authority] was this logic: born in the Americas, he could not be a true Spaniard; *ergo*, born in Spain, the peninsular could not be a true American [Mexican]."[16] Mexican politician, conservative ideologue, and historian Lucas Alamán (1792–1853)[17] would, in retrospect, view the manner in which Bourbon colonial Mexico discriminated against the Mexican-born creole population as one of the key causes behind the Mexicans' eventual push for independence: "There were sixty thousand Spaniards born in Europe residing in New Spain in the year of 1808. They occupied all the main jobs in the administration, the church, the judiciary, and the army: they controlled commerce almost exclusively. . . . [The result] was a declared rivalry between them [the European Spaniards and their Mexican counterparts], that albeit hidden for a long time, it was feared could break out in a baneful fashion, given the chance."[18]

The expulsion of the Jesuits from all of Spain's dominions in 1767 also resulted, moreover, in the proliferation of a number of seminal patriotic texts, as certain notable exiled Spanish-American professors, including Francisco Xavier Clavigero (1731–1787), set about producing works of great scholarship about the geography and history of their faraway homeland. Clavigero's *Ancient History of Mexico*, published between 1780 and 1781 from his exile in Italy, and which he described as "a history of Mexico written by a Mexican,"[19] served to initiate an intellectual process of national reappraisal that would ultimately give way to what David Brading came to define as "creole patriotism."[20] With the rejection of Spain serving as a cornerstone of Mexican creoles' incipient national identity came a drive to find in Mexico's ancient Mesoamerican civilizations cultural origins that distinguished them not only from Spain, but also from other emerging independent Spanish-American nations. Early Mexican nationalism would thus, as analyzed by Brading, incorporate the following leading themes—"the exaltation of the Aztec past, the denigration of the [Spanish] Conquest, the xenophobic resentment against the *gachupines* [a pejorative term for Spaniards], and the devotion to Our Lady of Guadalupe"—resulting in a developing national consciousness that was "based in large measure upon a repudiation of their Spanish origins and fostered by an identification with the Indian past."[21] Prolific diarist and pamphleteer, as well as perennial congressman and incorrigible gossip, Carlos María de Bustamante, following on from Servando Teresa de Mier, would make it his patriotic mission, notwithstanding his Galician ancestry and his contempt for contemporary indigenous peoples, to link independent Mexico with its Aztec past. He presented the three-hundred-year-long colonial period as a dark and tyrannical parenthesis in the nation's historical narrative,[22] whilst publishing a series of biographical treatises that exalted the lives of Mexico's ancient indigenous emperors and warriors.[23]

Although the *pronunciamiento* of Iguala of February 24, 1821, which succeeded in bringing an end to Mexico's devastating eleven-year civil war of independence, made a point of celebrating Mexico's Spanish legacies, customs, and affinities (whilst gunning for independence),[24] by the mid-late 1820s, Hispanophobia had become a resonant trait of early Mexican national identity. This was, in part, the result of decades of discriminatory Bourbon legislation, but it also stemmed from King Ferdinand VII's refusal to recognize Mexico's independence (the Spanish government would not do so until 1836), and Spain's open hostility to independent Mexico. This included Spain's bombing of the port of Veracruz from the island garrison of San Juan de Ulúa—which remained Spanish until November 1825—as well as a conspiracy in 1827 to hand Mexico back to Spain, and a failed military expedition to reconquer the country in the summer of 1829.[25] The repudiation of all things Spanish—expressed in a number of *pronunciamientos* during the mid-1820s[26]—would culminate in the passing of a raft of expulsion laws in 1827–29, which, in turn, resulted in the forced departure of thousands of Spaniards from Mexico.[27] Although Mexican officialdom has, in particular since the late nineteenth century, sought to present Mexicanness as a positive fusion of the country's Hispanic and indigenous traditions, celebrating the country's hybrid, syncretic, or *mestizo* characteristics within a *raza de bronce* interpretation of *Mexicanidad*,[28] Hispanophobia, first openly evident during the War of Independence and later in the 1820s, as Marco Antonio Landavazo reminds us, has remained for over two hundred years "practically a defining element of Mexican consciousness . . . , something like an incorrigible bad habit, a spurious expression of Mexicans' mental baggage, a mentality."[29]

Mexicans who went abroad were forced to reflect on what made them different from the people of the lands they visited, and they also started to write about what was distinctive about them and their homeland. Seasoned politician, six-times minister of war, and arch-spin-doctor of the *santanistas*, José María Tornel (1795–1853),[30] following the eighteen months he spent in Baltimore in 1830–31, was duly impressed with the American way of life. He praised the Americans' industriousness, their technological advances, and their country's wealth. Baltimore had, in 1831, he marveled, a thriving stock exchange, gas-lit streets and theaters, and the beginnings of a gigantic railway that would link the city to Pittsburgh. Having said this, Tornel could not help noting with a degree of pride that stemmed from his home in a Catholic country where slavery had been abolished on September 16, 1829, that the only place in Baltimore where blacks and whites were allowed to stand side by side was in the city's Catholic cathedral. In seeing white masters and black slaves take the Holy Communion together, he wrote:

> *In the United States this is truly extraordinary, because the people of color never alternate with those whose skin is white; and thus, only the Catholic religion grants humanity its dignity, without imposing differences based on the variety of one's epidermis. Not even in the theater can whites mix with blacks and mulattos; but God, in his Catholic temples, calls to the same table a mother of duchesses and a slave. For me never was the religion of my fatherland (mi patria) more philanthropic or kind as it was this day.*[31]

As Lucas Alamán would note in a letter to Santa Anna in 1853, echoing Tornel's Catholic vision of Mexicanness, the Catholic faith was "the only common bond that ties all Mexicans together."[32]

Caught up in Tornel's reaction to the American "other" were two further themes that would, alongside Mexican Hispanophobia and Aztec

FIGURE 7. José María Tornel. Courtesy Nettie Lee Benson Latin American Collection, University of Texas at Austin

pride (or neo-Aztecism), eventually become key components of early Mexican nationalism, namely: Catholicism viewed as an essential element of Mexican national identity, and an ambivalent love-hate stance toward the United States. Equally important, in particular for the way Mexicans would understand the Texans' agency in seeking to become independent from Mexico, was Tornel's condemnation of slavery.

Catholicism, and in particular, *guadalupanismo* (the cult of the Virgin of Guadalupe), were defining identity markers from even before the War of Independence. Mexican Roman Apostolic Catholicism, with its autochthonous calendar and saints, featured Mesoamerican religious practices that had been, over time, assimilated and integrated in its hybrid religious celebrations, processions, liturgical events involving the veneration of local Indian icons, cults, and practices. This resulted in Mexico having its very own distinctive national church and traditions.[33] The fact that, moreover, the Virgin Mary had chosen to make her apparition to a poor Indian just outside of Mexico City in 1531 spiritually transformed

Mexico's indigenous-*mestizo* people into something akin to a chosen race. The Indian Juan Diego became a Mexican Moses with the Virgin's miraculous image imprinted on his cape representing the Mexican Ark of the Covenant. *Guadalupanismo* would become a powerful expression of Mexican national identity after Miguel Sánchez (1596?-1674) published in Spanish in 1648, and in Nahuatl a year later, his *Image of the Virgin Mary, Mother of Guadalupe*. As David Brading reminds us: "The devotion [of the Virgin of Guadalupe] united Indians and creoles, rich and poor, in common devotion. . . . The strength and progress of the cult derived from its inextricable intertwining of religious fervor with patriotic enthusiasm. Sharply divided by race, class, customs, and even language, the inhabitants of New Spain had little to bind them together save their common identity as children and subjects of Our Lady of Guadalupe."[34] It is no coincidence that when the Mexican War of Independence erupted on September 16, 1810, Father Miguel Hidalgo y Costilla's rallying call to arms started with the cry: "Long live Religion! Long live Our Very Saintly Mother of Guadalupe!"[35]

The importance of the tie that was forged between Guadalupan Roman Catholicism and Mexican national identity would be reflected in the way that the first four Mexican constitutions (1814, 1824, 1836, and 1843) officially described Mexico as a Roman Catholic country and forbade the toleration of any other religion. It would also find an emphatic expression in the waves of the more than three hundred *pronunciamientos* that were launched in between 1833 and 1834 in opposition to Congress's anticlerical measures, depicting the politicians' attempts to secularize society (by ending certain Church privileges and activities, expelling key outspoken bishops, and confiscating targeted ecclesiastical wealth and properties) as being profoundly *unpatriotic* or antinational. As voiced in the pro-clerical *pronunciamientos* of 1833–34, Congress's attack against "the religion of our ancestors" made it "the duty of every Mexican to act to save the fatherland (*patria*)," sacrificing themselves for their "Sacred Religion."[36] This equation—Catholicism-Mexicanness—would similarly feature in the laws that were passed governing who could colonize the northern territories of Coahuila y Texas. As early as the summer of 1821, on the eve of Mexico's independence from Spain, when Stephen F. Austin moved to Texas to take up his deceased father's colonization concession at the head of three hundred families, it was made clear that these families would have to enter "from Louisiana, [be] all Roman Catholics, of good customs" and be prepared to "respect the constitution [that] established that the religion of the land *was and would be in perpetuity* 'the one true Roman, Catholic, and Apostolic faith.'"[37] Furthermore, once the law of February 13, 1823, was passed, the requirement for colonists to be Roman Catholics, with toleration of no other religion, would be made explicit.[38] This would lead Mexican historian Josefina Zoraida Vázquez to note that the "colonists not only entered Texas as Catholics but also freely accepted religious intolerance."[39] That they subsequently ignored such a stipulation, contravening the terms of their colonization concessions and the constitutional laws of the incipient Mexican nation, would be interpreted in Mexico, and once the Texas Revolution got under way in 1835, as evidence of the insurgent colonists' foreignness and heretical antinational sentiments.

The contradictory US love-hate element of early Mexican national identity evident in Tornel's impressions of Baltimore would be explained by historian Edmundo O'Gorman in the following terms in his seminal 1977 book on Mexico's traumatic history: Mexicans "wanted to enjoy the prosperity of the United States, but without renouncing their traditional way of being for considering this to be the essence of the new nation. . . . Thus they wanted the benefits of modernity, but not modernity itself."[40] Tornel was duly impressed by Baltimore's thriving tobacco market, the prodigies free commerce had brought with it, and the manner in which the city was surrounded by a host of industrial activities. He counted sixty mills, twelve textile factories, several paper, iron, and glass manufacturers, a copper foundry, two theaters, two museums, five markets, fifty primary schools, a public library, ten different banks, and an observatory. It was a city in "perpetual movement."[41] Tornel's awe of the United States' rapid technological and industrial progress would be shared by many Mexicans, including Lorenzo de Zavala, as will be discussed shortly. However, once it became evident that the US government was behind the Texan movement for independence, and went on to declare war on Mexico in 1846, sending its army to the very heart of the Mexican Republic, hoisting the Star Spangled Banner over the National Palace in the main square of Mexico City on September 16, 1847, most Mexicans' admiration for the United States would become indelibly and understandably dented.

However, in the case of Tornel, perhaps unusually, his enthusiasm for all things American was dampened *before* the Texan revolution began.

In being Mexico's minister plenipotentiary in the United States, he was able to witness at close hand how American officials such as Martin Van Buren, Anthony Butler, and David Brent were maneuvering to find ways of purchasing Texas, whilst Zavala and Cuban-born José Antonio Mejía were involved in illegal transactions with the Galveston Bay and Texas Land Company.[42] Tornel actually warned the Mexican government as early as 1830 that "there is no doubt that the majority [of Americans] wish to acquire those states that lie to the south and west of the United States."[43] By 1837, reacting to events in Texas, he would become convinced that "Once they [the Americans] have decided what will most satisfy their greed, they prepare for the right moment to close in on the object of their desire, projecting a certain abandonment and lack of interest that is far from being a true reflection of their real intentions. Once the circumstances seem opportune, they do not think twice about the means to employ to achieve their final aim."[44] Americans may have been industrious, modern, and prosperous, but that did not detract, in Tornel's mind, from the fact that, unlike the Mexican people, "Selfishness is a vice that cannot be separated from the character of the Anglo-American people."[45]

For liberal Yucatecan politician-cum-Texan vice-president Lorenzo de Zavala (1788–1836), his visit to the United States in 1834, albeit confirming his open admiration for the country, made it clear to him, by contrasting one nation with another, what Mexicans were like. Whilst Andrés Reséndez's point that the period in question was "a world of exceedingly fluid identities," is evidently valid, accounting in no small measure for someone like Zavala going from supporting Mexico's independence from Spain in the early 1820s to advocating Texas' independence from Mexico in 1835,[46] Zavala was still able to highlight cultural and behavioral traits that differentiated, in his mind, the nationals from one country from those of the other. Zavala claimed following his trip that the Americans were "hard-working, active, reflexive, circumspect, religious through a multiplicity of sects, tolerant, stingy, free, proud, and perseverant." Mexicans, on the other hand, were, in his own words, "lazy, intolerant, generous bordering on the extravagant, vain, warrior-like, superstitious, ignorant, and enemies of all responsibility." In his view:

> *The American works, [whilst] the Mexican has fun; the former spends hardly anything, the latter until he has nothing left; the one completes the*

> *most arduous of tasks, the other abandons them after the first few obstacles; the one lives in his house, adorns and furnishes it, protecting it from the weather; the other spends his life in the street, avoids being indoors at all costs, and in a region where there are no seasons does not look after his home. In the States of the North everybody is a proprietor tending to augment their wealth; in Mexico the few who are, do not look after their property or even dilapidate it.*[47]

He also thought that the United States was a far better place to live in than Mexico because it thrived on a free economic model, had a small regular army, enjoyed religious freedom as well as freedom of the press, had far fairer justice, penitentiary, and electoral systems, rested on robust meritocratic values, and had an educated population that benefited from a society in which wealth was evenly distributed. There were even more beautiful women in the United States than there were in Mexico![48] Having said this, Zavala would observe, like Tornel, how people of color were segregated and degraded in the United States, praise Tornel and mulatto

FIGURE 8. Manuel de Mier y Terán. Courtesy Special Collections Library, University of Texas at Arlington

president Vicente Guerrero for abolishing slavery in 1829,[49] and condemn the "antiliberal" slavery laws of Louisiana, South Carolina, and Georgia, whilst celebrating those northern states, such as New York, Pennsylvania, and Ohio, where slavery had, in fact, been abolished.[50]

Of course Zavala was the exception. From advocating in his American travelogue that Mexicans—to whom he dedicated his book—should endeavor to emulate the United States in order to overcome their innate barbarism, Zavala would, after speculating in Texan land, go on to actively support the Texas Revolution.[51] The Texan problem, first flagged by General Manuel Mier y Terán (1789–1832), following his 1828 inspection of the region, would have quite the opposite effect on the Mexican intelligentsia. Mier y Terán was shocked to find that, as a result of their laws of colonization (but also the impossibility of controlling the influx of illegal American migrants) "the Americans, . . . here they are the majority."[52] As will be argued presently, events in Texas, rather than inspire Mexican liberals to—as Zavala had hoped—give up their backward ways, served to awaken a national sense of pride and consciousness in them, contributing meaningfully to what would become a resonant form of Mexican nationalism. One, it may be noted, that would add a new ingredient to Mexicanness—American-phobia.

TEXAS: CATALYST OF EARLY MEXICAN NATIONALISM

The realization, from the perspective of the Mexican government, that there was a problem with Texas, only started to dawn on the minds of the republic's president and ministers once Mier y Terán's 1828 letters from Nacogdoches started to arrive in the National Palace. Mier y Terán's impressions made for uncomfortable reading. "As one travels from [San Antonio] Béjar to this town [Nacogdoches]," he wrote on June 30, 1828, "Mexican influence diminishes, so much that it becomes clear that in this town that influence is almost nonexistent." The Mexicans were no longer in a position to determine how the region was governed. On the one hand, there were no longer enough Mexicans to influence how the region was run. "The ratio of the Mexican population to the foreign is one to ten," he observed. Moreover, the few Mexicans that remained in Texas belonged to "what people everywhere call the abject class [*la clase ínfima*], the poorest and most ignorant." The North Americans residing in Nacogdoches, in contrast, "run an English school and send their children north for their education. The poor Mexicans neither have the resources to create schools, nor is there anyone to think about improving their institutions and their abject condition." Truth was, there were hardly any Mexican "authorities and magistrates." And Mier y Terán was seriously disturbed by "the foreign colonists' attitude toward our nation." They thought Mexico "consists of nothing more than blacks and Indians, all of them ignorant." Mier y Terán feared the worst: "From this state of affairs an antipathy has emerged between Mexicans and foreigners that . . . if timely measures are not taken, Tejas will put down the entire federation." Meanwhile, there was no stopping the constant arrival of more and more foreign settlers, and "lands are being settled without anyone's knowledge." Furthermore, most of the North Americans "hold slaves who, now having perceived the favorable intent of Mexican law with regard to their tragic state, are becoming restless to throw off their yoke, while their masters believe they can keep them by making [the yoke] heavier. They commit the barbarities on their slaves that are so common where men live in a relationship so contradictory to their nature: they pull their teeth, they set dogs upon them to tear them apart, and the mildest of them will whip the slaves until they are flayed."

In a letter dated July 7, Mier y Terán followed up these considerations with a staggeringly stark portrait of how Mexico had little or no control over what was happening in the region: "Foreigners . . . have this frontier of our federation open to them without [fulfilling] the requirements of the law." They settled "where it suits them, and they take over whatever land they desire without the *alcalde*'s approval and in defiance of the laws of colonization and of the rights of prior ownership." Mier y Terán was certain that the North Americans knew their settlements were illegal, but ultimately did not care because, "they rely on their numbers so that eventually they might be recognized as owners of the land they occupy."[53] By the time he presented his alarming formal 1829 report to the Mexican government, Mier y Terán had come to believe that the United States was putting together an army of fifty thousand men to invade Texas and that it would be impossible for the few Mexican troops scattered in the province to resist.[54]

It would be in response to Mier y Terán's recommendations that Lucas Alamán, acting as minister of relations under General Anastasio

Bustamante's 1830–32 government, promulgated the colonization Law of April 6, 1830, that, as a desperate measure, forbade the entrance of any more US settlers. As Alamán noted in the proposal he presented before Congress on February 8, 1830, justifying this draconian resolution:

> *If we examine the current situation in Texas . . . we will find that the majority of the population is already [made up of] citizens [*naturales*] of the United States of the North; that these occupy the frontier posts of the coast and the river mouths; that the number of Mexicans that lived in that region is insignificant compared to the North Americans who have come to settle all over the fertile lands;* being worthy of note that most of them have done so without having gone through the required processes established by our laws, or violating contracts that were duly signed. *The Mexican population is stationary, whilst theirs augments, being worthy of note the sheer number of slaves they have brought with them, and which they own without having manumitted them, as stipulated in Art. 2 of the law of July 13, 1824. This numeric superiority . . . [and] the fact that they have become the owners of the best areas, and that they have been able to carry out their actions with impunity, without it having been possible to oblige the colonists to comply with the contracts they signed . . . or prevent them from settling in the frontiers and in other locations from which they are forbidden [from doing so] by current laws and orders, and, above all, that this influx of adventurers has been tolerated, has all resulted in their preponderance in Texas, whose Department could almost be said to belong no longer to the Mexican Federation . . . and which, it would appear, is close to be taken away from us and annexed by the United States of the North.*[55]

The April 6, 1830, colonization law was, not surprisingly, impossible to implement and, as Pedro Santoni reminds us: "Not only was Mexico incapable of enforcing the major stipulations of the accord, but the decree also heightened resentment among American colonists in Texas."[56]

Nevertheless, what becomes evident from both Mier y Terán and Alamán's views on Texas at the time is that there was little doubt in their minds: (1) that the great majority of settlers were foreign and not Mexican; (2) that they originated mainly from the United States; (3) that they were colonizing Texas illegally; (4) that they were not abiding by Mexico's laws (5) that they were bringing in slaves; and (6) that if they were not backed by the United States, it remained the case that the United States was keen on either purchasing or annexing the region by force. From this we can discern that the Mexican political class's understanding of the Texan problem was, in the first instance, juridical, that they had no doubts whatsoever as to Mexico's legal claim to the region, and that they clearly believed there was such a thing as a Mexican nation and people, something the recent surge of colonists did not belong to, conform with, or was willing to be part of. It was a case of somehow putting a stop to the torrent of slave-owning American settlers from hemorrhaging across the border and illegally occupying *Mexican* land, breaking *Mexican* laws, and abusing *Mexican* generosity. As Tornel would put it: "It was a grave mistake to open the door to the Americans, and this grave mistake was not corrected until we were suddenly faced with all of its consequences." The ambition of the Americans, combined with the Spaniards and Mexicans' misguided generosity, had had galling results: "How much we have contributed ourselves to our own ruin and dishonor."[57]

That Texas legally belonged to Mexico was something that, at least in Mexico, there was no doubt. As accepted across Spanish America, in becoming independent from Spain, the different republics that emerged after ten to fifteen years of war appropriated the land that had previously been Spanish. In so doing, they retained the territorial boundaries the Spanish authorities had established around the different viceroyalties and captaincies-general. Thus, the Kingdom of New Spain became Mexico, the Captaincy General of Guatemala became the United Provinces of Central America (after 1823), the Captaincy General of Venezuela and the Viceroyalty of New Granada became Greater Colombia, and so on. The legal term given for this territorial transfer was *uti possidetis juris*.[58]

Needless to say, although Venezuelan liberator Simón Bolívar did acknowledge in his famous 1815 Jamaica letter that creole patriots like him were "neither Indian nor European, but a species midway between the legitimate proprietors of this country and the Spanish usurpers," noting in so doing that the indigenous peoples of the Americas were the actual rightful owners of the very land they were fighting for—finding himself thus at war both "against the rights of the natives" and "against the [Spanish] invaders"[59]—for the government of Independent Mexico, the American Indian tribes that inhabited Texas were at no point seen as the "legitimate proprietors" of Texas.[60] Early Mexican nationalism celebrated and identified with the country's historic indigenous civilizations, with José María Morelos's insurgents having adopted as their symbol the familiar mythical Aztec cactus-perched, snake-eating eagle that marked the chosen site of Tenochtitlan.[61] However, the proponents of early Mexican nationalism or creole patriotism did not associate the American Indian tribes that lived in Texas and the north of Mexico generally with their glorious Indian ancestors. They did not even grant them the considerations Indian communities were awarded in central and southern Mexico, i.e. those that were formed into *repúblicas de indios* (Indian republics) and granted communal lands during the colonial period.[62] The American Indians that Spanish and Mexican authorities and settlers had battled with ever since the first colonizers supposedly "discovered" the region were quite simply and repeatedly referred to as *indios bárbaros*, and were not seen to have any claim on the land.

Furthermore, the Spanish sale of Florida to the United States in 1819 made perfectly clear which lands were now American and which continued to belong to Spain, becoming part of Mexico following independence. As noted by Josefina Zoraida Vázquez, "The signing of the Adams-Onís Treaty [February 22, 1819] . . . established a clear border and set to rest the US claim that Texas was part of Louisiana."[63] Whilst it is true that American diplomats would try to delay the ratification of the treaty, with some pretending that Texas was part of the 1803 Louisiana Purchase,[64] and both countries would go on to sign a further boundary treaty in January 1828, agreeing to send their respective commissions to "explore, map, and mark the entire length of the borderline,"[65] the 1819 Treaty of Limits was understood in Mexico as unmistakable and nonnegotiable. It is a view Tornel would assert in his 1837 interpretation of the Texan conflict, quoting Luis de Onís's lengthy and detailed demarcation of Texas' borders.[66] Aware, as early as 1830, that there were colonists who were deliberately ignoring the Adams-Onís boundary, or claiming that parts of Texas west of the Sabine River belonged to Louisiana, Tornel translated Henri Joutel's 1684–88 diary of French explorer La Salle's last expedition to find the mouth of the Mississippi River. In his preface, which he pointedly dedicated to none other than the 1828 inspector of Texas, Manuel de Mier y Terán, Tornel stated that he had taken on the arduous task of translating Joutel's seventeenth-century diary in order to disseminate information on the original and historical American territories that had belonged to France, and to "shine light on certain facts, [subsequently] obscured by the passing of time and the well-known determination [of some] to protect [their claims] by means of novel and disorderly aspirations."[67] If there still was any doubt about the Mexican nation's sovereignty over Texas, the fact that minister plenipotentiaries such as Joel Poinsett and Anthony Butler negotiated with the Mexican government in the hope that it would accede to sell Texas, first in 1827 for $1 million, and later for $5 million during Andrew Jackson's presidency, demonstrated that the US government quite clearly recognized that Texas belonged to Mexico.[68]

With it therefore being clear in the minds of the Mexican political class that Texas was Mexican and that, as a result, it was governed by Mexican laws, subsequent claims that Texas was an empty wilderness, part of a wild frontier, free to be settled upon and conquered by freedom-loving, self-reliant pioneers would not be taken lightly. Whilst Texans would argue that they were seceding in 1835 as part of a struggle against Mexican tyranny, Mexicans would view their government's attempts to restore some form of control over the region, especially after 1830, as a natural response to a situation that had, quite simply, gotten out of hand.

With it having become evident from Mier y Terán's report that illegal US immigrants were entering the region at will, ignoring the shrinking Mexican authorities that could be found there, the need to assert Mexican control was an increasingly pressing concern. Of course, where the lack of control Mexico City bore on the region was most obvious was in its inability to halt or prevent the land speculation fever that gripped the province with a whole array of illegal (and as Tornel would have it, antinational) sales, purchases, and transactions. Regardless of Alamán's colonization Law of April 6, 1830, land speculators, both from north and south of the border, as shown in Miguel Soto's chapter in this volume, feverishly went about selling and buying what was not theirs to sell to or buy from American nationals who were supposedly barred from crossing the border into Mexico. Lorenzo de Zavala's dealings with the Galveston Bay and Texas Land Company, to note but just one example, earned himself the somewhat handsome sum of $100,000 by issuing an unspecified number of certificates for leagues and labors of land to Poinsett, for 4,428 acres, and to Butler, for an additional 177.[69] Tornel, writing as minister plenipotentiary in Baltimore at the time, could not have been more indignant, nor, for the purpose of the current study's interest in early Mexican nationalism, more patriotically offended by Zavala's actions. In a letter he addressed to Mier y Terán on February 5, 1831, he stated that Zavala was "canonizing crime, insulting his fatherland [*patria*]." Zavala's unforgivable and "most fatal" crime was to have sold, together with Cuban-born Col. José Antonio Mejía, "a great chunk of Texas, towards Galveston Bay." He was, at times, speechless with wrath and bemusement. How could a countryman of his commit such "open treason"? Dreading the impact the uncontrolled and uncontrollable immigration of Americans was having on Texas, Tornel feared Zavala and Mejía's transactions and advertisements could only dramatically worsen matters. He lamented quite openly that neither he nor his consuls could "stop Americans from embarking for Texas." He urged Mier y Terán to take resolute military action.[70] However, Mier y Terán was unable to prevent what appeared to him as tragically inevitable: the loss of Texas, or as he put it in an 1831 letter to Alamán, its "North American-ization."[71] On July 2, 1832, Mier y Terán committed suicide by plunging into his sword on the very same spot where Mexican liberator Agustín de Iturbide had been executed eight years earlier, in the main square of the village of Padilla.

Thus from the Mexican perspective, when the Texas Revolution began, it was seen to be waged by foreigners who had no right to be there in the first place, and who were up in arms against the Mexican government because it, as was noted by one newspaper on May 6, 1836, "does not allow and opposes the robbery and depredation . . . of its [nation's] fertile lands."[72] However, as has been eloquently argued by Josefina Zoraida Vázquez, 1830s Mexicans were also convinced that slavery was at the heart of the Texans' push for independence.[73] As was noted by none other than Santa Anna, on February 16, 1836, as he arrived in Villa de Guerrero, "There exists in Texas a considerable number of slaves, introduced here by their owners under certain legal pretexts; but who, according to our laws, should be free. Will we tolerate for much longer that these poor people suffer the pain of the chains in a country whose kind laws protect man's liberty without making distinctions of color or race?"[74] He was to see his role in the Texan campaign as that of a leader whose duty it was to ensure that the "laws of the Republic [that] prohibit slavery . . . are everywhere respected."[75]

From as early as 1821, on the eve of Mexico's independence, Miguel Ramos Arizpe, at the head of a group of Mexican deputies in the Spanish Cortes (parliament) in Madrid, drafted a colonization law that remained in place until 1824 which, as noted in its twenty-eighth Article, prohibited the importation of slaves into Spanish territories and emancipated those that had been introduced there. This legislation was to be seconded by the colonization law the Junta Nacional Instituyente approved in January 1823, which took on board the recommendations a previous colonization commission had made to the Mexican Congress in July 1822 calling for banning the sale and purchase of slaves and declaring children born of slaves free when they reached the age of fourteen. The colonization law of August 1824, moreover, went on to reiterate that the importation of slaves into Mexico was prohibited, as stipulated in the July 13, 1824, decree. From a Mexican perspective, slavery was thus presented as being anathema to the new values liberals wanted to embrace as their incipient nation joined the international arena as a free and sovereign state. Insurgent leader José María Morelos, who together with Miguel Hidalgo y Costilla is still celebrated as one of Mexico's founding fathers, had already advocated in Article fifteen of his foundational *Sentiments of the Nation* (1813) that slavery as well as racial discrimination ("*distinción de castas*") should be forever banned in Mexico.[76] In a similar vein, Iturbide's 1821 Plan of Iguala, in no small measure thanks to Afro-Mexican insurgent Gen. Vicente Guerrero's representations, declared in the first line of its opening address that the Mexican people—referred to as *Americanos* in the actual document—were not only those born in the country, but also included those Europeans, Asians, and *Africans* who lived there.[77]

However, with the 1824 Federal Constitution in place, the matter of implementing the government's antislavery measures fell to the state-constituent congress of Coahuila y Texas. With Stephen F. Austin and the Anglo-American settlers lobbying the state legislature forcefully so that it exempted the region from having to implement any proposed emancipation laws, the state authorities opted not to enforce them. Austin, in fact, proposed that the "Anglo-American colonists be allowed to introduce slaves until 1840, at which time they would free the male grandchildren of slaves at age twenty five and females at age fifteen."[78] In Austin's mind, "Texas must be a slave country. Circumstances and unavoidable necessity compel it. It is the wish of the people there and it is my duty to do all I can, prudently, in favor of it."[79] Mier y Terán was aware of this and had informed the government in Mexico City, as early as April 1828, as he made his way to Nacogdoches, that "the most persistent goal" for the American colonists was "to obtain permission for the introduction of slaves. Without them they say that their settlement cannot prosper."[80]

When the Mexican government finally abolished slavery completely in Mexico on September 16, 1829, the Coahuilan and Texan authorities, under pressure from the fast-growing population of American slave-owning settlers, once more pleaded to be exempted. Governor José María Viesca, convinced that if he tried to implement the September 16th decree they would incite major disturbances, adopted a pragmatic stance and interceded with President Guerrero on their behalf. Guerrero agreed to exempt Texas from enforcing the abolition of slavery, but made it clear that not one more slave was to enter the state.[81] This arrangement, whereby the state of Coahuila y Texas was exempted from enforcing the Mexican government's abolitionary laws, would remain intact as long as Mexico was governed by a federal constitution that allowed, by its very devolutionary nature, state legislatures, in some instances, to opt out of implementing decrees that came from the remote federal government in Mexico City. However, once events in 1835 made it clear that the 1824 Federal Constitution was to be abolished and replaced with a centralist charter that,[82] in turn, would inevitably bring an end to such exemptions, the slave-owning colonists had no option but to gun for secession so as to keep their slaves. Carlos María de Bustamante was unequivocal on the matter; the Texans' determination to hang onto their slaves was "the sole and only motive why Texas . . . sought to separate itself from Mexico."[83] Certainly appearing to confirm Bustamante's opinion was the point Robert M. Williamson (a.k.a. Three-legged Willie) made in his address to the secessionist assembly that gathered in San Felipe de Austin on July 4, 1835, that Santa Anna was going to "compel you into obedience to the new form of Government; to compel you to give up your arms; to compel you to have your country garrisoned; *to compel you to liberate your slaves.*"[84] Section nine of the Constitution of the Republic of Texas of March 17, 1836, may also add credence to the Mexicans' view that the Anglo-American Texans' decision to secede from Mexico was ultimately driven by their slave-owning entrepreneurial interests:

> *All persons of color who were slaves for life previous to their emigration to Texas and who are now held in bondage shall remain in the state of servitude, provided the said slave shall be the bona fide property of the person so holding said slave as aforesaid. Congress shall not pass laws to prohibit bringing their slaves into the Republic with them and holding them by the same tenure by which such slaves were held in the United States; nor shall Congress have power to emancipate slaves; nor shall any slave holder be allowed to emancipate his or her slaves without the consent of Congress, unless he or she shall send his or her slave or slaves without the limits of the Republic. No free person of African descent, in whole or in part, shall be permitted to reside permanent in the Republic without the consent of Congress.*[85]

Likewise, Texas' decision to secede from the United States on February 1, 1861, to join the Confederacy on March 2, 1861, because of its "solidarity with its sister slave-holding states,"[86] would similarly give credence to the Mexican view that slavery was a major driving force in Texan patriotism. If this interpretation of the Texans' agency comes as a surprise to some, this may be due in no small measure to the fact that, as noted recently by Phillip Thomas Tucker, "In order to uphold the time-honored stereotype of freedom fighters, [US] historians have minimized the fact that many soldiers of 1835–36 were either slave-owners, defenders of the right to maintain slavery, or aspired to own slaves one day."[87]

And so, for Mexicans such as Alamán, Bustamante, and Tornel, the Texan rebels were slave-owning, land-grabbing illegal immigrants who had flooded into Texas challenging the laws of the land. That they were foreigners, emphasized through their alterity,[88] or otherness, that they spoke English and not Spanish, that they were not Catholic, that they owned slaves, and that they held the Mexicans and their government with contempt, created a "them" and "us" distinction in the Mexicans' minds that, of itself, induced the Mexicans to develop their own idea of who they were and what they were like in contrast to the hostile or rebellious American colonist "other." Tornel had no doubt about the fact that the American squatters who were rebelling against Mexico were foreign: "For the colonists of Texas, the name *Mexican* is and has been an execrable name and there has not been an insult or violation that our compatriots have not suffered finding themselves reduced to being treated as foreigners in their own country."[89] It is this view of the Texan rebels as foreign criminals that would also justify Tornel's notorious decree of December 30, 1835, whereby "Foreigners landing on the coast of the republic or invading its territory by land, armed with the intention of attacking our country, will be deemed pirates and dealt with as such."[90] Santa Anna would, of course, agree, and the decree gave legitimacy to his decision to have the more than four hundred prisoners of Goliad controversially executed on March 27, 1836, on the grounds that "this is no war among brothers like the ones we have unfortunately had to suffer. But it is not a war between nations either, in which . . . prisoners are respected and even exchanged. These foreigners are bandits that have attacked the territory of the Republic to steal a part of it . . . ; that is why the Supreme Government has declared, with reason, that they are pirates, and orders that they are treated and punished as such."[91]

News of the Texan Revolution, albeit treated initially as a minor rebellion in the Mexican press,[92] had the added effect of awakening an early form of Mexican nationalism. Regardless of the remoteness of the region, that most Mexicans did not live in Texas, had never been to Texas, or even intended to move to Texas, the news that "foreigners" were rebelling to "steal" a portion of territory that belonged to *their* nation gave rise to the expression of an early form of Mexican nationalism. This can be seen in a plethora of patriotic articles, speeches, and writings, especially once Santa Anna's army started its march north from San Luis Potosí on December 22, 1835. As studied by Michael P. Costeloe, news of the Mexican victory at the battle of the Alamo was celebrated with resonant national pride (even though there were some newspapers that, critical of Santa Anna, did question the victory's "real value in the campaign against the Texan rebels").[93] Representative of what can be seen to have been an emergent Mexican national consciousness, a lead article such as the one that featured in *La lima de Vulcano* on March 22, 1836, entitled "LONG LIVE MEXICO! LONG LIVE ITS INVINCIBLE LIBERATOR!" celebrated "the enthusiastic exultation and happiness" that had been seen "on the face of every good Mexican" when news of the Alamo had reached the capital the day before, and exalted the triumph of "our national flag." What is more, it distinguished the foreign rebels, who had "bitten the earth *they* profaned" with "*their* impure blood" flowing "in atonement of *their* great insults" from "*our* valiant men." "Mexico," this newspaper proclaimed, had "been vindicated." "Mexico," it repeated, had "received a proper satisfaction." The rebels lay defeated by "the brave army of the fatherland [*patria*]." "These fools," it laughed, "do not know Mexicans."[94] For the writers of *La lima de Vulcano*, like those who also celebrated the Mexican victory in *El Cosmopolita*, *El Nacional*, *El Mosquito Mexicano*, *El Santanista Oaxaqueño*, *El Censor*, *El Cometa*, and *El Diario del Gobierno*, to name but a few, there was a discernible sense of national pride. They, by contrast, *did* know Mexicans. The Mexican press, in reaction to events in Texas, was unquestionably starting to promote and project an assertive vision of nationhood with exclamations hailing "ETERNAL PRAISE TO THE INVINCIBLE ARMY OF MEXICO!"; congratulating "all Mexicans for such a triumph," "THE ARMY OF MEXICO!,"[95] "the fatherland [*patria*]," and "brave General Santa Anna!!!"[96]. And then, as Costeloe noted, "In the atmosphere of xenophobia toward North Americans and confidence in their army and, above all, in Santa Anna, the defeat at San Jacinto came as an even greater blow to their national pride."[97] Once voiced, though, this national pride did not disappear, accounting for the Mexican government's refusal to recognize Texan independence until forced to do so by defeat in the Mexican-American War (1846–48).

British minister plenipotentiary Richard Pakenham, reporting back to Lord Aberdeen six years after Texas had become the Lone Star republic, was perfectly aware that the Texan problem stirred up patriotic sentiments whenever he broached the subject with Mexican officials: "I feel obliged to say that the question of Texas is, from a feeling of national pride or conceit, a sore subject with almost every Mexican; and that it would try the strength and popularity of any administration however enlightened and disinterested that should recommend the final relinquishment of what is still considered a part of the national domain."[98] Following Britain's recognition of Texan independence in 1840, and its subsequent diplomatic attempts to persuade the Mexican authorities to follow suit, an angry José María Bocanegra, responding as minister of relations in 1842, stressed that the Mexican government could "in no way . . . our line of conduct change . . . to carry on with our war in Texas until our rights over that part of the Republic's territory are vindicated."[99] Possible proof that this sense of national pride was not the exclusive domain of the few is that when General José Joaquín de Herrera's moderate liberal 1844–45 government, decided to adopt a pragmatic approach toward Texas and weigh its options, including recognizing the region's independence from Mexico, the press, in general, virulently turned against it, facilitating General Mariano Paredes y Arrillaga's rise to power in December 1845.[100]

The origins of the Mexicans' American- or Yankee-phobia, which alongside Hispanophobia would eventually become another common trait of Mexican national consciousness, albeit firmly (and understandably) consolidated as a result of the 1846–48 Mexican-American War, can first be traced back to the way Mexicans became convinced, rightly or wrongly, from very early on, that the United States government was pulling the strings behind the Texans' bid for independence. Tornel, writing in 1837, nine years before the Mexican-American War actually began, was adamant after what had happened in Texas that "the dominant thought of the United States of America, has been for the last fifty years, in other words, since its political infancy, to occupy great swathes of territory that were originally Spanish, and which now belong to the Mexican nation."[101] In fact, as Santa Anna got ready to leave the capital to head for San Luis Potosí to put together the expeditionary army with which he planned to crush the Texan rebels in the fall of 1835, Pakenham found, having gone to pay the Mexican warrior-president a visit, that:

> *Of the policy, which it appears not to be unreasonable to attribute to the American government with relation to Texas;—that of allowing events to take their course until the settlers are able to effect a separation from Mexico, and then, as it were, acquiescing in their annexation to the Northern Union, he [Santa Anna] seemed to be perfectly aware, and he asserted, as a proof of their desire to obtain possession of that province, that a short time ago persons commissioned by the government of the United States had waited upon him at his country residence near Veracruz, and offered to purchase Texas from his government for a sum of eighteen million dollars, with a present of one million to himself if he should cause the bargain to be concluded—which proposal he had rejected with the indignation which it deserved.*[102]

Carlos María de Bustamante was not oblivious either to the Americans' machinations and ambitions. On June 23, 1835, he noted in his diary that rumor had it Pres. Andrew Jackson was planning on raising a twelve thousand-strong army to conquer Texas. When Bustamante then made his views known in Congress, just over three months later, on October 6, concerning the US government's plans to annex Texas and was accused of scaremongering by deputy Antonio Pacheco Leal, he replied: "The North Americans' pretensions over Texas are as scandalous as they are public and well known by everybody in every household, by the hundreds who go to market [everyday], and by the government's own newspapers, and even by the government itself as evidenced by the actions it is taking to prevent [the Americans'] advances and involvement." As he jotted down prophetically in his October 27 entry, the manner in which the US government "scandalously" protected the invasion of Texas by "so-called adventurers" would inevitably lead to war between the two countries.[103] Although, as Marcela Terrazas has stressed, there was nothing definite about the US annexation of Texas in 1835,[104] in the long run, the Mexican-American War of 1846–48 would ultimately see the Mexicans' fears confirmed, ensuring that a deeply entrenched mistrust of the United States would become part of Mexican national identity.

CONCLUSION

If one takes the Texan Declaration of Independence of March 2, 1836, at face value, something Vázquez has argued much of the historiography has done "uncritically," perpetuating in so doing "the self-serving Texan version" of the event,[105] the Texans rebelled essentially to free themselves from the military tyrannical government in Mexico City. They argued that the Mexican government had "ceased to protect the lives, liberty and property of the people." Moreover, with the 1824 Constitution "no longer [having] a substantial existence, and the whole nature of the government [having] been forcefully changed, without their consent, from a restricted federative republic, composed of sovereign states, to a consolidated central military despotism," resulting in the "spirit of the constitution" having "departed," they had been subjected to horrendous acts of tyranny, "the combined despotism of the sword and the priesthood." This oppression, in part meted out by the government in the state of Coahuila from whom Texas had long wanted to be separated, as well as "a jealous and partial course of legislation, carried on at a far distant seat of government, by a hostile majority, in an unknown tongue, had become unbearable. "One of [their] citizens" (i.e., Stephen F. Austin), moreover, was unjustly "incarcerated in a dungeon," and they suffered from the absence of a fair justice system as well as the lack of "any public system of education." To add insult to injury, in recent months "the military commandants, stationed among us," had inflicted "arbitrary acts of oppression and tyranny … trampling upon the most sacred rights of the citizens." The Texans had also been denied their "right of worshipping the Almighty according to the dictates of [their] own conscience." It was thus that they were "forced to the melancholy conclusion that the Mexican people [had] acquiesced in the destruction of their liberty." The "necessity of self-preservation," as they termed it, decreed their "eternal political separation from Mexico."[106]

Tornel would look back in 1837 and unpick the Texans' Declaration of Independence with a tangible sense of disbelief and affront. He was flabbergasted that the Texans could claim they believed they were fighting for liberty when they kept slaves and had opened "a new market of human meat in Texas, in defiance of all Mexican laws." He did not believe the Texans' alleged federalist ideals either. To the claim that the Texans were opposed to a centralist system, he pointed out that the American colonizers had not previously objected to Spanish colonial rule, or Iturbide's empire, or the triumvirate, none of which had been in fact federalist. The federalist stance, he argued, was an excuse. That they wanted independence was in itself proof of this.[107] He considered that the allegation that they had neglected the improvement of education in Texas to be in bad faith. It was generally accepted, Tornel stressed, that the local town councils were responsible for taking care of the education in their respective communities with the funds they obtained through municipal and regional taxes and contributions: "If they did not allocate the funds to the education of their children, the fault was theirs." Furthermore, the Texans had two representatives in Congress, and they never voiced this concern. Tornel, as minister of war, also strongly objected to the accusation that the Mexican army had committed unnecessary acts of oppression and tyranny in Texas. In his mind, the reality of the situation had been quite the opposite: The American colonists had come to Texas armed, they had lived entirely how they pleased, not respected the law, refused to pay taxes, and challenged and attacked the Mexican authorities. The Mexican army's actions were part of an attempt to "ensure laws were abided by and to repress crime." Regarding religion, he noted that the Americans knew full well when they came to Texas that the Roman Apostolic Catholic faith was the only tolerated one in the Mexican nation. If they objected to this, he retorted, "Why did they not stay in their own country, or construct temples in the solitude of the West?" When they first settled in Texas, they had conformed with the Spanish and Mexican authorities' stipulations. To argue that the defense of Protestantism was a valid justification was in Tornel's mind irrelevant. Ultimately, however, Tornel was convinced the war was the result of US expansionism and had been promoted and supported from Washington.[108]

The independence of Texas and its consequence, as Josefina Vázquez has asserted, was "the war between Mexico and the United States." The two conflicts were, in her mind, "without doubt fundamental events in the history of both countries. For Mexico they meant the end of a future [Mexicans had envisioned] on the basis of the wealth of New Spain and eighteenth-century expansionism, and for the United States its consolidation as a continental power."[109] For Mexico, though, they also resulted in a national awakening, the beginning of the emergence of a more clearly defined, albeit heterogeneous and often contested, sense of national identity. One that, as highlighted by the confrontation with the American "other," in general spoke Spanish, was Catholic and Guadalupan, proud of its historic indigenous heritage, at times knee-jerkingly Hispanophobic, outspokenly abolitionist, and now—anti-American.

Mexican national identity took time to develop; or to put it differently, an interpretation of what it meant to be Mexican that resonated with the majority of the population took time to develop. Some would argue to this day that it is still impossible to provide a uniform fit-all definition of *lo mexicano*.[110] However, shared historical experiences did mold shared views. Local tastes in food that developed into a distinctive national cuisine also mattered, as did a growing autochthonous musical repertoire that would, with time, come to be associated with Mexicanness. Mexican sounds, smells, and sights, all played a part in instilling in the population a sense of what it meant to be Mexican, as did the authorities' concerted efforts, such as organizing patriotic fiestas and ceremonies.[111] Nevertheless, the Mexican-American War had a major impact; a national Mexican consciousness started to be forged as a result. For those Mexicans who witnessed the arrival and advance of the US military forces, who actually experienced firsthand an empirical encounter with the American "other," the question of who they were and why they had been defeated became all-important. As noted by Charles A. Hale, "Out of crisis came a fresh analysis of the great national problems and new proposals for their solutions." This soul-searching quest to answer why the United States had won the war—which brought with it a whole range of considerations about the Mexican character as well as the country's political institutions—did not bring unity to Mexico. "On the contrary," as Hale reminds us, "it gave rise to a profound schism which was to control the country's destiny for two decades."[112] And yet, the war, the defeat, the inevitable comparison that Mexicans made between their country and the one they had been at war with, initiated a process of a national reappraisal that, in the long run, would give rise to a generalized, albeit contested, sense of national identity.[113]

However, this very Mexican national identity that started to grow out of the ruins of the war and Mexico's traumatic defeat was not built on nothing, out of the blue. Instead, as has been argued here, it was erected on those earlier blocks or markers of national identity that the Texan Revolution had inadvertently provoked back in 1835. In the words of an aging Tornel, writing in 1852, "The revolution of Texas . . . seriously perturbed the march of the [Mexican] nation." It had given rise to one of Mexico's worst catastrophes, he noted, the 1846–48 war. To think about the Texas Revolution still made him fear for the future of his homeland. And in so doing, Tornel made a point of listing what was dear to him as a Mexican: "The glory of our race, the language and religion of our parents, everything that we are today, everything we own today, all that we are worth today."[114] They were concepts—a *mestizo* race, the Spanish language, the Catholic religion—that would, alongside Neo-Aztecism, Hispanophobia, and a distrust of the United States, with time be used by others to define Mexicanness, with the Texas Revolution having served, in a sense, as a catalyst for early Mexican nationalism.

NOTES

1. Otero, quoted and translated in Pedro Santoni, *Mexicans at Arms: Puro Federalists and the Politics of War, 1845–1848* (Fort Worth: Texas Christian University Press, 1996), 232. For Otero, see Melissa Boyd, "The Career and

Ideology of Mariano Otero, Mexican Politician (1817–1850)," (PhD diss., University of St. Andrews, 2012).

2. Archivo Histórico de la Secretaría de la Defensa Nacional (henceforth referred to as AHSDN): Exp. XI/III/1–116 [1–15], vol. V, ff. 1225–28, Minutes of a general meeting "en que se ventilase la importantísima cuestión de la guerra," (Mexico City, May 20, 1847).

3. Antonio López de Santa Anna, *Manifiesto del general de división, benemérito de la patria, Antonio López de Santa Anna, a sus conciudadanos, 24 de marzo de 1848* (Mexico City: Imp. de Navarro, 1848), reprinted in Genaro García, ed., *Documentos inéditos o muy raros para la historia de México. Antonio López de Santa Anna* (Mexico City: Porrúa, 1991), 59:210.

4. See Josefina Zoraida Vázquez, both *Mexicanos y norteamericanos ante la guerra del 47* (Mexico City: SepSetentas, 1972), 27–49, and *La intervención norteamericana 1846–1848* (Mexico City: SRE, 1997), 131–132. For other studies that argue that the 1846–48 war served as a watershed in the awakening of a clear national consciousness in Mexico, see Andrés Reséndez Fuentes, "Guerra e identidad nacional," *Historia Mexicana* 47:2 (octubre-diciembre 1997): 413; Jesús Velasco Martínez and Thomas Benjamin, "La guerra entre México y Estados Unidos, 1846–1848," in *Mitos en las relaciones México-Estados Unidos,* ed. María Esther Schumacher (Mexico City: FCE, 1994), 113; and Andrés Delgadillo Sánchez, *San Luis Potosí durante la guerra contra Estados Unidos de Norteamérica. Identidad nacional, símbolos y héroes patrios 1846–1848* (San Luis Potosí: Editorial Ponciano Arriaga, 2012).

5. See Lucas Alamán, *Historia de Méjico. Desde los primeros movimientos que prepararon su independencia en el año de 1808 hasta la época presente*, 5 vols. (Mexico City: Imp. de J. M. de Lara, 1849–52); Juan Suárez y Navarro, *Historia de México y del general Antonio López de Santa Anna. Comprende los acontecimientos políticos que han tenido lugar en la nación desde el año de 1821 hasta 1848* (Mexico City: Imp. de I. Cumplido, 1850); and José María Tornel y Mendívil, *Breve reseña histórica de los acontecimientos más notables de la nación mexicana* (Mexico City: Imp. de I. Cumplido, 1852). For a study on the publication and reception of Alamán's *Historia de Méjico*, see Michael P. Costeloe, "La Historia de México de Lucas Alamán: Publicación y recepción en México, 1849–1850," *Memorias de la Academia Mexicana de la Historia* 38 (1995): 105–27. For analyses of Tornel's *Breve reseña histórica*, see both María del Carmen Vázquez Mantecón, "José María Tornel y Mendívil," in *Historiografía mexicana.* Vol. 3. *El surgimiento de la historiografía nacional*, ed. Virginia Guedea (Mexico City: UNAM, 1997), 357–89; and Will Fowler, *Tornel and Santa Anna: The Writer and the Caudillo, Mexico 1795–1853* (Westport, CT: Greenwood Press, 2000), 255–62. For the Santa Anna dictatorship's attempts to instill a sense

of patriotism in the population between 1853 and 1855, see Carmen Vázquez Mantecón, *Santa Anna y la encrucijada del Estado. La dictadura (1853–1855)* (Mexico City: Fondo de Cultura Económica, 1986), 271–80, and Will Fowler, *Santa Anna of Mexico* (Lincoln: University of Nebraska Press, 2007), 299–302. For the Mexican national anthem, see Guadalupe Jiménez Codinach, *La guía del himno nacional mexicano* (Mexico City: SEP/Artes de México, 2005).

6. Benedict Anderson, *Imagined Communities: Reflections on the Origin and Spread of Nationalism* (London & New York: Verso, 2006), 50. Emphasis in original.

7. Raymond Buve, "Ayuntamientos and Pronunciamientos during the Nineteenth Century: Examples from Tlaxcala between Independence and the Reform War," in *Malcontents, Rebels, and Pronunciados: The Politics of Insurrection in Nineteenth-Century Mexico,* ed. Will Fowler (Lincoln, NE: University of Nebraska Press, 2012), 129.

8. Eric Van Young, "Of Tempests and Teapots: Imperial Crisis and Local Conflict in Mexico at the Beginning of the Nineteenth Century," in *Cycles of Conflict, Centuries of Change,* eds. Elisa Servín, Leticia Reina, and John Tutino (Durham & London: Duke University Press, 2007), 27.

9. Eric Van Young, *The Other Rebellion: Popular Violence, Ideology, and the Mexican Struggle for Independence, 1810–1821* (Stanford: Stanford University Press, 2001), 3.

10. Lesley Byrd Simpson would capture this idea with his appositely entitled book: *Many Mexicos* (New York: Putnam's Sons, 1941).

11. For creole patriotism see David Brading, *The First America: The Spanish Monarchy, Creole Patriots, and the Liberal State 1492–1867* (Cambridge: Cambridge University Press, 1991), and *The Origins of Mexican Nationalism* (Cambridge: Centre of Latin American Studies, 1985). For the army's nationalist rhetoric see my *Military Political Identity and Reformism in Independent Mexico: An Analysis of the Memorias de Guerra (1821–1855)* (London: ILAS, 1996), and *Tornel and Santa Anna: The Writer and the Caudillo, Mexico 1795–1853* (Westport, CT: Greenwood Press, 2000), 213–15.

12. An excellent study on military recruitment in independent Mexico is José Antonio Serrano Ortega, *El contingente de sangre* (Mexico City: INAH/Instituto Mora, 1993).

13. Alexander von Humboldt, *Political Essay on the Kingdom of New Spain: The John Black Translation* [Abridged] (Norman and London: University of Oklahoma Press, 1988), 45.

14. We still do not have concrete literacy figures for the period, although the studies by eds. Dorothy Tanck de Estrada and Anne Staples in *Historia de la Alfabetización y de la Educación de Adultos en México* (Mexico City: SEP/INEA:

El Colegio de México, n.d.), offer some figures; e.g., eight of 32 schoolgirls were able to sign with their names (Tanck de Estrada, "Reformas borbónicas y educación utilitaria 1700–1821," 98). Given that 90 percent of the population lived in the countryside (Anne Staples, "Leer y escribir en los estados del México independiente," 135), certainly places into context any urban figure of, for instance, 20.6 prisoners capable of reading and writing between 1828 and 1835 (Tanck de Estrada, "La alfabetización: Medio para formar ciudadanos de una democracia 1821–1840," 132). Also see Dorothy Tanck de Estrada, *La educación ilustrada 1786–1836* (Mexico City: El Colegio de México, 1977) and Anne Staples, *Recuento de una batalla inconclusa: La educación Mexicana de Iturbide a Juárez* (Mexico City: El Colegio de México, 2005).

15. See Title III, articles 11–24, in 1836 Constitution: Felipe Tena Ramírez, *Leyes fundamentales de México 1808–2002* (Mexico City: Porrúa, 2002), 408–10.

16. Anderson, *Imagined Communities*, 65, 58.

17. For Lucas Alamán, José Valadés' 1938 biographical study remains an essential point of reference, José C. Valadés, *Alamán: estadista e historiador* (Mexico City: UNAM, 1977). A succinct but noteworthy study is Andrés Lira, *Lucas Alamán* (Mexico City: Cal y Arena, 1997). We await the publication of Eric Van Young's new biography, but a preview of his findings may be sampled in his article "Vidas privadas y mitos públicos: Lucas Alamán y la independencia Mexicana," *Memoria de las revoluciones en México 20/10*, No. 9 (otoño 2010), 43–54.

18. Lucas Alamán, *Historia de México*, vol. 1 (Mexico City: Publicaciones Herrerías, 1938 [first printed as *Historia de Méjico* in 1849]), 54, 57.

19. Francisco Xavier Clavigero, *Historia antigua de México* (Mexico City: Porrúa, 2003 [first published in Italian as *Storia antica del Messico* in 1780–81]), xvii.

20. See by D. A. Brading both *The Origins of Mexican Nationalism* (Cambridge: Centre of Latin American Studies, 1985) and *The First America: The Spanish Monarchy, Creole Patriots, and the Liberal State, 1492–1867* (Cambridge: Cambridge University Press, 1991). Also see my encyclopaedic essay on "Mexico," in *Nations and Nationalism. A Global Historical Overview, vol. 1, 1770–1880*, eds. Guntram H. Herb and David H. Kaplan (Santa Barbara, CA: ABC-CLIO, 2008), 344–357.

21. Brading, *The Origins of Mexican Nationalism*, 3.

22. Will Fowler, *Mexico in the Age of Proposals, 1821–1853* (Westport, CT: Greenwood Press, 1998), 105.

23. Bustamante's glorification of pre-Hispanic Mexico can be found in the following exemplary texts: Carlos María Bustamante, *Galería de antiguos príncipes mexicanos* (Puebla: Oficina del Gobierno Imperial, 1821); *Juguetillo Nono, Antigüedades mexicanas. Historia del primer monarca conocido del reyno tulteco*

(Veracruz: Imp. Constitucional, 1821); *Manifiesto histórico a las naciones y pueblos del Anáhuac* (Mexico City: Imp. de Valdés, 1823); and *Para inmortalizar el valor heroico de los indios cascanes por causa de su libertad de la tiranía española* (Mexico City: Imp. de Galván, 1827).

24. The Plan of Iguala can be found in the Archivo General de la Nación (henceforth referred to as AGN), Impresos oficiales, vol. 60, núm. 62. A transcription of the text can be accessed online at the St. Andrews/AHRC web-based pronunciamientos database at: http://arts.st-andrews.ac.uk/pronunciamientos/dates.php?f=y&pid=740&m=2&y=1821. For the Plan of Iguala, see Nettie Lee Benson, "Iturbide y los planes de independencia," *Historia Mexicana* 2:3 (enero-marzo, 1953): 439–46; Christon I. Archer, "Where Did All the Royalists Go? New Light on the Military Collapse of New Spain, 1810–1822," in *The Mexican and Mexican American Experience in the 19th Century*, ed. Jaime E. Rodríguez O. (Temple, AZ: Bilingual Press, 1989), 24–43; Jaime E. Rodríguez O., "The Transition from Colony to Nation: New Spain, 1810–1821," in *Mexico in the Age of Democratic Revolutions, 1750–1850*, ed. Jaime E. Rodríguez O. (Boulder: Lynne Rienner Publishers, 1994), 97–132; Alfredo Ávila, *En nombre de la nación. La formación del gobierno representativo en México* (Mexico City: CIDE/Taurus, 2002), in particular 196–201; Jaime E. Rodríguez O., "Los caudillos y los historiadores: Riego, Iturbide y Santa Anna," in *La construcción del héroe en España y México (1789–1847)*, eds. Manuel Chust and Víctor Mínguez (Valencia: Universitat de Valéncia, 2003), 309–35; Ivana Frasquet, *Las caras del águila. Del liberalismo gaditano a la república federal Mexicana (1820–1824)* (Castelló: Universitat Jaume I, 2008), in particular 29–88; Ivana Frasquet and Manuel Chust, "Agustín de Iturbide: From the Pronunciamiento of Iguala to the Coup of 1822," in *Forceful Negotiations: The Origins of the Pronunciamiento in Nineteenth-Century Mexico*, ed. Will Fowler (Lincoln, NE: University of Nebraska Press, 2010), 22–46; Timothy E. Anna, *The Mexican Empire of Iturbide* (Lincoln, NE: University of Nebraska Press, 1990), 1–26; Timothy E. Anna, "Agustín de Iturbide and the Process of Consensus," in *The Birth of Modern Mexico 1780–1824*, ed. Christon I. Archer (Wilmington, DE: SR Books, 2003), 187–204; and Timothy E. Anna, "Iguala: The Prototype," in *Forceful Negotiations*, 1–21.

25. For the fraught Mexican-Spanish relations of 1823–30, see Antonia Pi-Suñer Llorens and Agustín Sánchez Andrés, *Una historia de encuentros y desencuentros. México y España en el siglo XIX* (Mexico City: Secretaría de Relaciones Exteriores, 2001), 32–41. Also see, for a study of the anti-Spanish stereotypes that were adopted in Mexican pamphlets of the time, Miguel Soto, "Imágenes y estereotipos durante la expulsión de los españoles de México," in *México y España en el siglo XIX. Diplomacia, relaciones triangulares e imaginarios*

nacionales, eds. Andrés Sánchez Andrés and Raúl Figueroa Esquer (Morelia, MI.: Universidad Michoacana de San Nicolás de Hidalgo, 2003), 195–206.

26. See, for example, the Plan of José María Lobato of January 23, 1824; the Plan de descoyotar en el Estado de Jalisco of August 7, 1827; and the Plan of Perote of September 16, 1828. The texts of all of these pronunciamientos can be consulted on the web-based St. Andrews/AHRC Pronunciamientos relational database: http://arts.st-andrews.ac.uk/pronunciamientos/. For three recent volumes that focus on the phenomenon of the nineteenth-century Mexican pronunciamiento, see *Forceful Negotiations,* as well as *Malcontents, Rebels, and Pronunciados: The Politics of Insurrection in Nineteenth-Century Mexico*, ed. Will Fowler (Lincoln, NE: University of Nebraska Press, 2012); and *Celebrating Insurrection: The Commemoration and Representation of the Nineteenth-Century Mexican Pronunciamiento*, ed. Will Fowler (Lincoln, NE: University of Nebraska Press, 2012).

27. See Harold D. Sims, *La expulsión de los españoles de México (1821–1828)* (Mexico City: Fondo de Cultura Económica, 1974) and Harold D. Sims, *The Expulsion of Mexico's Spaniards 1821–1836* (Pittsburgh: University of Pittsburgh Press, 1990).

28. It was during General Porfirio Díaz's long rule (1876–1910) that a number of historians such as Vicente Riva Palacio and, in particular, Justo Sierra, started writing conciliatory national histories and school textbooks that quite openly depicted Mexican nationality as a positive *mestizo* fusion of both Spanish and indigenous cultures. See Vicente Riva Palacio, *México a través de los siglos*, 5 vols. (Mexico City: Imp. J. Ballescá y Compañía, 1887–1889) and Justo Sierra, *Historia patria* (Mexico City: SEP, 1922). Of course, not everybody adopted such an upbeat take on *mestizaje*. Octavio Paz, in his canonical *Laberinto de la soledad* (1950), argued that the violent birth of modern Mexico—he would stress this was both a literal and figurative act of rape—had resulted in a people condemned to loneliness who neither wanted to descend from a rapist Spanish father-figure represented by conquistador Hernán Cortés or a raped (and treacherous) Indian mother-figure embodied by Cortés' interpreter and mistress—La Malinche. See Paz, *El laberinto de la soledad* (Madrid: Cátedra, 2003), 202–27.

29. Marco Antonio Landavazo, "Languages of Nationalist Violence: Notes on Mexican Hispanophobia," *Political Violence and the Construction of National Identity in Latin America*, eds. Will Fowler and Peter Lambert (New York: Palgrave Macmillan, 2006), 48, 50.

30. For Tornel, see María del Carmen Vázquez Mantecón, *La palabra del poder. Vida pública de José María Tornel (1795–1853)* (Mexico City: UNAM, 1997), and my *Tornel and Santa Anna*.

31. José María Tornel, "La ciudad de Baltimore en 1831," *El Mosaico*

Mexicano, vol. 3 (1840), 330–34. The complete run of *El Mosaico Mexicano* is held in the Hemeroteca of the Biblioteca Nacional, UNAM, Mexico City.

32. Lucas Alamán to Santa Anna, March 23, 1853, inserted in *El pensamiento de la reacción Mexicana. Historia documental. Tomo primero (1810–1859)*, ed. Gastón García Cantú (Mexico City: UNAM, 1994), 314.

33. Indian gods were equated with the saints. For example, Quetzalcóatl was equated with Saint Thomas; the Zapotec god, Cocijo, with Saint Peter. Catholic churches and shrines were erected on the sites of the old Indian cults. Where possible, the Catholic calendar was made to coincide with the pre-columbian one. Probably the most evident example of this was the way in which Mexico's ritual of the Day of the Dead was assimilated by the Mexican Catholic Church and incorporated into the festivity of All Saints. Similarly, the Indian goddess Tonantzin was equated with the Virgin of Guadalupe, whose apparition in 1531 was witnessed precisely on Tonantzin's sacred hill of Tepeyac. The Virgin of Guadalupe even inherited from her pre-columbian incarnation a mystical association with the cactus-based drink *pulque*. The fact that she presented herself to an Indian, Juan Diego, and that her complexion, miraculously imprinted on his cape, had indigenous traits, gave her an emblematic significance in the syncretic culture that developed in Mexico that no other figure or myth came to espouse. In a sense, she epitomized what would become one of the core aspects of Mexican identity: *mestizaje* (the fusion of Spanish and Indian cultures). See William B. Taylor, *Magistrates of the Sacred: Priests and Parishioners in Eighteenth-Century Mexico* (Stanford, CA: Stanford University Press, 1996) and Matthew D. O'Hara, *A Flock Divided. Race, Religion, and Politics in Mexico, 1749–1857* (Durham: Duke University Press, 2010).

34. The cult of the Virgin of Guadalupe (*guadalupanismo*) was and remains the most powerful expression of Mexican national identity. Following the publication of Miguel Sánchez's 1648 study on the apparition of the Virgin Mary on the hill of Tepeyac in 1531, the creole clergy of New Spain propagated the belief that Our Lady of Guadalupe was the Queen of Mexico. She provided the creole priesthood with an autonomous sacred foundation for their Church and mother country. Her image, miraculously imprinted on the cape of a humble Indian, Juan Diego, preserved and venerated at the holy mount of Tepeyac, was a clear sign that the Virgin Mary would protect the Mexican people. Her *mestizo* features and her associations with the Indian goddess Tonantzin served to transform her into the object of devotion of Indians and creoles, rich and poor alike. The cult of the Virgin of Guadalupe became widespread over time as a result of the intertwining of religious fervor and patriotic enthusiasm. In a country divided by race, class, customs, and language, the inhabitants of Mexico had little to bind them together except their shared

identity as children and subjects of Our Lady of Guadalupe. *Guadalupanismo* and Mexican nationalism became one and the same thing. Quote is from D. A. Brading, *Mexican Phoenix. Our Lady of Guadalupe: Image and Tradition Across Five Centuries* (Cambridge: Cambridge University Press, 2001), 74.

35. Fernando Serrano Migallón, *El grito de independencia. Historia de una pasión nacional* (Mexico City: Porrúa, 1995), 13.

36. Plan of Huejotzingo, June 8, 1833, included in St Andrews/AHRC pronunciamientos web-based database.

37. Josefina Zoraida Vázquez, "The Colonization and Loss of Texas: A Mexican Perspective," in *Myths, Misdeeds, and Misunderstandings: The Roots of Conflict in US-Mexican Relations*, eds. Jaime E. Rodríguez O. and Kathryn Vincent (Wilmington, DE: Scholarly Resources, 1997), 49. For an engaging biography of Stephen F. Austin, see Gregg Cantrell, *Stephen F. Austin: Empresario of Texas* (New Haven: Yale University Press, 1999).

38. Marcela Terrazas y Basante & Gerardo Gurza Lavalle, *Las relaciones México-Estados Unidos 1756–2010. Vol. I. Imperios, repúblicas y pueblos en pugna por el territorio 1756–1867* (Mexico City: UNAM/SRE, 2012), 141.

39. Vázquez, "The Colonization and Loss of Texas," 49.

40. Edmundo O'Gorman, *México. El trauma de su historia* (Mexico City: UNAM, 1977), 33.

41. Tornel, "La ciudad de Baltimore en 1831."

42. For Tornel's US correspondence, see Archivo de Secretaría de Relaciones Exteriores de México (henceforth referred to as ASREM), Exp. 6–19–6; also see José María Bocanegra, *Memorias para la historia de México independiente. 1822–1846*, vol. 1 (Mexico City: Fondo de Cultura Económica, 1987 [originally published in 1892]), 548–53.

43. José María Tornel to Minister of Relations, Baltimore, March 6, 1830, reproduced in *Documentos de la relación de México con los Estados Unidos (31 de diciembre 1829–29 de mayo de 1837)*, vol. 2, ed. Carlos Bosch García (Mexico City: UNAM, 1983), 189.

44. José María Tornel, *Tejas y los Estados Unidos de América en sus relaciones con la república mexicana* (Mexico City: Imp. de I. Cumplido, 1837), 10.

45. Ibid., 12.

46. Andrés Reséndez, *Changing National Identities at the Frontier: Texas and New Mexico, 1800–1850* (Cambridge: Cambridge University Press, 2005), 1.

47. Lorenzo de Zavala, *Viaje a los Estados Unidos del Norte de América* [originally published in Paris: Imp. de Decourchant, 1834] in Lorenzo de Zavala, *Obras* (Mexico City: Porrúa, 1976), 7–8.

48. Having said this, although he noted that "North American women have lovely colors, large and lively eyes, and well-formed hands and feet," Mexican

women still succeeded, in his mind, in walking more elegantly and voluptuously! See ibid., 80.

49. For a combative but sadly inaccurate study of Vicente Guerrero, see Theodore G. Vincent, *The Legacy of Vicente Guerrero, Mexico's First Black Indian President* (Gainesville: University Press of Florida, 2001).

50. Zavala, *Obras*, 22, 23, 25–28, 39, 44, 48, 73, 80, 92, 103, 159, and 175.

51. For Zavala's land speculation in Texas, see Margaret Swett Henson, *Lorenzo de Zavala. The Pragmatic Idealist* (Fort Worth: Texas Christian University Press, 1996).

52. Manuel de Mier y Terán, *Texas by Terán. The Diary Kept by General Manuel de Mier y Terán on His 1828 Inspection of Texas*, trans. John Wheat, ed. Jack Jackson, with botanical notes by Scooter Cheatham and Lynn Marshall (Austin: University of Texas Press, 2000), 103.

53. Ibid., 96–101, 104–05.

54. Josefina Zoraida Vázquez and Lorenzo Meyer, *The United States and Mexico* (Chicago: University of Chicago Press, 1985), 33.

55. Lucas Alamán, "Iniciativa que presentó al Congreso el 8 de febrero de 1830," quoted in Jesús Velasco Márquez, "La separación y la anexión de Texas en la historia de México y Estados Unidos," in *De la rebelión de Texas a la guerra del 47*, ed. Josefina Zoraida Vázquez (Mexico City: Nueva Imagen, 1994), 142–143.

56. Santoni, *Mexicans at Arms*, 25.

57. Tornel, *Tejas y los Estados Unidos*, 25–26.

58. According to the Argentine government, it is precisely because of the *uti possidetis juris* principle that the Malvinas Islands (Falklands) belong to Argentina and not to Britain, which seized them in 1833 by force.

59. Simón Bolívar, "Jamaica letter," September 6, 1815, included in translation in *Selected Writings of Bolívar*, eds. Vicente Lecuna and Harold A. Bierck Jr. (New York: Colonial Press, 1951), 1: 110.

60. These were the Apache, Atakapa, Bidai, Caddo, Cherokee, Coahuiltecan, Comanche, Coushatta, Jumano, Karankawa, Kickapoo, Koiwa, Kitsai, Tawakoni, Tonkawa, and Wichita tribes. See David La Vere, *The Texas Indians* (College Station: Texas A&M University Press, 2004).

61. The eagle, the cactus, and the snake would feature in the center of the Mexican green, white, and red flag as of 1824, having first figured in Iturbide's 1821 banner, only without the snake. See Enrique Florescano, *La bandera mexicana. Breve historia de su formación y simbolismo* (Mexico City: Fondo de Cultura Económica, 1998).

62. For a study on how the incipient Mexican State negotiated with established (and recognized) indigenous communities in Oaxaca and Yucatán

during the early national period (unlike the way the Mexican State dealt with the "barbarous Indians" of the north), see Karen D. Caplan, *Indigenous Citizens: Local Liberalism in Early National Oaxaca and Yucatán* (Stanford: Stanford University Press, 2010). Also see by Peter F. Guardino, *Peasants, Politics, and the Formation of Mexico's National State. Guerrero, 1800–1857* (Stanford: Stanford University Press, 1996), and *The Time of Liberty: Popular Political Culture in Oaxaca, 1750–1850* (Durham: Duke University Press, 2005); and Michael T. Ducey, *A Nation of Villages: Riot and Rebellion in the Mexican Huasteca, 1750–1850* (Tucson: University of Arizona Press, 2004).

63. Vázquez and Meyer, *The United States and Mexico*, 31

64. Luis G. Zorrilla, *Historia de las relaciones entre México y los Estados Unidos de América, 1800–1958* (Mexico City: Porrúa, 1977), 1:91–117.

65. Reséndez, *Changing National Identities*, 19.

66. Tornel, *Tejas y los Estados Unidos*, 14–17.

67. *Diario histórico del último viaje que hizo M. de la Sale* [sic] *para descubrir el desembocadero y curso del Missicipi* [sic], trans. by José María Tornel (New York: José Desnoues, 1831), 4.

68. Terrazas y Basante & Gurza Lavalle, *Las relaciones México-Estados Unidos*, 184. Also see Miguel Soto, "Texas en la mira. Política y negocios al iniciarse la gestión de Anthony Butler," in *Política y negocios. Ensayos sobre la relación entre México y los Estados Unidos en el siglo XIX*, eds. Ana Rosa Suárez Argüello & Marcela Terrazas Basante (Mexico City: UNAM/Instituto Mora, 1997), 19–63.

69. Henson, *Lorenzo de Zavala*, 51.

70. José María Tornel to Manuel de Mier y Terán, Baltimore, February 5, 1831, reproduced in Bocanegra, *Memorias para la historia de México*, 1:550–552.

71. Mier y Terán to Alamán, April 1831, quoted in Enrique Krauze, *Siglo de caudillos* (Barcelona: Tusquets, 1994), 116.

72. *Diario del Gobierno*, May 6, 1836.

73. Vázquez, "The Colonization and Loss of Texas."

74. Dispatch of February 16, 1836, Villa de Guerrero included as an appendix in Antonio López de Santa Anna, *Manifiesto que de sus operaciones en la campaña e Tejas y en su cautiverio dirige a sus conciudadasnos el general Antonio López de Santa Anna, 10 de mayo de 1837* (Veracruz: Imp. Liberal, 1837), reprinted in *Documentos inéditos o muy raros para la historia de México,* Vol. 59*: Antonio López de Santa Anna*, ed. Genaro García (Mexico City: Porrúa, 1991), 160.

75. Santa Anna to Minister of War [José María Tornel], Cuartel general de [San Antonio] Béjar, March 8, 1836, included as an appendix in ibid., 179.

76. José María Morelos, "Sentimientos de la nación o puntos dados para la

constitución," Chilpancingo, September 14, 1813, reproduced in Ernesto de la Torre, *La independencia de México* (Madrid: Mapfre, 1992), 250–251.

77. "Plan de Iguala," my emphasis.

78. Vázquez, "The Colonization and Loss of Texas," 48, 50, 53.

79. Austin to Wiley Martin, May 30, 1833, quoted in ibid., 70.

80. Mier y Terán, "Ideas about the colony," *Texas by Terán*, 56.

81. Ibid., 58–59.

82. For the change to centralism, see Michael P. Costeloe, "Federalism to Centralism in Mexico: The Conservative Case for Change, 1834–1835," *The Americas* 45 (1988): 173–185.

83. Carlos María de Bustamante, *Continuación del Cuadro Histórico. El gabinete mexicano durante el segundo período de Bustamante hasta la entrega del mando a Santa Anna* (Mexico City: Fondo de Cultura Económica, 1985 [originally published in 1842]), 2:14.

84. Williamson quoted in Wilfrid Hardy Callcott, *Santa Anna: The Story of an Enigma Who Once Was Mexico* (Hamden, CT: Archon Books, 1964), 124 (my emphasis).

85. "Constitution of the Republic of Texas. March 17, 1836," in *Laws of the Republic of Texas* (Houston: Office of the Telegraph, 1838), 2:19.

86. "Confederate States of America.—A Declaration of the Causes which Impel the State of Texas to Secede from the Federal Union," February 2, 1861.

87. Phillip Thomas Tucker, *Exodus from the Alamo: The Anatomy of the Last Stand Myth* (Philadelphia & Newbury: Casemate, 2009), 9.

88. See Emmanuel Lévinas, *Alterity and Transcendence*, translated by Michael B. Smith (New York: Columbia University Press, 1999 [originally published in French in 1970]).

89. Tornel's quote taken from *Diario del Gobierno*, November 3, 1835.

90. Translated in Richard Bruce Winders, *Crisis in the Southwest: The United States, Mexico, and the Struggle over Texas* (Wilmington, DE: SR Books, 2002), 25.

91. Santa Anna to José Urrea, [San Antonio de] Béjar, March 24, 1836, in AHSDN: Exp. XI/III/1–116 [1–15], vol. III, ff. 718–719.

92. News of the rebellion barely made an impact on the press until November 1835, and even then, the majority of early articles that mentioned the uprising did so without much of a sense of urgency. The first main piece on the rebellion featured in the *Diario del Gobierno*, November 7, 1835.

93. Michael P. Costeloe, "The Mexican Press of 1836 and the Battle of the Alamo," *Southwestern Historical Quarterly* 91 (April 1988): 533–43.

94. *La lima del Vulcano*, March 22, 1836. My emphasis.

95. *El Nacional*, March 21, 1836.

96. *El Mosquito Mexicano*, March 22, 1836.

97. Costeloe, "The Mexican Press of 1836," 543.

98. Richard Pakenham to Lord Aberdeen, Mexico City, August 29, 1842. Public Record Office, London, Foreign Office Papers (henceforth referred to as FO) 50/154.

99. José María Bocanegra to Richard Pakenham, Mexico City, September 23, 1842, FO 50/155.

100. Michael P. Costeloe, *The Central Republic in Mexico, 1835–1846: Hombres de Bien in the Age of Santa Anna* (Cambridge: Cambridge University Press, 1993), 276–79.

101. Tornel, *Tejas y los Estados Unidos*, 3.

102. Richard Pakenham to Lord Palmerston, Mexico City, December 15, 1835, FO 50/93.

103. For Carlos María de Bustamante's 1822–48 diaries, see *Diario histórico de México 1822–1848 de Carlos María de Bustamante*, eds. Josefina Zoraida Vázquez and Héctor Cuauhtémoc Hernández Silva, 2 CD-ROMs (Mexico City: CIESAS/El Colegio de México, 2001 & 2004).

104. Terrazas Basante & Gurza Lavalle, *Las relaciones México-Estados Unidos*, 195–97. Dr. Terrazas gave a particularly engaging lecture on this issue to the Research Seminar of the Department of Spanish of the University of St. Andrews on October 10, 2012, entitled "La independencia de Texas: ¿un conflicto internacional?"

105. Vázquez, "The Colonization and Loss of Texas," 77.

106. "The Texas Declaration of Independence (March 2, 1836)," can be accessed online at: http://www.lsjunction.com/docs/tdoi.htm.

107. Renowned radical federalists such as Valentín Gómez Farías and José Antonio Mejía, who initially backed the Texan revolt because they believed it was, indeed, a show of federalist resistance to the abolition of the 1824 Constitution, eventually withdrew their support when it became evident that what the Texans were after was, in fact, independence. See Will Fowler, "Valentín Gómez Farías: Perceptions of Radicalism in Independent Mexico, 1821–1847," *Bulletin of Latin American Research* 15:1 (1996): 44.

108. Tornel, *Tejas y los Estados Unidos*, 65–69.

109. Josefina Zoraida Vázquez, "¿Dos guerras contra Estados Unidos?" in *De la rebelión de Texas a la guerra del 47*, ed. Josefina Zoraida Vázquez (Mexico City: Nueva Imagen, 1994), 9.

110. For evolving interpretations of Mexican national identity, see Francisco Bulnes, *El porvenir de las naciones hispanoamericanas ante las conquistas recientes de Europa y los Estados Unidos* (Mexico City: Imp. de M. Nava, 1899); José Vasconcelos, *La raza cósmica* (Mexico City: Porrúa, 2003 [originally published

in 1948]); Octavio Paz, *El laberinto de la soledad*; Guillermo Bonfil Batalla, *El México profundo. Una civilización negada* (Mexico City: Editorial Grijalbo, 1987); and Roger Bartra, *The Cage of Melancholy: Identity and Metamorphosis in the Mexican Character* (New Brunswick: Rutgers University Press, 1992).

111. A number of noteworthy studies have focused on different kinds of fiestas and how the so-called *juntas patrióticas* played a key role in instilling Mexicans with a sense of national pride through the celebration and commemoration of what were deemed key foundational events, such as the beginning and the end of the War of Independence on September 16 and 27, respectively, or military victories such as Santa Anna's triumph of Tampico on September 11, 1829. See *¡Viva Mexico! ¡Viva la Independencia! Celebrations of September 16*, eds. William H. Beezley and David E. Lorey (Wilmington, DE: SR Books, 2001); Michael P. Costeloe, "The Junta Patriótica and the Celebration of Independence in Mexico City, 1821–1855," *Mexican Studies/Estudios Mexicanos* 13:1 (1997): 21–53; Will Fowler, "Fiestas santanistas: La celebración de Santa Anna en la villa de Xalapa, 1821–1855," *Historia Mexicana* 52:2 (2002): 391–447; Flor de María Salazar Mendoza, *La junta patriótica de la capital potosina. Un espacio político de los liberales (1873–1882)* (San Luis Potosí: Editorial Ponciano Arriaga, 1999); Flor de María Salazar Mendoza, "The Independence Celebrations in the cities of Morelia and San Luis Potosí, 1829–1876: Politics and Speeches" (Ph.D. diss., University of Bristol, 2007); Verónica Zárate Toscano, "Héroes y fiestas en el México decimonónico: la insistencia de Santa Anna," in *La construcción del héroe en España y México (1789–1847)*, eds. Manuel Chust & Víctor Mínguez (Valencia: Universitat de Valencia, 2003), 133–53; Verónica Zárate Toscano, "Las conmemoraciones septembrinas en la Ciudad de México y su entorno en el siglo XIX," in *Política, casas y fiestas en el entorno urbano del Distrito Federal. Siglos XVIII-XIX*, ed. Verónica Zárate Toscano (Mexico City: Instituto Mora, 2003). Also see, albeit for the second half of the nineteenth century, William H. Beezley, *Mexican National Identity: Memory, Innuendo, and Popular Culture* (Tucson: University of Arizona Press, 2008).

112. Charles A. Hale, *Mexican Liberalism in the Age of Mora, 1821–1853* (New Haven: Yale University Press, 1968), 37.

113. Josefina Zoraida Vázquez, *Una tragedia que reafirmó la identidad. La guerra del 47* (Mexico City: Centro de Estudios de Historia de México, 1983).

114. Tornel, *Breve reseña histórica*, 135.

FIVE

"TIME'S NOBLEST EMPIRE IS THE LAST"
Texas Annexation in the Presumed Course of American Empire

Amy S. Greenberg

"IT'S BEEN SAID that 'painting can illustrate, but not invent,'—and that its highest power consists of copying nature," wrote the *New York Commercial Advertiser* in 1836. But after witnessing Thomas Cole's five-part visual epic, *Course of Empire*, which burst onto the New York art scene mere weeks after voters in the newly independent Republic of Texas overwhelmingly approved an annexation referendum, reviewer "A" of that paper was driven to a different conclusion about the power of art. "Art is capable of loftier deeds—that, instead of . . . merely . . . 'point[ing] a moral or adorn[ing] a tale,'" painting "itself may weave the web of the story" and "produce the moral."[1]

Thomas Cole was already one of America's "most eminent artists" when *Course of Empire*, "the result of the toil and study of three years," was unveiled in the gallery at Clinton Hall in October of 1836. Like his other famously luminous landscapes, these paintings partook in what one scholar has called a "magisterial gaze," inviting viewers to visually possess the landscape from a lofty perspective and "illimitable horizon that they identified with the destiny of the American people."[2] Whatever they shared in perspective, the canvases that made up *Course of Empire* differed markedly in subject matter and tone from other works of the Hudson River School. These were heavily allegorical, even didactic works. Portraying "the gradual progress of man from the rude savage of the wilderness, to the highest and most palmy state of civilization, and then to mark the change which comes over the proudest efforts of humanity," the paintings immediately caused a sensation, not only because of the enormous scale of the "nobly imagined, beautifully executed" canvases, but because in a period when the average working man made about $300 a year, Thomas Cole had the audacity to charge an unheard of fifty-cent admission to the private exhibit.[3]

FIGURE 9. *The Savage State* by Thomas Cole. Courtesy New York Historical Society

FIGURE 10. *The Arcadian or Pastoral State* by Thomas Cole. Courtesy New York Historical Society

FIGURE 11. *The Consummation of Empire* by Thomas Cole. Courtesy New York Historical Society

FIGURE 12. *Destruction* by Thomas Cole. Courtesy New York Historical Society

FIGURE 13. *Desolation* by Thomas Cole. Courtesy New York Historical Society

But rapturous acclaim for the five "original" and "bold" compositions, "intended as a representation of the growth, greatness, decay, and destruction of a community," drowned out grumbling over the price of admission.[4] "These pictures are very nobly imagined, beautifully executed, and cannot be looked at without a feeling of strong interest," wrote the *New York Evening Post*.[5] The review from the *Gazette* in Alexandria, Virginia, was even more effusive in its praise of "the aerial perspective and beautiful harmony of the tints," apologizing at the end of a very long article that "we have been perhaps prolix in describing the subjects of these interesting works, but we are greatly mistaken if they are not destined to produce a very strong sensation, both here and elsewhere."[6] "We have no hesitation in saying that they place the artist in the highest rank of living painters," offered the *New-York Spectator*. "And they are not less remarkable for the force, the spirit, and ingenuity, with which the idea is developed, than for their beauty and excellence considered merely as pictures."[7]

Viewers were united in proclaiming Cole's paintings "deeply interesting and solemnly instructive," as described by the *New York Commercial Advertiser*:

> *To the moralist, the patriot, and the statesman, they convey, in a manner forcible and vivid, a lesson full of instruction. Who can turn from the pastoral scene, where all is peace and loveliness—where earth, air, and sky all harmonize with the useful, innocent and happy occupation of man, to the scene of horror and devastation, where the heavens are rent with the storm, and man more savage than the raging elements, is hurling to earth the works of art—assaulting the helpless females, and dealing death to his fellow men and not feel an ominous foreboding, and his mind prepared for the last solemn scene in that nation's history. . . . And if we look back to the magnificent city . . . see what it once was, and what it has now become—a tale is told—a lesson is taught—and a moral enforced by the pencil of the painter, which eminently prove the power and the intellectual independence of his art.*[8]

Cole was hardly subtle with his lesson and moral. In newspaper advertisements touting the exhibit, Cole quoted the relevant verse from "Childe Harold's Pilgrimage," a poem by British Lord Byron that provided the title and inspiration for his visual epic:

> *There is the moral of all human tales;*
> *'Tis but the same rehearsal of the past.*
> *First freedom and then Glory—when that fails,*
> *Wealth, vice, corruption—barbarism at last.*
> *And History, with all her volumes vast,*
> *Hath but one page.*[9]

As Cole wrote to his patron when first thinking about the allegorical series, "The philosophy of my subject is drawn from the history of the past, wherein we see how nations have risen from the Savage state to that of Power & Glory & then fallen & become extinct."[10] And yet, as he admitted to his diary, it wasn't only the past that was on his mind. As "Texas Committees" organized around the United States to send money and volunteers to Texas in August of 1835, it appeared to Cole "that the moral principle of the nation is much lower than formerly—much less than vanity will allow—Americans are too fond of attributing the great prosperity of the country to their own good government instead of seeing the source of it in the unbounded resources and favorable political opportunities of the nation. It is with sorrow that I anticipated the downfall of pure republican government. . . . The hope of the wise & the good will have perished—and scenes of tyranny & wrong, blood & oppression such as have been acted since the world was created—will be again performed."[11]

Thomas Cole was generally skeptical of political parties, but his sympathies lay with the Whigs, and he had particular contempt for Andrew Jackson. The 1841 death of the first Whig elected president, William Henry Harrison, he wrote, was the most lamented "since the death of Washington."[12] Cole had not previously painted an explicitly political canvas, but the events of the mid-1830s cried out for critique, and Cole offered one. At the same moment that American historians, led by George Bancroft, proclaimed that their national experiment was so exceptional that the nation's progress would be linear, a story of endless improvement, and not cyclical as Byron suggests, Cole demurred. America would fall just as surely as had Rome.[13]

Cole's paintings have provided a fertile field for art historians, many of whom have explored the meaning of his European and classical imagery in the social and cultural framework of the developing United States. Far fewer have placed Cole's work in a political framework, and those who have focused on the domestic rather than the foreign context, identifying the rampant speculation, urban poverty, and financial insecurity of the era, as well as Jackson's imperious actions, as the objects of Cole's ire. [14]

Yet no one has noted the obvious: Territorial expansion was the cause of imperial collapse. The third of the five canvases, *Consummation of Empire*, features a conquering emperor, returning from faraway lands with slaves, tribute, and an elephant. The gateway is surmounted by a gold statue celebrating war. The harbor is clogged with ships of trade, and hanging from the temple on the right is a banner bearing the imperial eagle, a symbol that recalled both Ancient Rome and the national seal of the United States. Canvas number four, *Destruction*, juxtaposes a stone warrior, primed for battle, but missing a head, with the suicide of a young woman fleeing rape at a soldier's hands. The course of empire in these paintings was clear, and clearly the result of imperialism itself: "wealth, vice, corruption—barbarism at last." This is a narrative about foreign policy, wrongly understood.[15]

Cole's *Course of Empire* was fantastically popular. At the same moment that both houses of Congress were inundated with petitions opposing the annexation of Texas, large crowds flocked to see the paintings when they went on display in New York. Cole cleared almost $1,000 in admission fees from the exhibition, which one critic called the "most successful . . . ever held in this city."[16] Nor is it too much to say that *Course of Empire* made Cole's career. In 1849, James Fenimore Cooper publically stated, "Not only do I consider the *Course of Empire* the work of the highest genius this country has ever produced, but I esteem it one of the noblest works of art that has ever been wrought."[17]

Whether or not viewers understood the "victorious general" in the third of the paintings to be Andrew Jackson, as one scholar has suggested, clearly the *Course of Empire* hit a nerve.[18] On one hand, the architecture, clothing, and other symbols clearly identify the empire in question as Rome. There were no classical ruins in the 1830s United States. Cole was painting the past.

But was he not also painting the present, and future? Cole himself compared the city in the canvases as containing "the essence of New York in its bustling diversity," and allegedly drew on the landscape of the Adirondacks for his backdrop and setting.[19] Why would the artist place figures resembling American Indians in canoes if his object was to represent ancient Rome? Is it any wonder that many viewers found it impossible to look at these canvases in 1836 without, as critics remarked, "feeling an ominous foreboding"?[20]

What this essay proposes to do is to allow *The Course of Empire* to fulfill the promise of art and "weave the web of the story." It will explore this "ominous foreboding" and consider how the Texas Revolution and possible annexation of Texas to the United States in the first year after independence fit into discourses about a US empire.[21] Opponents of annexation of Texas repeatedly drew on the "course of empire" and the fate of the Roman Empire, in particular, to connect the growth of the United States to inevitable collapse, while supporters of Texas independence and annexation in 1837 celebrated the dawn of a new age, and birth of a new history, in which the course of empire, as visualized by Cole, was no longer relevant. In the process those who embraced Texas elucidated a clear and coherent vision of America's Manifest Destiny for the first time, a vision that would ultimately justify annexation in 1845.

In recent decades, historians have embraced the idea that the United States has always been imperialist. Although at one time the standard narrative of American foreign policy started with Washington's farewell address, with the father of our country warning his fellow citizens about the dangers of expansion, it is now more likely to begin with Thomas Jefferson longing for Louisiana and Florida.[22]

One of the many things this new narrative elides is the strength, indeed prevalence, of anti-imperial ideology during the first decades of this country's history. Until the 1790s, there was a widespread understanding, drawn from the writings of the great Enlightenment philosopher Baron de Montesquieu, that extended territory was incompatible with good, virtuous, republican (with a small r) government. While the always-visionary Jefferson mused over a future "empire of liberty," his assumption that republics could not expand beyond certain limits underlay both the Articles of Confederation and opposition to the Constitution. Some scholars have argued that the ratification of the Constitution in 1787 undermined the Montesquieuian vision of extended territory equating with political collapse by endowing federalism with the mechanism for expanding government and territory simultaneously. Americans need not fear Roman precedent: Indeed, Rome's growth from republic to empire could be instructive. It's no coincidence that the authors of the Federalist Papers took the name "Publius," the founder of Rome, in order to associate the Constitution with the dynamic growth of Rome. The Constitution promised a future marked by growth and expansion, in contrast to the stagnation of the 1780s.[23]

But the Montesquieuian vision lived on long after the ratification of the Constitution. In an 1801 letter to James Monroe, Thomas Jefferson wrote that it was impossible to know just how much the republic might grow. "However our present interests may restrain us within our own limits, it is impossible not to look forward to distant times, when our rapid multiplication will expand itself beyond those limits and cover the whole northern, if not the southern, continent, with a people speaking the same language, governed in similar forms and by similar laws."[24]

But a close examination of Jefferson's exact wording about expansion: "people speaking the same language, governed in similar forms and by similar laws" suggests that what Jefferson and other expansionists in the very Early Republic imagined was not one state, spanning the continent, but a series of smaller satellite states set up by Americans, or other Europeans inspired by the American Revolution, separate from one another politically, but sharing a similar culture and politics. In short, Jefferson's vision of the settlement of the great continent looked quite different from the ultimate shape of the American empire.

Federalist opponents of Jefferson's expansionism embraced the Montesquieuian critique and turned to history in order to prove that extended territory spelled the death of a republic. After learning that Jefferson proposed to purchase the Louisiana Territory from France in 1803, Massachusetts Federalist Fischer Ames wrote his good friend Thomas Dwight, "Surely it exceeds all my credulity and candor . . . to suppose even they [Jefferson's supporters] can contemplate a republican form [of government] as practicable, honest or free, if applied when it is so manifestly inapplicable to the government of one third of God's earth. It could not, I think, even maintain forms."[25] When a nation shared language, values, and experiences, it prospered. Extended empires, like that of ancient Rome, or modern Britain, fractured and collapsed, in the same way that the bridge in *The Course of Empire: Destruction* collapses under the weight of the army.

The 1820s saw the birth of a continental vision for the future growth of the United States as expansionists, including Henry Clay, and the author of the Monroe Doctrine, John Quincy Adams, worked to purchase Texas from Mexico. Yet the Texas Revolution in the middle of the 1830s provoked a similar response, and much the same anti-imperial critique as had the Louisiana Purchase in 1803.

At the same time, the Texas Revolution proved to be a galvanizing event in the formation of the ideology of American empire. Events in Texas drove both supporters and opponents of annexation to conceptualize two visions of Manifest Destiny that in scope and scale were unprecedented. Looking closely at how Americans at the time understood the Texas Revolution and potential annexation in 1836–37 can lead to a more nuanced understanding of the true course of American empire, and specifically the genesis of the ideology of Manifest Destiny.

"By every foot of land that we add to the union, we weaken, we disunite, and we dissolve! Satis superque! [Enough!]" So warned the editor of the *New York Courier and Inquirer* in November of 1835 after reporting on the many American volunteers heading to Texas. Only Latin could fully express the threat that Texas posed to the nation. "Satis superque! should even now be our motto—we are already well nigh too large for self-government, we already comprehend too many jarring interests! Increase to us is ruin! Like the Roman Empire, we shall fall to pieces imperceptibly from a mere want of moral cement to keep together our component atoms."[26] That the United States was emulating older empires was abundantly clear to Mexican intellectuals during the Texas Revolution. Manuel Eduardo de Gorostiza, Mexican minister to the United States shortly after the conflict, condemned America's "race of migratory adventurers," while José María Tornel, secretary of war during the Texas campaign, compared the United States to "Alexander" and "Napoleon" and "the barbarous hordes of a former age" in "its desire, its frenzy to take control of that which rightly belongs to its neighbors."[27]

Critics within the United States also pointed to ancient precedent, combining Montesquieuian fears of extended territory with a critique of the manhood of the participants. In June 1836, the *Vermont Telegraph* wrote of Texas, "We are daily more and more convinced that this is a war of conquest, a bloody and wicked plot of land speculators and land pirates to fill private purses, and to extend and establish the dominion of slavery. Volunteers are now enlisting in the Southern States, to be paid in land in Texas, six hundred acres to each who enlists for the war! A more unprincipled, ferocious work, was not carried out in the days of Alexander or Julius Caesar."[28]

Many in the United States feared that Texas would be the genesis for a new Empire of Slavery. "One who Knows" reported to the *Alexandria Gazette* in April of 1836 that "the advocates of disunion and secession" favored a "scheme of establishing an independent Empire in Texas, to serve as a nucleus for a Southern Confederacy."[29] The *New York Herald* also anticipated Texas forming the core of "a distinct and separate empire, distinct in habits, interest, and policy, as well as in climate and productions."[30] In a series of essays first published in the *National Gazette*, and republished in an 1836 pamphlet *The Origin and True Causes of the Texas Insurrection, Commenced in the Year 1835*, abolitionist Benjamin Lundy most clearly enunciated this view when he condemned the "insatiate and all grasping views" of the Texans and those who supported them, arguing forcefully that the true purpose of the Revolution was to "extend the bounds of the Texian empire to the bounds of the Rio Grande" and to the Rocky Mountains.[31]

But a far greater fear than Texas giving birth to a new empire of slavery on the Rio Grande was that annexation of Texas would lead to the internal collapse of the United States. As John Quincy Adams asked his congressional colleagues in May 1836 (in a speech that he called "the most noted that I ever made"), "Are you not large and unwieldy enough already . . . Is your Southern and South-Western frontier not sufficiently extensive?"[32] Critics of Texas annexation in the United States pointed to ancient precedent, with the intention of showing, like Cole, the inevitable course of empire. From 1835 to 1837, readers of popular periodicals in the United States could contemplate the moral of Rome's decline and fall in stories such as *The Knickerbocker Magazine*'s maudlin "Downfall of Nations," a lengthy investigation of the rise and fall of the great empires of the past. Rome, once an "empire more extensive than any other on historic record," was "overwhelmed by conquest," and sunk "under the results of victory." America's fate would be different, the author suggested, but only if the "enlightened conditions of a community insures the perpetuity of her institutions." In other words, if the United States replicates Rome, it too will fall. "A Day at Carthage," by Mordecai Noah, also closed with a warning to American readers: "Ambition—proud, anxious, restless ambition—might here receive a salutatory lesson."[33]

Partisan newspapers made the connection directly. "There is a certain extent to which the territorial possessions of a community may be safely extended, under a wise and energetic administration of government—beyond that, empires and republics are in equal hazard of discord and dismemberment," argued the Norwich, Connecticut, *Courier*, in April of 1837. "The very weight and extent of the [Roman] empire caused it to break in pieces." Clearly it was the "height of folly for any community, and especially for a Republic to aim at acquisition of extensive territory."[34]

This anti-imperial critique was a common trope at the many public meetings held in opposition to the annexation of Texas in 1837. Public meetings have no clear equivalent today, but they were something like political rallies that were publicized ahead of time, featured enthusiastic public speakers of some note, usually offered up a number of resolutions which were adopted after receiving sufficient applause or cheers from the audience, and often drew crowds in the thousands.[35] The primary ways that American citizens could embrace, or reject Texas, without traveling to the territory itself, was through the gendered vehicles of petitioning Congress and attending public meetings. And they did both of these things with gusto. Although the "ladies" of Nashville were "invited to attend" a meeting in favor of Texas in February of 1836, because of their public and often unruly nature (drinking before, during, and after was common), public meetings were attended almost exclusively by men.[36]

Petitioning, by contrast, was an activity embraced by women. Throughout the second half of 1836, and through 1837, petitioners, many of them female, bombarded both houses of Congress with petitions opposing Texas annexation. "Ladies" were "very busy in going from house to house soliciting signatures to memorials praying Congress to prevent the unholy Union" of Texas with the United States, a Massachusetts paper noted with regret. "Dear creatures, if they would stay at home and see that their babies are taken proper care of, how much better they would appear!"[37]

But they did not stay home. In Lorraine County, Ohio, 241 ladies submitted a petition against the annexation of Texas to the Senate in September 1837, while the *Providence Journal* marveled that "two misses, yet in their teens, with pencil in hand, called on a respectable and intelligent lady, the wife of a professional gentleman, requesting her to sign a petition to Congress, against the admission of Texas into the Union. . . . With such female petitions no doubt the table of both houses of Congress will be loaded." The tables were indeed loaded. On a single day, in September 1837, John Quincy Adams, now a firm opponent of the annexation of Texas, presented "from the different States, 117 remonstrances against the annexation of Texas to the Union. Other gentlemen offered a great many more." By December 1837, "numerous" petitions were the order of business on a regular basis. In the aftermath of the passage of the gag rule tabling, without consideration, all antislavery petitions, the anti-Mexico petition campaign became incredibly heated. It was an orchestrated campaign that threatened, at points, to paralyze Congress. While the majority of these petitions were written by abolitionists and specifically addressed the threat of the spread of slavery, they also spoke to the danger that extended territory posed to the republic.[38]

The anti-slavery and anti-imperial critiques were linked at public meetings as well. At a "large and respectable meeting of the inhabitants of Oxford Township and its vicinity" on the twenty-second of August 1837, Pennsylvanians resolved "that we view with apprehension any accession of territory to our widely extended empire, insomuch as our limits are already so expanded, as to bring into action conflicting interests and feelings, which greatly embarrass the operations of government, engender feelings so hostile in one part of the union to other portions of it, as on more than one occasion to threaten an explosion from which the most fearful results might justly be dreaded; and we conceive that the annexation of Texas would greatly multiply the elements of discord, a consequence we earnestly deprecate."[39]

The citizens of Canton, Ohio, reached a similar conclusion when they resolved to oppose the admission of Texas into the Union in November of 1837 "because it would, without any corresponding benefits, needlessly extend our already sufficiently extended territory."[40] So did the attendees at a public meeting in Worcester, Massachusetts, held in the summer of 1837. "Mr. Jefferson said there was ample territory in our Union in his day, to sustain the growth of one hundred generations, and since that time, Louisiana and Florida have been added by purchase, to increase the extent of our over-grown republic." There was no need to add Texas.[41]

This same critique was evident in the widely reported and highly influential 1837 public letter against annexation written by America's foremost Unitarian preacher, William Ellery Channing, to Whig leader Henry Clay, the former secretary of state under John Quincy Adams, and likely candidate for the presidency in 1840. "Some crimes, by their magnitude, have a touch of the sublime; and to this dignity the seizure of Texas by our citizens is entitled. . . . The pirate seizes a ship. The colonists and their coadjutors can satisfy themselves with nothing less short of an empire," Channing proclaimed.[42]

Most scholars have focused on Channing's critique of the potential that Texas Annexation posed to strengthening the "Slave Power," a phrase first used by abolitionist Lydia Maria Child in 1833 in reference to the threat Texas posed to the republic.[43] But an imperial critique is equally evident. "Did this country know itself, or were it disposed to profit by self-knowledge, it would feel the necessity of laying an immediate curb on its passion for extended territory," he wrote. "Already endangered by our greatness, we cannot advance without imminent peril to our institutions, union, prosperity, virtue, and peace."[44]

What is particularly interesting about Channing's letter is not his Montesqueian critique, which, as we've seen, was widespread, but his recognition of the place of Texas in America's Manifest Destiny. "We talk of accomplishing our destiny. So did the late conqueror of Europe [meaning Napoleon]; and destiny consigned him to a lonely rock in the ocean, the prey of an ambition which destroyed no peace but his own." A similar fate faced America. "I have alluded to the want of wisdom with which we are accustomed to speak of our destiny as a people. We are *destined* (that is the word) to overspread North America; and intoxicated with the idea; it matters little to us how we accomplish our fate. . . . Why can't we rise to noble conceptions of our destiny?"[45]

Channing not only critiqued the destiny of the United States to absorb Texas, but offered, instead, an alternate vision of America's "sublime moral empire" that in many ways was indistinguishable from the ideology of Manifest Destiny that the *United States and Democratic Review* promulgated two years later in "The Great Nation of Futurity," and which only gained the name "Manifest Destiny" in the middle 1840s. Channing wrote,

> *when we look forward to the probable growth of this country; when we think of the millions of human beings who are to spread over our present territory; of the career of improvement and glory open to this new people; . . . of the vast field in which the experiment is to be made of what the unfettered powers of man may achieve; when we think of all this, can we help for a moment surrendering ourselves to bright visions of our country's glory; before which all the glories of the past are to fade away? Is it presumption to say, that, if just to ourselves and all nations, we shall be felt through this whole continent, that we shall spread our language, institutions, and civilization through a wider space than any nation has yet filled with a like beneficent influence. Are we prepared to barter these hopes, this sublime moral empire, for conquests by force? Are we prepared to sink to the level of unprincipled nations?*[46]

Channing clearly embraced American exceptionalism, and the contention, first presented in Bishop George Berkeley's 1726 *Verses on the Prospect of Planting Arts and Learning in America*, that America would be seat of the last, greatest empire. "Westward the course of empire takes its way; The first four Acts already past, A fifth shall close the Drama with the day; Time's noblest offspring is the last." Although Berkeley composed the verses to promote a college he hoped to found in Bermuda, in the 1830s they were embraced by Americans enamored of their own shining destiny, and appeared in children's schoolbooks, poetry, and orations. The *New Bedford Mercury* had noted back in the 1820s that Berkeley's contention that "Time's noblest empire is the last," contained

> *not only a precious promise, but a solemn injunction of duty. . . . The four first acts—the Empires of the former world and of former ages—the Assyrian, the Persian, the Grecian, the Roman Empires—were Empires of conquest. . . . The Empire which his great mind, piercing in to the darkness of futurity, foretold in America was the Empire of Learning and the Arts. . . . Well may this be termed nobler than conquest.*[47]

But the fate of Texas to the destiny of the nation was just as obvious to those supporters of conquests by force as it was to the critics who instead dreamed of a sublime moral empire and warned that extension of territory would lead to internal collapse. Both supporters and opponents agreed that foremost among the conquerors was Andrew Jackson. Not long after becoming president in 1828, Jackson wrote that he "had long since been aware of the importance of Texas to the United States" and vowed "to keep my eye on this object and the first propitious moment make the attempt to regain the Territory." He saw the annexation of Texas as an "essential component of his dream of empire" and spent seven years attempting to purchase it from Mexico.[48]

The Texas Revolution offered him a chance to fulfill America's destiny, but only if he was willing to embrace the image of that emperor on the bridge in *Course of Empire: Consummation*. The Montesquieuian critique against extended empire was employed by Jackson's opponents in part because it resonated with charges that "King Andrew I" was a despot whose tyrannical actions, whether foreign (Texas), or domestic (withdrawing deposits from the Second Bank of the United States, threatening to march the army on South Carolina when the state proposed to nullify a federal tariff), were undermining the liberties of the people.[49] The rhetorical scholar Lyon Rathbun has argued that the anti-imperial critique was so effective in 1836 that it prevented Jackson from publicly embracing annexation. He was too worried about the election of his successor, Martin Van Buren, and the fate of his own legacy to embrace Texas, as much as he wished to, and Texas remained independent.[50]

This is not to say that all supporters of Texas annexation worried about the resonances with Ancient Rome; far from it. The *Nashville Banner* confirmed news of victory at San Jacinto and admitted, "The great, noble, and magnificent principles of the 'antique Romans,' those conquerors and masters of a world for a thousand years, we admire, revere, and honor."[51]

Supporters of Texas annexation happily turned the anti-imperial critique on its head, embracing territorial expansion, and Manifest Destiny, in the name of a martial vision of manhood. Consider for a moment the moving War of 1812 panorama offered in February of 1836 in New York by William J. Hannington, the esteemed creator of entertaining "dioramas" (a series of large-scale paintings attached on vertical rollers so the scenes unfolded from left to right in front of a seated audience). Every evening, starting at 7:30 at P. T. Barnum's American Museum, visitors could enjoy the thrill of "Hannington's New Moving Dioramas," an "allegorical representation of the Treaty of Ghent, and Triumph of America," in which "the whole spectacle is represented in the style and costume of the ancient Romans." The diorama featured an obelisk "erected to the glory of the American heroes of the last war" and a representation of the American capital building "to localize the scene as having been laid in Washington," regardless of the Roman costume of the participants. "The admiring spectator will observe with delight the motion of men and horses, as natural as life, keeping time with the martial music," the advertisement offered.[52] While the War of 1812 might seem, at first glance, to have little to do with Ancient Rome, Hannington could think of no better way to celebrate the course of American empire than to dress it in Roman garb.

Six months later, Hannington produced a diorama featuring the Texas Revolution (at the Marble building adjacent to the American museum: doors open at 7, performance begins at half past eight). This celebration of the "glorious achievement of 'our' brave countrymen in Texas" (note the slip of identifying the Texans as Americans), included not only a key naval battle from the War of 1812, but three scenes focused on the "glorious victory at the battle of San Jacinto." No Roman garb was evident, but plenty of celebration of martial virtue. The first scene offered "the Mexican Army attacked by the Texians. A general battle ensues, in which the Texians are triumphant." The scene changed to "the battle ground after the engagement, strewn with killed and wounded Mexicans," and finally viewers saw "The Texas camp by moonlight." Admission was twenty-five cents (only half of the cost of Cole's *Course of Empire*), and for children under twelve: twelve-and-a-half cents.[53]

A similar celebration of martial manhood and American empire could be found in less spectacular settings. Consider, for a moment, the cover page of the *Tallahassee Floridian*, on Sunday, September 2, 1837. On one page readers could enjoy poetry with classical resonances, the more or less

Admittance 25 Cents!

UNEQUALLED ATTRACTIONS!!

THREE NEW PIECES of Extreme Interest
ARE ADDED TO
HANINGTON'S GRAND MOVING

DIORAMAS,

Illustrative of GENERAL HOUSTON'S GLORIOUS VICTORY at the BATTLE OF SAN JACINTO, in Texas; the whole forming

EIGHT DISTINCT PIECES!

WITH APPROPRIATE MUSIC,

AT THE CITY SALOON, Marble Buildings, opposite St. Paul's Church, (next door to the American Museum,)

Doors open at 7 in the Evening. Performance to commence at ½ *past* 8.

ORDER OF THE VARIOUS MOVING SCENES,

GRAND DIORAMIC SCENE I.

ANIMATED VIEWS IN SWITZERLAND

Daybreak, Meridian, Setting Sun, and Moonlight.

The scenery abounds with the romantic and picturesque, for which that country is so justly celebrated. The rowing and sailing of boats; the shepherd attending his flocks; and other animated objects, cannot fail to gratify the curious.

GRAND DIORAMIC SCENE II.

Interior of the Monastery of St.Gallen, Switzerland,

With the Funeral of a Monk by torch light.

GRAND DIORAMIC SCENE III.

EXHIBITION OF THE ACTION BETWEEN THE

UNITED STATES FRIGATE CONSTITUTION,

CAPTAIN JAMES HULL.

AND H. B. M. SHIP GUERRIERE,

JAMES R. DACRES, Esq. Commander, Fought August 16th, 1812, which resulted in the capture of the latter vessel, after a hotly contested engagement of 30 minutes, and loss of 15 killed, 62 wounded, and 25 missing. The loss on board the Constitution was, total killed and wounded, 14.

GRAND DIORAMIC SCENE IV.

MOONLIGHT, SEA VIEW, STORM, & SHIPWRECK

In this very interesting scene, vessels are seen tacking from side to side in a manner truly nautical, others sailing before the wind—in the course of the representation a storm arises, the sea becomes agitated—the deep reverberations of thunder are heard, accompanied with lightning and torrents of rain. A vessel appears as if beating off a lee shore, she fires signals of distress, and is answered from the fort, from which a life-boat is sent to her assistance—the crew are saved, but the vessel is lost.

GRAND DIORAMIC SCENE V. The awful & devastating

CONFLAGRATION

OF A LARGE PART OF THE CITY OF NEW-YORK,

On the Inclement night of the 16th December, 1835.

THE WHOLE TO CONCLUDE WITH

Gen. Houston's Glorious Victory

At the Battle of SAN JACINTO, in Texas; comprising several scenes of the utmost interest.

GRAND DIORAMIC SCENE VI.

THE MEXICAN ARMY ATTACKED BY THE TEXIANS!!

A Battle scene in which the Texians are triumphant. Gen. Houston and Staff are seen in the foreground

GRAND DIORAMIC SCENE VII.

The Battle Ground after the Engagement.

Strewed with the killed and wounded Mexicans.

GRAND DIORAMIC SCENE VIII.

THE TEXIAN CAMP BY MOONLIGHT.

Removal of the wounded and burial of the dead, with appropriate Music—the Army passes in front, some resting after their severe toil, others cooking by the camp fires; the distant country and river San Jacinto are seen in the background, illuminated by the pale light of the Moon, forming a scene replete with interest and beauty.

Professor of the Piano, ...Monsieur Foures, from Paris.

Admittance to the whole, 25 cents—Children under 12 years, when accompanied by their parents or guardians, 12½ cents. [Turn over.

FIGURE 14. DIORAMAS clipping. Courtesy Dolph Briscoe Center for American History, University of Texas at Austin

true story of a man rejuvenated by his sojourn in Texas, and an unapologetic celebration of the arts of war, all of which connected events in Texas with the future course of the United States. The poem, "The Texian," placed the heroes fighting for "Freedom's Cause" in the classical pantheon on laurel-wreathed warrior heroes. "Where havoc wields her reddest brands, His step will be the lightest, Where steel is grasped by heroes' hands, His blade will be the brightest. In Freedom's cause, defying death, He'll march with the deserving; For Freedom twines the only wreath—Whose form is worth preserving."

A neighboring column offered the well-known story of Ephraim "Deaf" Smith (reprinted from the *Southern Literary Messenger*). Smith, a "native of the state of New York" who went to Texas at age twenty-two "in very feeble health. His constitution was soon renovated by the effects of a good climate and active exercise. He married a Mexican woman, by whom he has two children." "Frank, open-hearted, honest (and) humane," the not really deaf, but hard of hearing Smith gained a reputation for his fighting prowess in key battles of the revolution. Yet this paragon of martial manhood, "like thousands of others," had been "unjustly and ignorantly regarded as fighting for the spoil of conquest" when "he has staked his life for liberty."[54]

Lest the message be lost on readers that Texas was an eminently healthy place to prove one's masculine virtues, they needed only let their eyes wander down the page to "Our Own Country," reprinted from *The Knickerbocker*. America, the article claimed with more than a little self-satisfaction, was marked by a "universal scramble for property, for the adoration felt for wealth—in the neglect of the fine arts—in the little reward that genius has hitherto received at the hands of our countrymen, while it is cherished everywhere else. But what more could be expected?" it rhetorically asked. "We have just finished laying the foundations of an empire. We have had two wars to fight, both fierce and bloody. The war-whoop is not yet over. . . . We will rear the fabric of free government to the skies. We will adorn and embellish it, and make it beautiful in the eyes of all men. . . . Imagination, even can not picture the destiny that awaits us, if we preserve our liberty and our Union. God will promise us a renowned existence, if we will but deserve it."[55] It should go without saying that this author did not believe "the destiny that awaits us" to be that of Thomas Cole's *Course of Empire*. But what more could be expected? The author had already confessed to neglecting the fine arts.

Mississippi Democrat John F. H. Claiborne's speech to the House of

Representatives in January of 1837 also linked the American empire to the masculine virtue of the men fighting in Texas, refuting images of Rome in the process. America need not fear "extended empire or centralism," Claiborne asserted, because great men were "baptizing with their blood the star-gemmed banner of a maiden empire. . . . Mr. Speaker, I need not tell the house that the tide of empire is sweeping to the West."[56]

The Mississippi legislature also rejected the analogy to Rome, because regardless of how great America might grow, its people would remain united. Unlike Rome, Americans "speak the same language; profess the same religion; are inspired by the same love of country; subject to laws of our enactments; united upon principle, not force."[57]

Supporters of Texas annexation who gathered at their own public meetings and proudly proclaimed America's Manifest Destiny drew on the same themes of masculine regeneration and a pro-imperial outlook. At a meeting in Washington, DC, in May of 1836, an orator embraced "Texas, the youngest daughter of the Republic," and was greeted with "great cheers" when he proclaimed, "Onward is the cry of the Pioneer; and again he plunges into the depths of new forests, again to open to the view new worlds, guided alone by that 'star of empire that westward takes its way.'" Nor would the "onward march of the pioneer" be stayed at the Rio Grande. "What, though the mighty Emperor of the Western hemisphere be already greater in extent than was that of the Mistress of the World at the very zenith of her power in the days of Trojans. It will be greater still. . . . Such is destiny."[58]

One attendee at a "magnificent" (and high-priced) fund-raiser "in honor of Texas, Texian liberty, and Texian defenders in the Congress of the United States," held at New York's American Hotel on the evening of July 18, 1836, mused that, "As with the old Romans when they grew strong, so the spirit of conquest is upon us, and you might as well stay the whirlwind or the storm as attempt to stay it. There is a grandeur and a sublimity in our view of empire which, reason as we may, will impel us onward till only oceans and Andes-mountains can stop our course. The Canadas and the Provinces, as well as Texas must belong to us. It is the destiny of things, and no man can stay it." Nor, since the "discovery of steam power" did the author fear "the extension of our empire." Thanks to the railroad, "an extension of empire is not such a calamity as empire was to Rome. . . . There is a destiny for America, great and glorious I am sure," he intoned. And invoking Berkeley's famous lines, he linked the empire of learning with that of conquest in a perfect formulation of Manifest Destiny nine years before the phrase was first penned in the *United States Magazine and Democratic Review* essay "Annexation" by John L. O'Sullivan. "If we but follow in the wake of that destiny with Religion and Liberty, and Law upon our banner, History will but copy on our record the words of prophesy—'TIME'S NOBLEST EMPIRE IS THE LAST.'"[59] Diorama creator William J. Hannington was present at the dinner. He seemingly concurred with this vision of destiny, but in a manner that problematized the idea that America's empire was any less warlike than Rome's: he offered a toast to the "fallen brave" along with the wish that "the massacre at the Alamo stimulate all freemen to avenge them."[60]

It would be difficult to argue that the anti-imperialists won this debate. True, a critique of empire helped delay annexation for eight years, but the debate over Texas allowed those in favor of annexation to elucidate and promote a fully formed ideology of Manifest Destiny (such as that voiced at the New York pro-Texas fund-raising dinner), for the first time. And of course, Texas was ultimately annexed. History is not kind to losers, and in general, those who opposed territorial expansion, from the Federalists in 1803 through the anti-imperialists of 1898, have found themselves marginalized in historical narratives precisely because the "course of empire," at least up until the moment of "Consummation," seems, in retrospect, so inevitable. I would like to suggest that the failure of scholars to see a critique of territorial expansion in Thomas Cole's work, despite the use of the word "empire" in the title, reflects this unwillingness to question the forward momentum of Manifest Destiny.[61]

As for Thomas Cole and his *Course of Empire* canvases, they were never as convincing as the artist intended. For every viewer who felt "an ominous foreboding" upon viewing the canvas, others felt none whatsoever because they denied its relevance to their own lives. "Parents," wrote one critic, "will bring their children here and explain to them the *Course of Empire*, and tell them stories of other lands." Nor was the pessimistic Cole particularly surprised by this. "Very few will understand . . . the philosophy" behind the series, he grumbled in a letter to his patron before the opening of the show.[62]

In an extreme irony, by the time Texas became the twenty-eighth state

FIGURE 15. *Progress, or the Advance of Civilization* by Asher B. Durand.

in the Union, the art world had moved to reject allegorical paintings as un-American. In 1845, the *Broadway Journal* dismissed *Course of Empire* as "sermons in green paint; essays in gilt frames" in which "the charm of nature is destroyed, the moment that the discovery is made, and we turn from them in disgust."[63] What the rising generation insisted on was the glory of pure nature, and the power of American landscapes, unmediated by history, untainted by European precedent, free from dour warnings of what was to come. Paintings would no longer "produce the moral," if ever they had. Landscapes such as Asher B. Durand's *Progress, or The Advance of Civilization*, commissioned by a railroad executive in 1853, looked to the West, in the direction of the setting sun, and openly celebrated American Manifest Destiny. Durand was just one of the landscape painters who rose to prominence after mentoring and encouragement by Cole. Thomas Cole died at the close of the US-Mexican War, and before the sad truth was revealed: although he would forever be revered as the father of the Hudson River School, Cole's progeny would reject him, just as surely as young America would reject old Europe, and they would do so in favor of the same exceptionalist worldview that *Course of Empire* fought vainly to critique.[64]

NOTES

1. "Cole's Pictures," *New York Commercial Advertiser*, December 12, 1836, 2.

2. "Cole's New Pictures," *New York Evening Post*, October 18, 1836, 2; Albert Boime, *The Magisterial Gaze: Manifest Destiny and American Landscape Painting, c. 1830–1865* (Washington: Smithsonian Institution Press, 1991), 38.

3. "Fine Arts," *Alexandria* (VA) *Gazette*, October 15, 1836, 2; "Mr. Cole," *New York Evening Post*, October 21, 1836, 2.

4. "Fine Arts," *Alexandria* (VA) *Gazette*, October 15, 1836, 2; "Cole's New Pictures," *New York Evening Post*, October 18, 1836, 2.

5. "Cole's New Pictures," *New York Evening Post*, October 18, 1836, 2.

6. "Fine Arts," *Alexandria* (VA) *Gazette*, October 15, 1836, 2.

7. "Mr. Cole's Pictures," *New-York Spectator*, October 17, 1836.

8. "Cole's Pictures," *New York Commercial Advertiser*, December 12, 1836, 2.

9. Lord Byron, "Childe Harold's Pilgrimage" (1812–18). Canto IV.

10. Cole to Luman Reed, September 18, 1833, in Louis L. Noble, *The Life and Works of Thomas Cole, N.A.* 3rd Edition (New York: Sheldon, Blakeman and Co., 1856), 176.

11. Thomas Cole, *The Collected Essays and Prose Sketches*, ed. Marshall Tymn (St. Paul, MI: J. Cole Press, 1980), 134–5.

12. Quoted in Angela Miller, *The Empire of the Eye: Landscape Representation and American Cultural Politics, 1825–1875* (Ithaca: Cornell University Press, 1993), 11.

13. On Bancroft see Eileen K Chang, *The Plain and Noble Garb of Truth: Nationalism and Impartiality in American Historical Writing, 1784–1860* (Athens, GA: University of Georgia Press, 2008), 159–75.

14. Angela Miller has argued that "internal dissolution and attack from without are two sides of the same coin, and, in the 1830s, those most concerned with the stability of the republic feared the former far more than the latter." Angela Miller, "Thomas Cole and Jacksonian America: The Course of Empire as Political Allegory," *Prospects* 14 (October 1989): 65–92, quote 80; See also Allan Wallach, "Cole, Byron and The Course of Empire," *Art Bulletin* 50 (1968): 375–9; Lucy Elizabeth Eron, "Visions of Empire: The Theory and Uses of Allegory in American Art from the Nineteenth Century to the Present," (MA Thesis, Art History, San Diego State University, 2011); Stephen Daniels, *Fields of Vision: Landscape Imagery and National Identity in England and the United States* (Princeton, NJ: Princeton University Press, 1993), 146- 73; for an alternate and very compelling reading, see Nick Yablom, *Untimely Ruins: An Archaeology of American Urban Modernity, 1819–1919* (Chicago: University of Chicago Press, 2009), 19–48.

15. I am indebted here to Angela Miller's analysis of these paintings in *Empire of the Eye*, particularly pages 25–37. Miller, however, does not consider the role of the Texas Revolution in inspiring Cole.

16. Tim Barringer, "The Course of Empires: Landscape and Identity in America and Britain, 1820–1880," in *American Sublime: Landscape Painting in the United States, 1820–1880*, eds. Andrew Wilton and Tim Barringer (Princeton: Princeton University Press, 2002), 97; on petitions, see Sam W. Haynes, *Unfinished Revolution: The Early American Republic in a British World* (Charlottesville: University of Virginia Press, 2010), 220–21; Justin H. Smith, *The Annexation of Texas* (New York: The Baker and Taylor Co., 1911), 53.

17. Quoted in Noble, *The Life and Works of Thomas Cole*, 167.

18. "Fine Arts," *Alexandria* (VA) *Gazette*, October 15, 1836, 2; Tim Barringer, "The Course of Empires," 52.

19. Lucy Elizabeth Eron, "Visions of Empire," (MA Thesis, Art History: San Diego State University, 2011), 39; Yablom, *Untimely Ruins*, 46. See also Barringer, "The Course of Empires," 51–2.

20. "Cole's Pictures," *New York Commercial Advertiser*, December 12, 1836, 2.

21. Today we're comfortable with a broad definition of empire that encompasses cultural imperialism. Oxford English Dictionary online, 2nd edition, 1989, *http://www.oed.com*. As Frank Ninkovich put it, empire exists when "an important aspect of a nation's life is under the effective control of a foreign power." But as commonly understood in the nineteenth century, "empire" had a more circumscribed meaning: It was about political sovereignty—an empire was "an extensive territory under the sway of an emperor or supreme ruler; or, an aggregate of subject territories ruled over by a sovereign state." Frank Ninkovich, *The United States and Imperialism* (Malden, MA: Blackwell Publishers, Inc., 2001), 5.

22. See, for example, Walter Nugent, *Habits of Empire: A History of American Expansionism* (New York: Viking, 2008); Fred Anderson and Andrew Cayton, *The Dominion of War: Empire and Liberty in North America, 1500–2000* (New York: Viking, 2005).

23. Lyon Rathbun, "The Debate over Annexing Texas and the Emergence of Manifest Destiny," *Rhetoric and Public Affairs* 4 (Fall 2001): 459–93; Gordon S. Wood, *The Creation of the American Republic, 1776–1787* (New York: Norton, 1969), 499–516, 593–619; Peter S. Onuf, *Statehood and Union: A History of the Northwest Ordinance* (Bloomington: Indiana University Press, 1987), 1–21.

24. Thomas Jefferson to James Monroe, November 24, 1801, *The Writings of Thomas Jefferson*, ed. H.A. Washington (New York: H. W. Derby, 1861), 4:420. On Jefferson's views of empire see Peter S. Onuf, *Jefferson's Empire: The Language of American Nationhood* (Charlottesville: University of Virginia Press, 2000).

25. Fischer Ames to Thomas Dwight, October 31, 1803. *Works of Fischer Ames* (Boston: T. B. Wait and Co., 1809), 109.

26. "The Texas Campaign," *Daily National Intelligencer*, November 4, 1835.

27. Cecil Robinson, *The View from Chapultepec: Mexican Writers on the Mexican-American War* (Tucson: University of Arizona Press, 1989), xliv, xliii.

28. Quoted in *The (*Boston*) Liberator*, Saturday, June 11, 1836, 96.

29. "Texas," *Alexandria Gazette*, April 6, 1836.

30. "Important from Washington," *New York Herald*, May 25, 1836.

31. Benjamin Lundy, *The origin and true causes of the Texas insurrection, commenced in the year 1835* (Philadelphia, 1836), 11.

32. John Quincy Adams, *Memoirs of John Quincy Adams, comprising Portions of his Diary from 1795 to 1848*, ed. Charles Francis Adams (Philadelphia: J.B. Lippincott, 1874–1877), 9:431; John Quincy Adams, "Speech of John Quincy Adams on the Joint Resolution for Distributing Rations to the Distressed Fugitives from Indian Hostilities in the States of Alabama and Georgia" (Washington, DC, 1836), 3. See also Rathbun, "The Debate over Annexing Texas," 469–70.

33. "Downfall of Nations," *Knickerbocker Magazine* VI (1), July 1835, 44–53 (quotes on 48, 52); M. M. Noah, "A Day at Carthage," *New-York Mirror*, March 28, 1835. See also "Original Sketches of Ancient Rome: A True Tale of the Coliseum," *New-York Mirror*, February 3, 1836; "Original Papers: Scenes in Europe. Rome—No. I," *The New-England Magazine* Volume 9, Issue 11, November 1835; "Original Papers: Scenes in Europe. Rome—No. II." *The New-England Magazine* Volume 9, Issue 12, December 1835, 447–56.

34. "Texas and the South," *Norwich (*MA*) Courier*, April 25, 1837.

35. On public meetings see Amy S. Greenberg, "Pirates, Patriots, and Public Meetings: Antebellum Expansionism and Urban Culture," *Journal of Urban History* 31 (July 2005): 634–50.

36. "Wednesday, February 10, 1836," *National Banner and Nashville Whig*, February 10, 1836, 3.

37. "Meeting," *Gloucester (*MA*) Telegraph*, August 26, 1847, 2.

38. "Female Politicians," *New York Commercial Advertiser*, August 4, 1837, 2; "From Washington," *Pennsylvania Inquirer and Daily Courier*, September 20, 1847, 1; *Norwich Courier*, January 3, 1837, 2; *Richmond Enquirer*, September 29, 1837, 3; Edward P. Crapol, "The Foreign Policy of Antislavery, 1833–1846," in *Redefining the Past*, ed. Lloyd C. Gardner (Corvallis: Oregon State University Press, 1986): 85–103, quote 89.

39. "Anti-Texan Meeting," *Pennsylvania Inquirer and Daily Courier*, Wednesday, August 30, 1837, Issue 51.

40. "Texas Meeting," *The Liberator*, December 29, 1837, 212.

41. "Texas from the Worcester Spy, Public Meeting," *The Liberator*, August 25, 1837, 37.

42. William Ellery Channing, *A letter to the Hon. Henry Clay, on the annexation of Texas to the United States* (Boston: James Munroe and Co. 1837), 20–21.

43. Edward P. Crapol, "The Foreign Policy of Antislavery," 103.

44. Channing, *Letter to the Hon. Henry Clay*, 23–4.

45. Ibid., 28, 61.

46. Ibid., 61; on the origins of the term Manifest Destiny see Greenberg, *Manifest Destiny and American Territorial Expansion*, 78–79.

47. "Time's Noblest Empire is the Last," *New-Bedford Mercury*, July 18, 1828, 1; on the transit of empire, and Berkeley, see Yablom, *Untimely Ruins*, 33–37.

48. Michael A. Morrison, *Slavery and the American West* (Chapel Hill: University of North Carolina Press, 1997), 14; Rathbun, "The Debate over Annexing Texas," 467. See also John Behlolavek, *"Let the Eagle Soar!" the Foreign Policy of Andrew Jackson*, (Lincoln, NE: University of Nebraska, 1985), 214–38; Robert Remini, *Jackson and the Course of American Democracy,1833–1845* (New York: Harper and Row, 1984), 357–360, 367–368.

49. Rathbun, "The Debate over Annexing Texas," 466. See also Harry L. Watson, *Andrew Jackson vs. Henry Clay: Democracy and Development in Antebellum America* (Boston: St. Martin's Press, 1998).

50. Rathbun, "The Debate over Annexing Texas," 467.

51. Quoted in "Texas," the *United States Telegraph*, May 25, 1836.

52. "Grand Exhibition of Hannington's New Moving Dioramas," *New York Commercial Advertiser*, February 13, 1836, 3. Originally cited in Angela Miller, "Thomas Cole and Jacksonian America: The Course of Empire as Political Allegory," *Prospects* 14 (October 1989): 65–92 (quote 75).

53. "The Fourth of July," *New-York Spectator*, July 4, 1836; "Powerful Attractions," *The New York Herald*, September 21, 1836.

54. "Deaf Smith," *Tallahassee The Floridian*, September 02, 1837, Issue 4, 1. On Deaf [Erastus] Smith, "The Harvey Birch of Texas," see "Express Mail News Latest from Texas," *Daily National Intelligencer*; February 4, 1837, 3; "San Antonio," *Telegraph and Texas Register*, December 9, 1836, 2; "From The Journal of a Texan Officer," *Boston Saturday Morning Transcript*; January 14, 1837.

55. "Our Own Country," *Tallahassee The Floridian*, September 2, 1837; Issue 4, 1.

56. "Speech of Mr. Claiborne, of Mississippi," *Mississippi Free Trader and Natchez Gazette*, February 24, 1837.

57. "Refuge of Oppression," *The Boston Liberator*, September 8, 1837.

58. "Sketches from the address of Mr. Custis, of Arlington, Delivered in the City Hall, the 24th of May, 1836," *United States Telegraph*, June 23, 1836, 1.

59. "Texian Festival in New York," *United States Telegraph*, July 27, 1836. This column was widely reprinted. See *Worcester Spy*, August 3, 1836, *Newburyport Herald*, August 5, 1836; *New Hampshire Statesman and State Journal*, July 30, 1836; "Annexation," *The United States Magazine and Democratic Review* (Washington, DC: Langtree and O'Sullivan, 1845) 17:5, 7, 9. Authorship of "Annexation" has been contested. Linda Hudson argues that it was journalist Cora Montgomery who invented the term "Manifest Destiny." Linda Hudson, *Mistress of Manifest Destiny: A Biography of Jane McManus Storm Cazneau, 1807–1878* (Austin: Texas State Historical Association, 2001).

60. "Texian Dinner," *New York Spectator*, July 21, 1836.

61. I believe this also reflects a clear preference for the domestic over the foreign in the larger field of cultural history.

62. Miller, *The Empire of the Eye*, 33; Cole to Luman Reed, March 26, 1836, *The Life and Works of Thomas Cole*, 217.

63. *The Broadway Journal*, New York, vol. 1, 1845: 103.

64. My analysis of Cole's place in the evolution of American landscape painting is largely drawn from Angela Miller, *Empire of the Eye*, 67–8; on Durand, see Elizabeth Kuebler-Wolf, "The 'Earlier, Wilder Image': Early Artists of the American West," in *The World of the American West*, ed. Gordon Morris Bakken, (New York: Routledge, 2011), 187–88; Tim Barringer, "The Course of Empires: Landscape and Identity in American and Britain, 1820–1880," 53–4. Frederick Church was Cole's best-known student, and his landscapes are arguably more celebratory of Manifest Destiny than are Durand's.

ABOUT THE CONTRIBUTORS

WILL FOWLER is professor of Latin American Studies at the University of St Andrews, Scotland, where he is the head of the School of Modern Languages. He is the author of *Mexico in the Age of Proposals, 1821–1853* (1998); *Tornel and Santa Anna, The Writer and the Caudillo* (2000); *Santa Anna of Mexico* (2007), *Latin America since 1780* (2002; 2nd edition, 2008), and *The Pronunciamiento in Independent Mexico (1821–1858)* (in press). He has published numerous articles on the early national period and edited twelve volumes on Mexican and Latin American political history, including *Gobernantes mexicanos*, 2 vols. (2008), and three volumes focused on the dynamics and culture of the *pronunciamiento* (1821–76).

AMY S. GREENBERG is the Edwin Erle Sparks professor of history at Penn State University. She is the author of four books on gender and politics in nineteenth-century America, and the relationship between the United States and the wider world, including *Manifest Manhood and the Antebellum American Empire* (1995) and *Manifest Destiny and American Territorial Expansion* (2012). Her most recent volume, *A Wicked War: Polk, Clay, Lincoln and the US Invasion of Mexico* (paperback 2013), received book prizes from the Western History Association, the Society for Historians of American Foreign Relations, and the Society for Historians of the Early American Republic. She holds a PhD from Harvard University, and a BA from the University of California at Berkeley.

SAM W. HAYNES is a professor of history and director of the Center for Greater Southwestern Studies at the University of Texas at Arlington. Specializing in Jacksonian America, nineteenth-century Texas, and the American Southwest, Haynes is the author of three books and several coauthored texts. His most recent book, *Unfinished Revolution: The Early American Republic in a British World* (2010), examined the role Great Britain played in the formation of an American national identity. He is also the author of *James K. Polk and the Expansionist Impulse* (1998) and the coeditor, with Cary Wintz, of *Major Problems in Texas History* (2002). For the past three years, he has served as managing editor of a website on the 1846–1848 conflict between Mexico and the United States. Entitled *A Continent Divided: the US-Mexico War*, the website is a collaborative digitization project between the Center for Greater Southwestern Studies and the UT-Arlington Libraries. He holds a BA from Columbia University and a PhD from the University of Houston.

GERALD D. SAXON, a Beaumont native, is an associate professor of history at the University of Texas at Arlington after having spent twenty-five years in library administration at the university, including seven years as dean of the library. He received his PhD in history from North Texas State University (now the University of North Texas) in 1979. He is currently working on a biography of Texas empresario Sterling Clack Robertson (1785–1842). His two most recent books are *Collecting Texas,* with Thomas Kreneck, published by the Book Club of Texas in 2010, and *Historic Texas from the Air*, with David Buisseret, Jack Graves, and Richard Francaviglia, published by the University of Texas Press in 2009.

ERIC R. SCHLERETH received his PhD in American History at Brandeis University and is currently an associate professor of history at the University of Texas at Dallas. He is the author of *An Age of Infidels: The Politics of Religious Controversy in the Early United States* (2013). His next book is a history of expatriation in North America from 1750 to 1870. He is also the author of several articles and essays, most recently "Privileges of Locomotion: Expatriation and the Politics of Southwestern Border Crossing" in the *Journal of American History* (March 2014) and "Religious Revivalism and Public Life" in *A Companion to the Era of Andrew Jackson*, published by Blackwell Publishing Company in 2013.

MIGUEL SOTO received his PhD in history at the University of Texas at Austin and is currently a professor of history at the Universidad Nacional

Autónoma de Mexico. He has written widely on early nineteenth-century US-Mexico border relations and is the translator and editor of the Spanish language edition of David Pletcher's *The Diplomacy of Annexation: Texas, Oregon and the Mexican War.* He is the author of four books and more than 40 articles and book chapters, among them *Transition and Political Culture: From Colony to Independent Mexico* (2004) and *Approaching History* (1998). His literary output also includes the following essays and books: "The Other Texas Loss: Sale and Trafficking of the Properties of Eleven Sites, 1828–1834," in the *Disputed Territory in the War of 1846–1848; Resistance and Assimilation of Mexican Communities* (2007); "Moderate and Radical Mexico and Spain," in *Mexico on Three Occasions: 1810–1910–2010; Towards Commemoration of the Bicentennial of Independence and the Centennial of the Mexican Revolution: Challenges and Prospects* (2007); and "Mariano Paredes y Arrillaga," with Will Fowler, coordinator, in *Mexican Rulers: 1821–2000* (2008).

INDEX